D0345579

The Pillars of the Post

Drawing by Vint Lawrence

The Pillars of the Post

The Making of a News Empire in Washington

By HOWARD BRAY

W · W · NORTON & COMPANY · *NEW YORK* · *LONDON*

FIRST EDITION

The text of this book is composed in photocomposition Avanta. Display type is typositor Perpetua. Manufacturing is by the Haddon Craftsmen. Book design by Marjorie J. Flock.

ISBN 0-393-01313-8

1 2 3 4 5 6 7 8 9 0

To Ann FOR HER LOVE, PATIENCE, STRENGTH, AND WISDOM

Contents

Foreword

In Evelyn Waugh's delightfully ironic novel, *Scoop*, Lord Copper, head of the Megalopolitan Newspaper Corporation, asserts: "The workings of a great newspaper are of a complexity which the public seldom appreciates. The citizen little realizes the vast machinery put into motion for him in exchange for his morning penny."

Lord Copper was right. When I began writing this book, I told a senior editor of the *Washington Post*, "I am trying to explain the workings of a significant, successful, and fascinating institution, the *Post*. I am telling the story through the interplay of the people who have crafted the modern *Post*. As I think about it, the story is almost Darwinian in the sense of the *Post*'s survival, rise to dominance, and adaptive and inventive character." The *Post* is worth study by more than journalists; it has been an important part of the history of our time and continues to be a powerful influence in the life of its community and nation.

While I focus principally on the *Post*, I include much more; the newspaper is only one element, the primary and most celebrated one, in a variegated communications empire that encircles the globe. The Washington Post Company owns other papers, broadcasting stations, magazines, and a major news service. They are part of this story, too.

• • •

I am grateful to the many women and men who graciously shared with me their knowledge and perceptions of the events described

The Pillars of the Post

herein. I am especially indebted to journalists Nick Kotz, Robert Maynard, J.Y. Smith, and Milton Viorst who read all or part of my manuscript, proving their friendship with tough criticism. Any errors of omission or commission, of course, are mine. Starling Lawrence, my editor, was always encouraging; Bob Lescher provided steady counsel. And Martha Smith and Sheila King Clarke remained my friends even after they finished typing the manuscript.

H. B.

The Pillars of the Post

ONE

Up from Bankruptcy

The instruments which shape the minds of citizens are not freely at the disposal of anyone who wishes to operate them. They are controlled, for the most part, by men or bodies who can afford either to create or employ them. And for the most part they are controlled by the vested interests which dwarf altogether the individual and leave him helpless, save as he can find some other association which makes it possible to express his experience of life. It is open to Mr. Eugene Meyer . . . to buy or start a newspaper like the Washington Post . . . the best the ordinary citizen can hope for is to creep into the correspondence columns.

—HAROLD J. LASKI, *American Democracy,* 1948

THE CHARTS FLASHING on the screen conveyed an account of extraordinary success. At the end of the long, red-carpeted room stood Katharine Graham. A tall, slender woman dressed in a simple manner, she commented upon the achievement. "I would be tempted," she told those gathered at the annual stockholders' meeting that sunny morning in May 1978, "to call the last two years almost miraculous years" for the Washington Post Company. In a few days, Mrs. Graham would be sixty-one; she had been running the Washington Post Company for close to fifteen years, and the past year had outbounded all the others.

The bars on the financial charts appearing behind her resembled a row of tall silhouetted buildings; those representing 1977 towered over the previous years. All of the vital signs of the giant corporation that she headed—operating revenues, net income, earnings per share, dividends, shareholders' equity—were bullish: 1977, which happened to be the centennial of the *Washington Post,* had been a great business year, indeed. The company's net profits had soared 45 percent over 1976, which itself had been a very good year. Her reward was a bonus of $150,000, on top of her $150,000 salary, and the enrichment of her immense holdings of stock.

Katharine Graham has been described by an admirer as "the most powerful woman since Queen Victoria." Whether Mrs. Graham fills this billing depends, of course, on one's definition and perception of power. Mrs. Graham governs a huge news business empire that reaches around the planet: Her *Washington Post* and *Newsweek* station correspondents throughout the world; the company holds a major interest in the *International Herald Tribune,* which informs the world's business and governing elite—including those in the Kremlin and the Imperial Palace in Peking—in Europe, Africa, and Asia, and 50 percent of a news service that dispatches the *Post's* top stories to some four hundred newspapers across America, in Europe, South Africa, Australia, India, and Japan. Most of the newsprint used by the *Post's* presses is produced in mills partly owned by the company. The newspapers the company owns in New Jersey and on Puget Sound and its television stations in Florida, Connecticut, and Michigan might be compared to colonies yielding riches to the mother country.

The Washington Post Company possesses vast economic power to achieve its corporate financial goals. But there is a concurrent power of far greater consequence. As Mrs. Graham put it, "The power is to set the agenda. What we print and what we don't print matter a lot. What leads the paper or the magazine impacts [sic] on events and people's awareness." Power, said Karl Marx more than a century ago, is control of the means of production. "Power in America today," says Arthur Schlesinger, Jr., "is control of the means of communication." Queen Victoria commanded the most awesome fleet in the world and an army that held India and much of Africa in rein. Katharine Graham commanded the means to influence people's hearts and minds. In this age, that is a greater power than Victoria's.

Sitting on the blue-skirted dais that May morning one seat from Mrs. Graham was her oldest son, Donald E. Graham, then general manager of the *Washington Post* and at thirty-three the heir apparent to the corporate throne. Other officers of the company were ranked at her sides. A few feet away in the front rows of the audience sat other company directors. Among them were her brother, Eugene Meyer III, a psychiatrist with a deeply-tanned ascetic face; Warren Buffett, an unimposing midwesterner who owned 10 percent of the company and had quickly impressed Mrs. Graham as a "financial wizard"; George J. Gillespie III, a partner in the eminent New York law firm, Cravath, Swaine & Moore, that had contributed several members to the Post Company's hierarchy; Nicholas de Belleville Katzenbach, President Kennedy's under secretary of state, President Johnson's attorney general, and now I.B.M.'s general counsel; Arjay Miller, once president of the Ford Motor Company; and John W. Sweeterman, whom Katharine Graham had deposed as publisher of the *Post* to make way for fresher leadership. Benjamin C. Bradlee, executive editor of the *Post* and a giant figure in modern newspaper lore, though not a director also was present. As he watched the glowing financial returns on the screen that morning, John Sweeterman, in from Florida retirement, might have thought back to those leaner times when *Post* reporters were badgered to get the final reproductive gasp from the carbon paper. The modern *Washington Post* was a Depression baby.

Sitting in her office, Katharine Graham told a visitor, "I can remember when we were number five." Like most other American cities, Washington had once had a clutch of competing newspapers. Washingtonians in 1933 could choose among the dominant *Evening Star,* the *Daily News,* the *Herald,* the *Times,* and the trailing and sickly *Washington Post.* Every sign was that the *Post* would die at the dissolute hands of its mentally unsound owner, Edward H. McLean. Unable to pay the International Paper Company for delivered newsprint, the once-profitable and influential *Post* was in receivership. The court had ordered it sold at auction on June 1, 1933, to satisfy creditors. Rumors flew that both wealthy Republicans and Democrats wanted control of the *Post* in order to wield political influence in the capital and to keep watch on the new president. The defeated president, Herbert Hoover, wanted Republican capitalist Lewis Strauss to buy the

Post. Newspapers were then and are now a rich man's game. Among the possible bidders, the *New York Times* reported, were Louis K. Liggett, the drug store magnate who was close to former president Calvin Coolidge, and ultrareactionary multimillionaire John J. Raskob, a Democrat who had opposed the party's choice of Franklin D. Roosevelt for president. Now Roosevelt was in the White House.

Evalyn Walsh McLean, the estranged wife of the owner of the *Post,* arrived for the auction on the steps of the *Post* building wearing the fabled Hope diamond, a deep-blue, forty-four-carat boulder. She bid $600,000, but dropped out as the offers increased for the decrepit printing plant, a pile of debts, and a valuable Associated Press franchise. An agent for William Randolph Hearst, the publishing giant who already owned the *Herald* and the *Times* as well as other newspapers elsewhere and who had tried privately to buy the *Post,* went to $800,-000. But a Washington attorney on behalf of an unidentified principal raised Hearst $25,000—and the auction was over; the *Post* was sold. Twelve days later, after the court dismissed Evalyn McLean's challenge to the sale, Republican Wall Street financier Eugene Isaac Meyer announced that he was the new publisher of the *Post.* Meyer hungered for the political platform of a newspaper in the capital. He had tried to buy the *Herald* in 1925. In 1929 he offered $5 million for the *Post* but was turned down; he had been ready to bid up to $2 million at the auction. Over the years he would pour more millions into the Post but it remained a superlative bargain. On the front page of his newly acquired property, Meyer declared his intention: "[to] make the *Post* an even better paper than it has been in the past. It will be conducted as an independent paper. . . ." The California-born Meyer, who had not a jot of newspaper experience, kept his word.

"I felt this was the best way I could make myself useful at a critical time," Meyer said of what he exuberantly regarded as a new career of public service. At fifty-seven, he could look back on intermittent employment in high-level federal financial posts starting with the wartime Wilson administration; in later years he served Presidents Hoover, Roosevelt, whom he often harshly criticized editorially, Truman, and Eisenhower.

Meyer, with his pince-nez glasses and bald dome, could afford the high-stakes newspaper game. He had inherited money and made a fortune investing daringly in copper, automobiles, oil, and railroads as the pre-World War I industrial boom swept America. During labor unrest Meyer dispatched to Chicago a man who posed as a reporter to spy on railroad strike organizers. He operated on the premise that owning shares in productive assets was preferable to holding bonds or debentures which represented indebtedness. Two years before Meyer bought the *Post,* his stock in Allied Chemical, an industrial giant that he had helped create, was worth about $43 million; Allied paid cash dividends throughout the Depression. These dividends, according to Meyer's biographer Merlo J. Pusey, "would enable him in later years to cover the heavy losses he was to suffer rehabilitating the *Washington Post.*"

The critical time Eugene Meyer spoke of engulfed the country. Depression wracked the industrialized nations; Franklin D. Roosevelt, in the Oval Office less than three months, labored to rescue America from social and financial catastrophe. During debate in the House of Representatives on F.D.R.'s proposal on gold buying, Congressman Louis T. McFadden from Pennsylvania asked rhetorically, ". . . [is it] not true in the United States today that the Gentiles have the slips of paper while the Jews have the lawful money." McFadden's slur, denounced by a colleague as "Hitlerian," came a few days before Meyer bought the *Post.* Although the two events were unconnected, McFadden had been a critic of Meyer's management of the War Finance Corporation during the Wilson administration, and unsuccessfully opposed his appointment in 1931 to the Federal Reserve Board. After the war a congressional committee investigated Meyer's use of his former Wall Street office to market Liberty bonds. He was cleared of any conflict of interest after proving that he received neither commissions nor expenses for this service which aided the government.

Still, both of Meyer's grandfathers were rabbis, and although he had long since dropped his Jewish ties, McFadden's religious hostility could not have escaped Meyer in the rising tide of anti-semitism. By the time Meyer became publisher of the *Post,* fifty thousand Jews had fled Nazi

Germany. In August the American Jewish Committee began writing to him about the degradation and economic ruin of Jews in Germany. For several days in November 1938 the *Post*'s front page reported the brutal outbreak of Nazi assaults on Jews in Germany and Austria. An editorial urged that Palestine be kept open as a homeland for Jewish refugees, a goal Meyer had supported for years, though he was not a Zionist and resented any attempt to identify him with Jewish political causes.

Over the next decade Meyer's losses at the Post sometimes would run more than $1 million a year. These were cushioned, however, by the income tax advantages for such debits. In the *Post*'s hungry years, Meyer personally appealed to other Washington businessmen to buy space in his paper. But he shrugged off the automobile dealers' removal of ads— their angry protest of an editorial siding with the General Motors sit-down strikers. When another Croesus, his friend Andrew Mellon, offered to buy the *Post* at a handsome profit to Meyer, the publisher politely said no, he preferred to continue the resurrection of the morning paper. "Indeed, the *Post* is for him, in a luxury sense, what steam yachts and strings of race horses may be for some other wealthy men," commented Erwin D. Canham of the *Christian Science Monitor*.

Eugene Meyer used his newspaper to influence people and the course of events in the direction of his ideal. In this constitutionally protected role—and through those less apparent but effective channels available to a rich and forceful businessman—Meyer possessed power on a scale beyond reach of most men.

"Power," Meyer philosophized late in life, "means different things under different conditions and in different contexts. . . . Power can be used as brute strength, or it can be used as the highest form of influence in connection with science or truth or eternal verities. . . . Ideas, I think, have more power than anything. They are intangible, but very powerful." He explained: "That is why I bought a newspaper—because it's a place where you can work in the field of ideas. If you study out the right ideas and translate them into language which others can understand, you exercise power very usefully and helpfully. The right ideas pursued in journalism, in government, or anywhere else are useful ideas." "People also like to be told what to think," Meyer went on. "If you give them the truth and back it up with clear explanations and sound arguments, you are exercising very great power in a very useful way." 'Very great power,' indeed. Nobless oblige underpinned the publisher's presumptions about 'right ideas' and something as elusive as 'the truth.' His conclusion, however, that people want 'to be told what to think' seemed to be the ultimate arrogance, even from as decent a man as Eugene Meyer. Meyer's investments in cash and energy in the *Post* in time began returning increases in circulation and advertising. He added new writers and features and the editorial page grew in stature. In June 1946 he named his son-in-law, Philip L. Graham, publisher of the *Post*. Like Meyer, Graham used the paper as a political power tool.

After concluding in the early 1950s that the country urgently needed a change in political control, Meyer applied his considerable power to the nomination and election of a president of his favor. The Democrats had occupied the White House for almost two decades and dominated the Congress nearly that long. After 1950 the Truman administration seemed fatally wounded by the continuing war in Korea and charges of corruption. General Dwight D. Eisenhower had impressed Meyer during World War II as a military leader who also displayed political mastery in dealing with America's allies. Meyer kept in occasional friendly touch with the general whom he and many others saw as presidential timber. In 1948 the *Post* serialized Eisenhower's best-selling *Crusade in Europe*.

In November 1951 Meyer, a lifelong Republican, and his editor J. Russell Wiggins, a close friend of Eisenhower's brother, Milton, journeyed to the outskirts of Paris where Eisenhower had his headquarters as supreme allied commander in Europe. Their purpose was to encourage him to run for the presidency on the GOP ticket. Over coffee Meyer, as Wiggins's personal notes tell it, "said we had come on no mission but to tender our good offices to do anything [or not do anything] that the general thought would be helpful to protect him from his friends or enemies . . . in any way that would be useful, that the general was a national asset that the *Post* was anxious to see safeguarded and used in [the] most effective way." Eisenhower expressed his conviction that it was important to keep military and political activities separate, particularly since the restoration of Western Europe's defenses depended on the support of both Congressional Democrats and Republicans.

From the outbreak of the Cold War the keystone of United States foreign policy was the building of a credible bulwark in Western Europe against the Soviet Union and communism. Meyer threw the force of the *Post* and his own considerable persuasive talent behind this effort. He championed Universal Military Training, a controversial proposal in Congress, whose advocates expected it to spur our allies to strengthen their own armies. In September 1947, with UMT in political trouble, Meyer met in Rome with Pope Pius XII to seek his help in offsetting the opposition of some American Catholic groups. These Catholics insisted that moral considerations involved in conscription be resolved first; Meyer, who had counseled Army Chief of Staff George C. Marshall on UMT, told the Pope that the higher priority was national security. The publisher tentatively solicited the vicar's support for the conscription plan but did not press the point. Meyer was accompanied on this private diplomatic mission by Alfred Friendly, a *Post* reporter who later became managing editor. As they were parting the Pope asked them to keep the conversation confidential, and Meyer assured him that they were not there as journalists. Meyer also worked energetically for the Marshall Plan for European economic recovery from the war. He testified for the plan in Congress and the *Post* ran many favorable articles on the program. Friendly took leave from the paper for more than a year to direct the program's information campaign.

In General Eisenhower, Meyer saw a president who could head off any isolationist retreat from Europe. By early 1952 the efforts of the pro-Ike, internationalist wing of the Republican Party accelerated to offset the head start of conservative Senator Robert Taft of Ohio. But Eisenhower remained at his job in Europe, discreetly relying on his friends at home to keep his political fires burning while he withheld a public declaration of his candidacy. His most vigorous backers included the chairman of the *Washington Post,* who became an intelligence gatherer and untitled campaign counselor for the general.

In his early days as a publisher Meyer became interested in the public opinion surveys of Dr. George Gallup, a pioneer in the field. The *Post* began carrying the Gallup Poll in 1935, and Meyer often suggested questions and comments to the pollster. Among the information that Meyer fed by frequent letters to his candidate in France were advance copies of the Gallup Poll. On February 8 Meyer airmailed to Eisenhower an advance report: "The Gallup Poll knows me as an old friend, so I ventured to take a liberty and asked what the coming release for next Wednesday, which we will get probably on Monday, will show. Ordinarily, they do not reveal these things ahead of time, but they do me an occasional favor. Strictly for your private information, Taft and you run a dead heat with the Republican voters. With the independents, you show a lead at forty-two against sixteen for Taft. . . ."

Meyer desired the election of a Republican Congress, as well as a Republican president. He thought that Taft would not be as effective as the popular general in picking up doubtful GOP congressional seats. Meyer also passed along to Eisenhower Gallup's judgment that his chances for the nomination were endangered by his supporters' overoptimism. He had his son-in-law, Phil Graham, check Gallup on the political situation in New Jersey, where the Taft people were assiduously working in the precincts. Graham reported to Herbert Brownell, a key Eisenhower strategist. Meyer counseled that the Eisenhower campaign write off in advance the primary election outcomes in Illinois and Ohio so that the newspapers would not overplay an anticipated Taft "romp" in these states. He suggested, too, that Ike ask Paul G. Hoffman, head of the European recovery program, to soften his description of Eisenhower as a "friend of business" because the characterization might "have some unfavorable results."

In March the *Post* started running excerpts from *The Man from Abilene,* a laudatory biography of the general. That month the paper endorsed Eisenhower—the first time the *Post* under Meyer had supported a presidential candidate. "Herbert Brownell, who would be Eisenhower's attorney general, said it was the most effective journalistic blow that had been struck for Ike," wrote Merlo Pusey, himself a *Post* editorial writer at the time. Pusey also described how Adlai Stevenson was uncertain about accepting the Democratic nomination to run against Eisenhower: "While Stevenson was still wavering over the nomination, Philip Graham told him it would be an 'act of arrogance' to turn it down. Stevenson agreed, and on this basis [*Post* reporter Edward] Folliard wrote an exclusive story saying that Stevenson would accept a draft from the convention." Graham's maneuvers in both presidential camps displayed his skill and daring on the political high wire. His acrobatics in 1952 were a precursor of his bolder feats in national politics in the years ahead.

The endorsement of Eisenhower provoked a split among the editorial staff between Eisenhower and Stevenson supporters. Herblock's cartoons which were critical of the Republican ticket were banned from the *Post* before election day. In mid-October President Truman denounced Eisenhower as the "captive candidate" of anti-Semitic and anti-Catholic forces. In a statement on the *Post*'s front page, Meyer branded Truman's remarks "outrageous and ridiculous."

On Meyer's eightieth birthday on October 31, 1955, hundreds of well-wishers gathered at a luncheon in the Willard Hotel. President Eisenhower was recuperating from a heart attack and sent congratulations through his vice president. The newspaper the next day portrayed a beaming Richard Nixon handing Ike's note to Meyer. Almost two decades after that felicitous moment, Richard Nixon would resign his presidency in abject disgrace, an unprecedented event encouraged by the *Post*'s Watergate coverage.

Meyer, who died at the age of eighty-three on July 17, 1959, came to journalism well past the midstream of his life. Journalism, however, was where his future wife, Agnes Ernst Meyer, began making a living after she finished putting herself through Barnard College—in spite of her father's outburst ("I would rather see you dead.") when she told him she intended to become a reporter. Agnes Ernst, a tall beauty, began working for the *New York Morning Sun* in 1907; she was the first woman reporter in the city room of that venerable journal. She remained a vigorous and progressive-minded reporter and commentator through most of her life. When she died in 1970 at the age of eighty-three, a *Post* staffer informally eulogized her: "Agnes Meyer was a gutsy old girl. She was warm, difficult, irresponsible, arrogant. She had one of the first-class minds of the century. She was extraordinary in every way. She kept her wits right up to the day she died." "Brunhilde with a typewriter," one of her friends called her.

In the spring of 1943 German forces were retreating in North Africa and the Japanese were being pounded back in the South Pacific. Agnes Meyer, then a fifty-six-year-old grandmother, had spent weeks beating around war plants and military bases reporting the losing fight against juvenile delinquency. Her Lutheran preacher ancestors would have said "Amen" to her scorching prose. Under a Seattle dateline, she wrote of "these forces of darkness . . . the invisible, nameless, but no less powerful underworld forces, the leeches, panderers and racketeers, as firmly entrenched here as in many of our big cities, that never fight in the open, but work relentlessly to keep their hold on the rich graft to be derived from the prostitution racket." Mrs. Meyer discovered the "Victory girls": "Many of them are girls with a curiously perverted sense of patriotism who would not think of having sex relations with a civilian but feel they are doing something patriotic for their country when they enter into such relationships with members of the armed services. Most of them scorn to accept money." The trouble, she reported, was that these generous young women were also giving away gonorrhea and syphilis.

Mrs. Meyer used the columns of the *Post*, the speaker's rostrum, and her ready access to the politically powerful as the pulpits of reform. She fought no small battles: She took on the Catholic Church for its opposition to federal aid to public education; exposed coal operators for their gross neglect of miners; attacked the evils of racial segregation; and denounced Red-baiting Senator Joseph R. McCarthy, as did the *Post*, before most other critics mustered the courage.

Eugene Meyer was skittish about his wife's bluntness in public lest her words be regarded as also the *Post*'s. The paper already was the target of critics who labeled it "the downtown Pravda" for its stout defense of civil liberties. Meyer was not anxious to add new enemies. On one occasion Meyer, who was leaving town, asked editorial writer

Alan Barth, an unshakable civil libertarian, to read a speech Mrs. Meyer was writing before it was made public to "keep her out of trouble." The publisher's wife invited Barth to tea. "I walked into the sitting room," he recalled, "and she told me 'I know "Euge" told you to read my speech to keep me from making waves, but I've already mimeographed it and sent it out so you don't have to feel embarrassed.' " "She was a Valkyrie, a big, overpowering woman like a super-dreadnought," said Barth with affection.

Eugene and Agnes Meyer lived in a large house that faced Henderson Castle, a fortresslike mansion that was built in 1888 by Senator John B. Henderson, the author of the Thirteenth Amendment, which barred slavery. For half a century the "Castle" was a center of Washington high society. But it became vacant and fell into decay. In 1947 Mrs. Meyer bought the mansion and its walled six-acre grounds as a trust for her twelve grandchildren.

She thought at one time of turning the site into a park with a planetarium to attract famous astronomer Harlow Shapley to Washington. On Agnes's seventieth birthday, in 1957, Shapley named a whirl of stars that he had discovered "the Agnes Spiral." But her son-in-law, Philip Graham, had other ideas for the property. "He wanted to develop the site with high rises and make a killing," according to Elizabeth Rowe, who headed the National Capital Planning Commission. Libby Rowe was a friend of the Meyers' children. Her husband, James Rowe, Jr., was one of Lyndon Johnson's advisors. Her brother-in-law, Alfred Friendly, was then the managing editor of the *Post.* The weed-choked Henderson property at the edge of the black ghetto stood idle as the city's shortage of decent housing for low-income families worsened. The tract lay within a proposed urban renewal area. Lawyers for the Meyer-Graham family succeeded in having the property excised from the renewal project. Mrs. Rowe found this hypocritical when the *Post* was urging full-speed-ahead on urban renewal elsewhere in Washington. The elimination of these six acres helped doom the overall project. In the late 1960s Katharine Graham, as one of her mother's trustees, responded favorably to a nonprofit organization's proposal to erect on the tract housing for the elderly and for low-income families. Mrs.

Meyer, confined by arthritis to a wheelchair in her home across from the site, sent word to the architects that the view from her second-floor window was not to be obstructed. They spent several months revising the plans to meet her objection. But the project died on the drawing board because of inadequate federal housing subsidies. A private developer bought the property for $2.5 million and erected 216 luxury town houses. Mrs. Graham regretted the outcome but she explained that there was no choice other than to do the best for Agnes's grandchildren.

Agnes Meyer could be an awesome personage, even stuck in a wheelchair. Writer Judith Viorst interviewed Mrs. Meyer a few years before her death. "She asked me whether I preferred cream or lemon with tea," the writer recalled. "I said 'cream'—and Mrs. Meyer served me lemon. She said she couldn't stand bangs that get down into the eyes—and I went home and cut off my bangs." Mrs. Meyer presented her granddaughter, Elizabeth "Lally" Graham, with three expensive dresses just before her wedding. Katharine Graham asserted that her daughter should not wear the long black gown because it was cut so low. Agnes declared she could wear it anytime she "damn well pleased." It was a "glorious scene," Lally related to a friend. Agnes, as usual, prevailed. She dominated Katharine.

"I'm goddamned glad Mrs. Meyer wasn't running the paper," asserted Frank Waldrop, who for many years edited the rival *Times-Herald*. "She would have been tough. While Eugene Meyer ran an honest newspaper and a literate newspaper, he did not run a popular newspaper. . . . Agnes Meyer," Waldrop continued, "contributed more humaneness to the *Post* than anyone I knew. She was alive and human. She understood what Eleanor Patterson [the *Times-Herald* publisher] understood: The typical Washington resident then was a girl about twenty-six, had to get a job, was away from home and one disastrous marriage (or one disastrous nonmarriage), had some education, and was lonesome. Patterson had a flawless eye for what would attract this model Washingtonian. Meyer never really understood what we understood so well: The hell with what the president thinks; what does the government clerk think?" Meyer was too much a man of power to be unconcerned about the thought processes of the man in the White

House. There was one thing, however, about the *Times-Herald* that he understood quite completely: He wanted to own it.

As World War II sparked the rapid growth of Washington, the *Post* began making a little money. Circulation and advertising climbed under Meyer's persistent demands that the newspaper had to be profitable and independent of his personal funds. Agnes even checked up on inattentive carrier boys and suggested to Eugene where the *Post* might increase subscriptions in the suburbs. Meyer's drive to make the newspaper a money-making proposition, said Al Friendly, was more existential than a financier's compulsion. "The paper in the black was for him an outward and visible symbol of inward and spiritual tidiness," Friendly remarked.

The *Post* had become an important and admired newspaper. But by 1953, twenty years after Meyer's takeover, the *Post* was getting less than 25 percent of the advertising and circulation of the four Washington newspapers—including by then the combined *Times* and *Herald.* Business manager John Sweeterman still had to okay even a five-dollar raise for a deserving reporter. Then in 1954, on St. Patrick's Day, Eugene Meyer and Phil Graham closed one of the truly great deals in American newspaper history. They set the company on the course of empire.

Eleanor Medill Patterson, a member of the families that owned the *Chicago Tribune* and the *New York Daily News,* had acquired the *Herald* and the *Times* from William Randolph Hearst and combined them into a ten-edition round-the-clock newspaper with more circulation than any other Washington paper; she was a fierce competitor for her erstwhile friend, Gene Meyer. When Mrs. Patterson took over the papers in 1935, their combined deficit was $1,363,000; ten years later their profit was more than $1 million. Cissy Patterson's newspaper echoed the isolationist and sometimes ranting conservative bias of the *Tribune* and the *Daily News* in contrast to the *Post*'s internationalist and moderate politics.

Mrs. Patterson died suddenly in 1948, leaving the *Times-Herald* to seven executives of the paper. Their collective management stumbled and things were complicated by a pressing need to pay estate taxes.

Meyer and Philip Graham, who with his wife, Katharine, had acquired the controlling stock of the *Washington Post* from the Meyers in 1948, quickly moved to buy, and probably erase, a competitor. The executives were close to accepting the offer when Cissy's cousin, Colonel Robert R. McCormick, publisher of the *Chicago Tribune,* countered with a better proposition, reportedly $4.5 million, that included his commitment to continue publishing the paper—an unlikely sequel to a successful bid from the *Post.* McCormick installed his niece, Ruth McCormick Miller, as publisher. She soon had the paper on the skids. McCormick stepped in as publisher in 1951 to salvage the situation; the *Times-Herald,* however, was bleeding millions of dollars, and he was in failing health. McCormick, who had a conservative's antipathy to Washington, "had lost his sense of adventure, it wasn't fun anymore," recalled Frank Waldrop. "He had heard 'the knock,' and wanted to get his affairs in order." Late in January 1954, McCormick signalled his willingness to sell to Meyer.

Waldrop, who was one of the seven inheritors of the *Times-Herald,* believed McCormick was willing to sell to his rival because Meyer had supported McCormick when the colonel tried to prevent a competitor to his *Chicago Tribune* from getting news through the Associated Press. Newspapers are, foremost, a business. The AP excluded a newspaper from its wire service if the paper competed with an AP member. The *Post* belonged to the AP and Eugene Meyer also had invoked this restriction in 1942 to bar Mrs. Patterson's *Times-Herald* from an important source of news. This interference with the free flow of news later was overturned by the Supreme Court on antitrust grounds. McCormick also respected Meyer as a fellow Yale man and a successful publisher.

Without hesitation Meyer and Graham agreed to McCormick's asking price of $8.5 million, with another $1 million for severance pay for *Times-Herald* employees. (The Justice Department did not examine the deal for possible antitrust violations, and Waldrop wondered whether Meyer's support of Eisenhower influenced Attorney General Herbert Brownell. Perhaps, but the sale still left three competing dailies in Washington, a fact which would weaken an antitrust case.)

The *Post* shrewdly incorporated from the *Times-Herald* two more pages of comic strips, several columnists whose world view was far to the right of the *Post*'s, and popular sports writers—a move that helped hold for the suddenly fattened *Post* an amazingly large share of the *Times-Herald*'s readership. Almost overnight, the *Post* took the lead in circulation among the three remaining dailies and headed toward the lead in advertising. The retention by the acquiring paper of so much of the former competitor's circulation was unprecedented. "After 1954," said Al Friendly, "the *Post* was safe as a newspaper." The *Times-Herald* deal, Friendly said, "was the key. Other properties helped make money, but the newspaper then was like the Rock of Gibraltar."

Katharine Graham, who had her father's business sense and was willing to risk much for big stakes, years later recalled that monumental event. "One of us was bound to go under," she said of the rivalry between the two newspapers. "Then by persistence and good luck the colonel sold to us. It gave us a base from which they could build." Her father and husband had "created something out of nothing, by gambling," she said. They gambled, though, with all the odds in their favor.

Philip Graham had barely turned schoolage when his father and schoolteacher mother moved with him from a tiny South Dakota mining town to the edge of the Everglades near Miami, then a city for only twenty-five years and with fewer than thirty thousand people. Ernest Graham, an engineer, supervised an experimental sugar plantation that later failed. But he emerged with land holdings that later left the family prosperous as Miami burgeoned. The senior Graham served in the state senate and lost a race for the Democratic gubernatorial nomination in 1943. His youngest son, Robert Graham, a millionaire real estate developer, was elected governor of Florida in 1978.

After graduating from the University of Florida, Phil Graham went to Harvard Law School, edited the *Law Review,* and graduated tenth in his class. He grew close to one of his professors, Felix Frankfurter; after Frankfurter later went on the Supreme Court Graham served as his law clerk. The tall, lanky, dark-haired lawyer met Katharine Meyer and quickly proposed. They were married in June 1940.

After Graham returned from the war, Gene Meyer brought the son-in-law he loved and admired into the family business. Graham was often in the newsroom, a vibrant man with lively ideas and an openness that appealed to the reporters. He brought them together with the top editors for drinks and long, informal lunches and freewheeling talk without regard for protocol. He was not one of the boys, of course, but the reporters liked to think of him that way. After the *Post* began digging into local police corruption, an honest cop sneaked to the *Post* nearly six hundred official records on three-by-five cards which indicated lax law enforcement. Phil and others on the staff spent all night reproducing the records in the paper's photo lab so the officer could slip them back into the police files in the morning. Another time he spotted a brief business item and sent the clipping to his city editor with a note, "This is worth looking into." The staff followed up the boss's lead and uncovered a savings and loan scandal in Maryland.

Before he joined Meyer, Graham seriously considered moving back to Florida to practice law and enter politics. He would have made a superb politician: creatively intelligent, future-minded, generous in spirit, physically attractive, articulate, restlessly conscientious, loyal, energetic. As it was he used those superlative qualities to improve the *Post,* expand into broadcasting, and buy *Newsweek;* and he used them politically with dramatic effect without ever holding any public office. He was a New Dealer who supported Republicians when that seemed the best route to achieve his aims. In the last years of his life Eugene Meyer watched with heavy heart as his beloved Phil slipped into an emotional whirlpool that would eventually consume him.

In time Graham became deeply enmeshed with Lyndon Baines Johnson. He was an inner-sanctum counselor and political operator for Johnson and used his paper's news columns, as well as the editorial page, to advance the Texan's ambitions. "I think my husband and Johnson had a lot in common," Katharine Graham reflected after Johnson's presidency. "They regarded a lot of issues in the same way. The main thing about them, as I look back on it, is that they both had a fascination with power, and with the use of power. I think Phil admired the way Senator Johnson ran the Senate, the way he got done what he wanted to get done." A close friend of Graham, Joseph Rauh, Jr., a leading liberal labor and civil rights lawyer, had a harsher view of the relationship: "Johnson played Phil like a harmonica. He was mesmerized by Johnson."

By the mid-1950s Johnson, the Senate majority leader, was reconnoitering his presidential possibilities. The seemingly unbreachable barrier between him and the presidency, which he recognized as clearly as anyone, was his southern connections and his record of voting to maintain the racial status quo in Dixie when the liberal wing of his party was championing federal laws to end racial injustice.

In 1954 the Supreme Court established a momentous new fact of political and social life by ruling an end to public school segregation. Massive resistance was the immediate answer in much of the South. When the Democrats convened in Chicago in August 1956 to nominate their presidential candidate they were sorely challenged to ward off a split over the segregation issue. Adlai Stevenson, who lost the election in 1952, was the front runner for renomination and anxious to hold southern support. Averill Harriman was the favorite of delegates who were pushing for tough enforcement of desegregation. Senator Johnson, with a bloc of southern delegates, was a potential compromise nominee.

The liberals demanded implementation by all public officials of the school desegregation decision as well as protection of voting rights, outlawing of the poll tax, and other civil rights measures. The majority position, supported by the Southern delegates, was bare of any pledge for direct enforcement of the Supreme Court's decision. Adopted over the objections of the enfeebled liberals, the Democratic plank declared:

> Recent decisions of the Supreme Court of the United States relating to segregation in publicly supported schools and elsewhere have brought consequences of vast importance to our Nation as a whole and especially to communities directly affected. We reject all proposals for the use of force to interfere with the orderly determination of these matters by the courts.

"It was ludicrous double-talk," charged Joe Rauh. "To some the second sentence meant opposition to vigilantes preventing desegregation; to others it meant opposition to executive and legislative action in support of desegregation. But no one could read it as an all-out endorsement and promise of enforcement of the Supreme Court's decision."

Phil Graham had a large and deft hand in fashioning the waffling plank. It did keep the Democrats intact, which was Johnson's goal, if not altogether satisfied. The party renominated Stevenson, but Johnson's reputation as a brilliant political strategist was magnified. Chicago was the prelude to Graham's further labors with Johnson to pass a civil rights act the following year. During this period Phil and Katharine Graham spent a weekend with Johnson at his ranch in Texas. It was her first close touch with Johnson. Johnson contended that Northerners were liberal theoreticians who didn't know how to deal practically with race relations. "He thought that I was a bit more liberal than my husband," Mrs. Graham recalled.

In the summer of 1957, the House passed a bill giving the government tough sanctions with which to enforce desegregation, and sent it to the Senate, the graveyard for such legislation because the Southerners controlled that chamber's machinery. Johnson saw the country as well as his own presidential aspirations advancing through enactment of legislation that responded to Negro and liberal pleas. He began maneuvering delicately to pass a bill restricted to protecting the right to vote. His strategy was to avoid goading the Southerners to filibuster the bill to death.

Johnson's tactic was to remove the injunction power that the House gave the Justice Department to enforce court-ordered desegregation, and to substitute jury trials when these orders were disobeyed. This, he correctly figured, would gain the bill's passage. Phil and Kay Graham had invited Justice Felix Frankfurter and Joe Rauh to spend the day at their country estate in Virginia—an hour from Washington. Over drinks after tennis, Rauh, who was Frankfurter's first law clerk, argued against Johnson's plan, which Graham and Frankfurter praised. Minus sanctions, asserted Rauh, it would make a mockery of desegregation. But Graham agreed with the Johnson thesis that other rights and benefits would soon follow if the right to vote were secured for Negroes.

As the fight in the Senate waxed hot, Johnson phoned Graham for help to lobby liberal opponents, and the publisher moved in with

Johnson until the bill passed. The Southerners went home and claimed victory, asserting that their states' resistance to desegregation of the schools had been confirmed. Rauh was convinced the act and the debate leading to it had set back school integration by several years. Nevertheless, the voting rights act of 1957 was the first civil rights law enacted by Congress since Reconstruction, and was the forerunner of a series of such laws. Graham's part in it, Johnson would say many times, was decisive. Editorially the *Post* endorsed the rising civil rights movement out of a dedication to justice. It was a pragmatic decision, too; Washington was becoming a predominently black city.

Lyndon Johnson had run a hobbled half-hearted campaign for the Democratic presidential nomination in 1956. But he was regarded as a more realistic candidate for 1960; Phil Graham among others so viewed him. The rising star in the polls, however, was the handsome, forty-one-year-old senator from Massachusetts, John F. Kennedy. One night in 1958 at columnist Joseph Alsop's Georgetown home—after most of the guests had left except for Kennedy and his wife, Katharine Graham and Alice Roosevelt Longworth, one of Washington's living artifacts—the *Post*'s publisher told Kennedy: "Jack, you're good. I'm sure you will be president some day, but I think you are too young to run now and I hope you don't." Graham was twenty-two months older than Kennedy. Kennedy replied that he was running for three reasons: He thought he was better than any other possible candidate, except Lyndon Johnson; if he didn't run someone else would, and most likely would be in office for eight years and probably dictate his successor; and if he stayed in the Senate intending to run one day, he would end up being "a lousy senator and a lousy candidate." The recollection of that evening was Mrs. Graham's. In her own mind, she was unsure if her husband supported Johnson from a true belief that the Texan would become president, or even nominee. "I think he didn't, because both Johnson and my husband were rather realistic about the possibility of a Southerner being nominated." In December 1959, however, Graham told associates that Johnson would win the nomination in a three-way battle with Kennedy and Adlai Stevenson. Privately Graham still urged Johnson to drive for the presidential nomination. He contributed five to ten thousand dollars to support that bid, according to Mrs. Graham; wrote speeches for LBJ; and drafted Johnson's July 5 statement announcing his candidacy. But the convention was six days away and John Kennedy's precision-tooled organization had the nomination all but clinched for their man.

Graham's mother-in-law had a different candidate. Twenty-four hours before the convention opened, seventy-three-year-old Agnes Meyer addressed seven thousand persons at a National Association for the Advancement of Colored People rally. Kennedy had spoken to the mostly black crowd and got only perfunctory applause. The mention of Johnson by various speakers drew boos. Negroes obviously were uncertain about their prospects with the Democrats. Mrs. Meyer read to the assemblage an endorsement by Eleanor Roosevelt of Adlai Stevenson, twice-before the party's losing candidate. The two socially conscious women had publicly argued with each other over the New Deal's welfare policies during FDR's early years; their mutual devotion, however, to the improvement of public education overshadowed their earlier differences. Until she voted for Stevenson in 1956, Mrs. Meyer was an unbudgeable Republican in the progressive fold. She told the NAACP rally on that sultry Sunday that she had abandoned the GOP because it lacked leadership. "Don't let Nixon forget on election day that he did nothing to help your cause for eight long years," she urged the audience in Los Angeles.

The next day the convention opened. With Kennedy virtually assured the nomination, the *Post* ran a front-page speculative story. The article was intended to propel a political agreement in which Phil Graham himself was an actor. The byline was reporter Richard Lyons's but the source was Graham. The writer seemed to be privy to Kennedy's innermost tactical thinking: "He had mulled over in his mind for some time now the problem of healing the pre-convention breach with Johnson. There is no doubt that Kennedy is fully prepared to come to working terms with Johnson, that he realizes the total necessity of doing so. . . . Kennedy knows that Johnson is vain and that he will be hurt by a defeat at the hands of a junior senator. But Kennedy also believes that Johnson is a big man, able to swallow defeat and to work with him for the good of the party and the good of the nation."

There was another Graham-inspired report the next morning: "The word—as well as the logic of the situation—is that Kennedy has decided to ask Johnson to run on the ticket and that he hopes the senator will accept . . . the arguments in favor of a bid to Johnson were most convincing to Kennedy." Johnson on the ticket, the article said, would add votes in all sections of the country, capture the Republican-leaning southern states, and heal the breach between the liberal and conservative wings of the party.

A week after the convention, Graham wrote a long memorandum to himself that detailed his intimate behind-the-scenes role in Kennedy's decision to offer second place on the ticket to Johnson, and the Texan's decision to accept. His intention most likely was to preserve the narrative for some future use, perhaps in his own memoirs. The publisher disagreed with Theodore H. White's description of the Los Angeles transaction in *Making of the President 1960;* he sent the author a copy of the memo. White, as Mrs. Graham recalled the episode, asked her if he could use the memo in his subsequent chronicle of the 1964 campaign. She acquiesced only to be "quite horrified" that White published it verbatim. Johnson by then was president. She thought it was too soon to tell the episode in such detail. Graham described how he and Post columnist Joseph Alsop urged Kennedy to offer Johnson the vice-presidential spot and to do so sincerely since Johnson was likely to accept. Graham moved back and forth between the Kennedy and Johnson hotel suites arguing this course. Other Democratic strategists were also counseling the same decision. Kennedy made the offer privately and Johnson accepted. Robert Kennedy was furious at Graham's description of him conducting a desperate attempt to get Johnson to change his mind because of liberal opposition to the Texan. Graham recited in the memo how he impatiently told John what his brother had done. Kennedy reassured Graham, "Bobby's been out of touch and doesn't know what's been happening." Robert Kennedy later told Mrs. Graham, "Phil didn't know us then. My brother and I would never have been apart." RFK, by then a senator, was bruised by the published report that he was out of "sync" with his brother at such a critical moment. In fact, he was acting on vacillating instructions from JFK, whose remark to Graham about Bobby may have been a ploy to avoid personal embarrassment. Graham was close to Johnson, and Johnson could not be budged in any event from his eager acceptance.

After his frantic intercession between Kennedy and Johnson, Graham hurried to find his wife in the convention hall to share the tale. He was trembling from tension and excitement; he held the story until they found a place to have a drink away from the convention hall babbling. Graham always ran at a frantic pace. He and Katharine had gone to Puerto Rico earlier in the year for a long vacation, but he wasn't sleeping well and Joe Alsop couldn't induce him to use sleeping pills to get some rest.

Before Kennedy was inaugurated telephone operators at the *Post* frequently heard Graham order, "Get me Palm Beach." Kennedy was in Florida resting from the campaign and organizing his administration. One of Graham's friends nicknamed him "Warwick" after the kingmaker of fifteenth-century England. Graham had a hand in the appointment of Douglas Dillon as secretary of the treasury. He urged that his friend David Bruce be sent to England as the American ambassador. But although his mental state was worsening, he had periods of tremendous effectiveness, in politics and business.

Phil Graham leaned across to his companion in the first-class section of the Los Angeles–bound airliner and read aloud from his yellow legal pad: "Bonn, Cairo, Rome, Athens . . . How does that sound to you?" he asked Erwin Knoll, an editor on the *Post.* "Terrific," replied the Vienna-born Knoll. "Can we find the people in thirty days?" the forty-six-year-old publisher asked. It was the autumn of 1961, and Graham, Knoll, and managing editor Al Friendly were on their way to work out an exchange of news agreement with the *Los Angeles Times.* The capitals Graham exuberantly ticked off were among those where the two newspapers considered basing correspondents. The joint venture initially provided that if the *Post* opened a bureau in Bonn, for example, the *Times* would place a correspondent in, say, New Delhi, and so on until the principal news centers of the globe were covered by either of the two papers. Each paper would receive the reports of the other's writers.

The time was ripe for both newspapers to be expansive. The *Post* had become the dominant of Washington's three dailies, and its preeminence was generating more wealth from advertising and circulation. Graham, who had taken over the *Post* when it was trailing the capital's other newspapers, was pumping more cash into better coverage and beefing up news-staff salaries. Five years earlier in an interview for a *Time* cover story, Graham expressed his dream of greatness for his paper: "I want independence and institutionalism. Before I die, I should like to see the *Post* like *La Prensa* of Buenos Aires, the *Times* of London or the *New York Times*. . . ." But at the time these words were spoken, the seven reporters on the *Post*'s national staff equaled only one-third the force in the *New York Times*' Washington bureau. The *Post*'s sole foreign bureau was in London. "We were assaulted by our Georgetown readership for lack of foreign coverage," recalled Al Friendly. "But we were broke until we bought the *Times-Herald*. It cost thirty to forty thousand dollars a year to send a correspondent abroad then." Even the expense of maintaining the lone London outpost riled executive vice-president John W. Sweeterman. There on business he asked the *Post*'s London correspondent, Murrey Marder, his impression of Walter Lippmann. Marder acknowledged his esteem for the eminent journalist. "Well," mused Sweeterman, "he contemplates the world from home." Graham knew that if his vision of greatness for the *Post* was to be realized, he would have to spend much more money for foreign reporting. "The genius of Phil Graham," reporter Chalmers Roberts said, "was in putting things together so they cost as little money as possible." Graham's idea to divide the costs of realizing his dream with the *Los Angeles Times* was brilliant. The timing was perfect.

Otis Chandler, a strapping, blond athlete, was thirty-two when he succeeded his father as publisher of the *Los Angeles Times*, a prosperous, politically potent, and parochial newspaper. He had been boss less than two years when the arrangement with the *Post* developed. The sixth generation of his family to preside over the *Los Angeles Times*, Chandler had a more urgent and less visionary motive for uniting with

Graham, namely the imminent invasion of his paper's territory by the *New York Times.* Two other newspapers rooted in the East published West Coast editions—the *Wall Street Journal* since 1929 and the *Christian Science Monitor* since 1960. These were specialized newspapers and not really competitive with Chandler's daily. The *New York Times,* however, with its deep bench of Washington and foreign correspondents and regional reporters throughout the United States, was threatening. Chandler's paper, like Graham's, didn't have anywhere near such journalistic power. Playing rough but by the rules of the newspaper game, the *New York Times* halted its syndicated news service to western clients, including Chandler, in order to make its new edition the exclusive outlet in the West. With Graham's help Chandler would have his own network of correspondents to serve his flagship paper and the smaller newspapers in southern California that he planned to acquire. (The *New York Times* western edition failed to get the advertising and circulation it needed to survive. After sixteen months and a $2 million loss, the edition died.) Both Chandler and Graham also expected that a world-girdling network of reporters and superior coverage from Washington would gain national prestige for their papers. At the same time, they saw a dividend in journalistic quality for the twenty or so newspapers that they anticipated would subscribe to their service. Their expectation was too conservative. The service eventually would have some four hundred newspaper clients around the world; started as a device for improving the founders' papers without intent of its making money, the service later became profitable.

The creation of the *Times-Post* news service came in Philip Graham's manic phase when he was undergoing period psychiatric care. It was the second of two super deals that he forged in 1961. "Even when he was mad, his judgment was better than anyone I ever knew," said Al Friendly, Graham's close friend and a large stockholder in the company. Earlier that year in March Graham bought *Newsweek.* Founded in 1933, ten years after *Time, Newsweek* was virtually insolvent three years later. Among those who saved it from bankruptcy were multimillionaires Vincent Astor and W. Averill Harriman, and F. D. R. brain-truster Raymond Moley. (In 1933 when Eugene Meyer bought the *Post* at auction, one bid had been submitted for Harriman and Astor, who would have made Moley editor had they gotten the paper.) After Astor's death in 1959, the controlling interest in *Newsweek* passed to his philanthropic foundation. The magazine was reported to be for sale. Among those who first counseled Graham to buy the magazine were two *Newsweek* staffers, Benjamin C. Bradlee and Kenneth Crawford. Uninterested at first in acquiring the magazine, Graham soon perceived the news weeklies "as a pretty important branch of journalism." Press tycoon Samuel Newhouse, John Hay Whitney, Doubleday, and others also reportedly coveted *Newsweek;* "I felt if any of those people got control it would have been a disaster," Bradlee said.

Graham and Frederick S. Beebe, his legal counsel, devised a strategy that depended on Averill Harriman selling them his 12 percent block of *Newsweek* stock. Al Friendly had been an aide to Harriman in 1949 when Harriman ran the Marshall Plan recovery program in Europe. Harriman was traveling in Italy, and Graham dispatched Friendly, without alerting Harriman, to persuade him to sell. Friendly phoned Harriman at 8 A.M. from the lobby of his hotel in Rome, went up to the old diplomat's room, pulled open the drapes, and announced, "I'm here to offer you $2 million for your *Newsweek* stock." They talked and Harriman accepted. At the editor's request, Harriman cabled the Astor Foundation trustees to recommend sale to Graham on the moral ground that the *Post* company would be a responsible publisher. After his own lobbying of the trustees, Graham paid $15 million for the magazine which included a 49 percent interest in a television station. Graham sold the television interest. There was $3 million in *Newsweek's* cashbox. So *Newsweek* actually cost Graham $9 million—only $75,000 of it in cash—an amazing bargain considering what the magazine was to become. Another bastion of the *Post* empire was in place.

In 1968 *Newsweek* pushed ahead of *Time* in domestic advertising. The next year brought record pre-tax profits. But then profits fell sharply and the 1974–75 recession further reduced the newsweekly's net. Rumors persisted that *Newsweek* was for sale, and CBS and Westinghouse made overtures to buy it, to no avail. As the recession passed, many advertisers could not buy time on television networks, which were fully booked. They turned to the national magazines, and *News-*

week thrived anew. By 1977, *Newsweek* and its related book operation were spawning annual profits approaching more than three times what Graham paid for the magazine.

After Lyndon Johnson was elected vice-president, Graham acted as his attorney in picking and buying a house suitable for his expanded social needs. The house he chose had antique paneling and parquet floors imported from France, sparkling chandeliers in the main rooms; the grounds included a topiary, a circular fountain, and a summer house. Another confidant of Johnson, Abe Fortas, whom he appointed to the Supreme Court, argued with Graham that Johnson would be hurt politically by this sumptuous display, but Johnson bought the place. A few days after John Kennedy was assassinated, Lady Bird Johnson phoned to invite Katharine Graham for a quiet evening at the Johnson home, now guarded by a legion of Secret Service agents. The Johnsons had not yet moved to the White House. The new president gazed at a portrait of the late Speaker Sam Rayburn and somberly told Mrs. Graham that the people he would miss as he entered his new office were Rayburn and her husband.

Melancholy clutched at the Johnsons and their few guests that night, but none could feel the gloom more deeply than Katharine Graham. Three months earlier, Phil had been in a suburban Washington sanatorium for treatment of the manic depression that had kept him on an emotional roller coaster for years. He seemed to be better, and his psychiatrist thought that a weekend at the Graham's country estate in Virginia would help. Phil and Katharine were there with just the servants. While she was elsewhere in the house, he fired a single shotgun blast into his head. His death catapulted her into the upper reaches of power in America.

Unlike Phil, Katharine Graham would use her power at arm's length from politicians. "She wasn't going to get into bed with anyone politically," said one of her closest friends. "That was her natural inclination but it was strengthened by the experience between Lyndon Johnson and Phil." Still, for several years the *Post* and Johnson would travel the same road on the most bitter issue of recent times—Vietnam. Vietnam had deep repercussions for the next decade at the *Post.*

TWO

Waist Deep in the Big Muddy

. . . American policy-makers believed they could transform Hanoi's perceptions and ultimately influence its performance simply by projecting the right impression about U. S. intentions. And this quite naturally put a high premium on appearances. Thus, it was considered distinctly unhelpful, if not actually destructive of American interests, for the press to suggest that U. S. strategy wasn't working as advertised or that the war effort was failing, for this could only invite public questioning. And it was the conventional government wisdom that this, in turn, could only invite questions in Hanoi about American staying power.

—PHILIP L. GEYELIN, EDITOR OF THE *Washington Post* EDITORIAL PAGE

EUGENE MEYER LISTENED ATTENTIVELY to the small, dark-haired Frenchman as they sat in the American's suite in the Hotel Ritz in Paris. It was the autumn of 1951. Pierre Mendes-France, a Social-ist deputy who would become premier in three years, stressed to the seventy-six-year-old chairman of the *Washington Post* France's agonizing predicament in Indochina. The costly struggle to retain her colonies threatened to bankrupt France. Meyer was sympathetic; his family's roots ran deep in Alsace. But more than familial ties motivated him. He was a tough, politically outspoken businessman and financier who believed that strong allies in Europe were essential to America's own security. After the Germans overran France in 1940, Meyer fired his editorial-page editor Felix Morley because of Mor-ley's conviction that the United States should stay out of Europe's quarrels.

As Meyer and Mendes-France talked, the war against Ho Chi Minh's nationalists was draining the cream of France's military manpower. "As long as we continue in Indochina there will be no French army in Europe," the politician warned. Meyer found this alarming. France was crucial to American strategy in Europe. Meyer regarded Europe as the main arena in the West's contest against communism. Southeast Asia was a distracting sideshow. Moreover, it was a huge region that was little understood by the men who directed the *Post.* "The war in Indochina is a bottomless pit that is soaking up most of the financial aid [to France] from the United States," Meyer concluded in an article he co-authored with his editor J. Russell Wiggins after their 1951 trip to Europe. In time, Americans replaced Frenchmen in Vietnam. The succession came fractionally, an inch at a time in the beginning, hardly perceptible to the American people.

But as our involvement deepened other critics for other reasons would again liken the embattled region to a "bottomless pit." The *Post* was not among them. Longer than most major newspapers the *Post* endorsed the government's disastrous policies in Vietnam; the distrust of government that was a legacy of Vietnam fueled the paper's pursuit of Watergate. At first, though, the newspaper reacted warily to an aggressive role in Indochina for this country.

By mid-April 1954, the French had their backs to the wall in Indochina. Admiral Arthur W. Radford, chairman of the Joint Chiefs of Staff, told members of the American Society of Newspaper Editors at the Pentagon that "free nations cannot afford to permit a further extension of the power of militant communism in Asia." The *Post* was dubious about any American armed venture to save the French. "American military men, with the possible exception of Admiral Radford, are almost uniformly gloomy about the outlook for military success in Indo-China . . . the American people, and their allies,need to be told frankly what the facts and the risks are. . . ." Next day the newspaper editors were briefed by a high government official, who under his strict ground rules was to be unnamed by the journalists in their stories so that he presumably could speak more candidly. "He had them enthralled by a speech that could not be more alarming," recalled Clayton Fritchey whose column runs in the *Post.* "It was a brilliant presentation of the situation in Indochina. When he finished the first question was, in effect, 'If it's as serious as you say, are we just going to sit still or send in troops?' Without hesitation he answered, "Send in the troops." With that Fritchey slipped from the meeting room and phoned an account that included the official's name to the Washington correspondent of the *London Telegraph*, who was not bound by the off-the-record agreement. When his story broke in the British press the high official was identified as Vice President Richard Nixon. Fritchey, a Stevensonian Democratic, believed that the disclosure helped deter the Eisenhower administration from an armed intervention. "I had the feeling that if we did go in to rescue the French, the editors would all have rallied around the flag," recalled Fritchey. Such a move was cut off, however, when a few key Senate Democrats including Lyndon Johnson voiced deep pessimism, the British were unwilling to go along and the French were too exhausted to prolong the war.

A few days before the French surrendered on May 2, 1954, the *Post* signalled its support for a larger American presence in Vietnam's future. "We cannot stand aside and abandon the French and the Associated States to an ignominious fate without suffering an erosion of our own vital interests in Asia . . . [the United States] has belatedly discovered that talk of massive retaliation is no answer to the kind of internal subversion abetted by China but parading under the banner of nationalism and anti-colonialism."

An uncertain truce stilled the guns in Indochina, the Korean war was over, and Stalin's successors in the Kremlin declared their goal to be coexistence with the West. At home industrial production had fallen sharply, and tax cuts were being urged to lift the economy out of a severe recession. A *Post* editorial asked whether the United States was "resilient enough to sieze the chance for abatement of the cold war if such chance exists?" The piece riled Philip Graham. "I would like to raise a warning signal against what seems to me a rush toward an uncritical acceptance of something called 'co-existence' in general United States thinking the last few months," publisher Graham told editorial-page editor Robert Estabrook in a two-page memo. Graham continued:

. . . A year or so ago it was clear to all of us that the Soviet system was one of total evil—one with which nothing but "self-enforcing" agreement could be made. That, in my opinion, has not changed. We ought to be very much on guard against the powerful pulls exerted by the temptations to revise that opinion. And how powerful they are. The fear of a hydrogen cataclysm; the burdens of armaments, selective service, taxation, a security system . . . all these evaporate once one embraces the fullest hopes of "co-existence." . . . "Co-existence," I submit, is every ounce a bastard idea, sired by Wish, and mothered by Cold-war weariness. . . .

The publisher urged that the *Post* "keep continually in front" of its readers the evil of Soviet totalitarianism; the need to possibly wage "local conflicts" against further communist expansion; and the "inevitability" of high defense spending. Graham also commended "peaceful and adroit subversion" of the Soviet Empire. It was a view held by many high government officials including senior executives of the Central Intelligence Agency who were among Graham's closest friends.

Graham's combative injunction laid down an editorial policy line that would encourage perpetuation of the dangerous tensions between the two superpowers. His premises in large measure eventually shaped the *Post*'s editorial view on the Soviet-American rivalry for more than a decade, even beyond his lifetime. There was an ironic twist in this. In defense of liberty the *Post* vigorously denounced Joe McCarthy's wild Red-hunting which threatened this country with the sort of political thought control practiced in the Soviet Union. Yet the cold war gospel, preached over and over by political leaders and widely embraced by the press, accomplished its purpose in part by creating a climate of public fear. In such an atmosphere the political freedom treasured by the *Post* was undermined by the government in the name of defending America from international communism.

April of 1961 was a terribly disquieting month for the infant Kennedy government: Civil war threatened France over President de Gaulle's announced withdrawal from rebellious Algeria; in Laos American military advisors went into combat with the right-wing government against communist elements in what would become a prolonged secret war for the United States; and the CIA-engineered invasion of Cuba had failed miserably. (The judgment of failure was not unanimous. Clayton Fritchey was an overnight guest at the White House and told a glum president,

"Don't feel so bad. You might have won; then where would you be running Cuba."

"That's the first bright thing I've heard," Kennedy laughed.)

In the wake of that disaster President Kennedy looked for more effective means to oppose the spread of communism in Latin America and Southeast Asia. One impediment was the fact that the United States was a party to international agreements barring intervention in the affairs of other countries. The *Post* viewed these treaties as obsolete in the face of shadowy dangers to America's own interests. "The United States is committed in a series of international undertakings to consultative and nonviolent methods in the settlement of disputes, and this country has paid obsequious service to the doctrine of nonintervention," stated an editorial alongside a Herblock cartoon of a straw-hatted Cuban with a rifle and a banner proclaiming, "Freedom Si, Castro No!" "Yet it could be altogether self-defeating," the editorial added, "to become so wrapped up in narrow legalisms as to miss the point." For the *Post* the point was that "the increasing communist grip in Cuba" had to be broken with American help if needed. The *Post* expressed regret at this country's long connection with the pre-Castro rightist dictatorship and recognized the need for social and economic reform in Latin America, but regarded the totalitarian left as posing "far greater dangers." The *Post*'s editorialists struggled with the dicey implications for the American conscience of a stepped-up United States game of "dirty tricks" against the enemy. What the paper wanted, however, was for the United States to play the game more efficiently than it had at the Bay of Pigs, "without one hand tied behind its back," which also meant far more secretly.

Columnist Stewart Alsop did not equivocate over conscience. He wrote in the *Post:* ". . . Fidel Castro cannot indefinitely be permitted to survive in triumph. . . . There is hardly anybody in the higher reaches of the Kennedy administration who does not agree that this commitment to Castro's destruction now in fact exists. . . . Some day, one way or another, the American commitment to bring Castro down will have to be honored," Alsop said. "The commitment can only be honored if the American government is willing, if necessary, to strike to kill, even if that risks the shedding of American blood."

In the fall before Alsop's commentary, CIA officials set in train plans to assassinate Castro. There were at least eight plots to murder the Cuban president, some involving Mafia chieftains, the Senate Intelligence Committee reported in 1976, fifteen years after the events.

Alsop, who died in 1974, was a highly regarded journalist with excellent contacts in the White House and the intelligence community. Richard Bissell, the CIA official who planned the assault on Cuba, was an old friend of his. Alsop may have used the words "destruction" and "kill" figuratively; in any case, his choice of words and references to the White House are fascinating to consider in the light of uncertainty over whether Kennedy knew of the plans to assassinate Castro. "Stewart wrote that because he believed it," recalled his brother, Joseph, who was his frequent writing partner. "It's garbage to think he knew about the Castro assassination plot. No one wanted to know about dirty tricks, and if you did you kept your mouth shut about them." Surely, though, fervid columns and impassioned editorials in the *Post* and other papers shaped American opinion against Cuba and encouraged prolonged hostility between the two countries. The Cuban veterans of the Bay of Pigs who invaded the Watergate a decade later believed that they were striking at those who might end this enmity.

As that inflamed April of 1961 was ending, President Kennedy—whose promised direct intervention (if necessary to thwart communism) in Latin America and whose declaration that the United States "did not intend to abandon" Cuba drew wide newspaper endorsement—sought to water down the First Amendment's freedom of the press guarantee. Addressing the American Newspaper Publishers Association, the president sounded an alarm: "Our way of life is under attack. . . . The survival of our friends is in danger." He went on:

And yet no war has been declared, no borders have been crossed by marching troops, no missiles have been fired. If the press is awaiting a declaration of war before it imposes self-discipline of combat conditions, then I can only say that no war has ever imposed a greater threat to our security. If you are awaiting a finding of "clear and present danger," then I can only say that the danger has never been more clear and its presence more imminent. . . . I am asking the members of the newspaper profession and the industry in this country to re-examine their own responsibilities—to consider the degree and nature of the present danger—and to heed the duty of self-restraint which the danger imposes upon all of us. Every newspaper now asks itself with respect to every story: "Is it news?" All I suggest is that you add the question: "Is it in the interest of national security?"

Kennedy's emotional appeal, a mistake he did not repeat, did not completely convince the *Post* that an urgent need for increased secrecy existed. Skeptical that censorship would have altered the outcome of the Cuban landing, the newspaper argued, "Such restraint as the press exhibited already has brought it some reproach from critics who think more information might have headed off the calamity." Nevertheless, the paper was susceptible to Kennedy's alarm that Armageddon was at hand.

Chalmers Roberts, a *Post* reporter, long afterwards wrote that President Kennedy had told him in advance of the CIA's part in the invasion, but Roberts did not inform his readers at the time. Phil Graham and editors Russell Wiggins and Alfred Friendly agreed to this self-censorship. "The fact was that Graham, Wiggins, Friendly, and Roberts found no fault with such a CIA operation and hoped it would succeed in what they perceived as the national interest." The four men had all been in air force intelligence during World War II; they had understood the exigencies of military secrecy. But as journalists they had already done occasionally what Kennedy was now urging the press to do regularly—on questionable premises and in quite nebulous terms. They didn't publish what they reliably knew about the secret CIA reconnaissance flights over Russia, a fact known to Moscow, until a U-2 photo plane was shot down in 1960. As Roberts revealed in 1977 the *Post* also did not print its authoritative information that the United States had tried to bribe members of the French Assembly in the early

1950s to vote for unification of the West European armies, an alliance warmly backed by Meyer and Graham.

When Kennedy addressed the newspaper publishers, he may have been thinking ahead to his desire to shield operations in another part of the globe from public knowledge and, therefore, possible questioning of his policies. Pierre Salinger, his press secretary, explained later that with the Cuban debacle fresh at hand and a crisis looming in Berlin, Kennedy was "not anxious to admit the existence of a real war in Southeast Asia."

Katharine Graham visited Vietnam in early 1965 when things seemed to be going better for Saigon and the Americans. She felt convinced that the administration was right in its conduct of the war and the premises of its policies. "Once you were there," she reasoned, "you had to do what was necessary to hang in." After a surprise mortar attack on February 7 killed 8 Americans and wounded 126 at the Pleiku base, Defense Secretary Robert S. McNamara declared "this was a test of will, a clear challenge of the political purpose of both the United States and the South Vietnamese governments." The conflict, the *Post* editorialized, "is not an isolated battlefield but a part of a long war which the Communist world seems determined to continue until every vestige of Western power and influence have been driven from Asia . . . withdrawal from South Vietnam would not gain peace, but only lead to another war." Mrs. Graham was in wholehearted accord with this interpretation. Some time later at a lunch in the *Post*'s executive dining room the discussion turned to the advisability of pulling out of Vietnam. The publisher put the question to a vote of the dozen or so persons around the table. City editor Steven Isaacs alone voted for withdrawal. "You're so stupid, you're not thinking," she rebuked him.

Through most of that longest war in American history, the *Post* defended the government's policies in Vietnam. "*Post* editorialists," commented *Time* in 1966 as the fighting grew more fierce and disillusionment grew at home, "have often done a better job of explaining President Johnson's Far Eastern policies than the president himself." Inside the *Post*, however, Johnson's handling of the war was beginning to sharply divide those writers. For the first time their publisher, Katharine Graham, was wavering on the war.

Lyndon Johnson had just been nominated by the 1964 Democratic National Convention in Atlantic City. Katharine Graham had attended the convention; she was exhausted and anxious to get back to her Virginia estate to relax. But her company's plane could not take off ahead of the president's Air Force One. She stood with her daughter, Lally, watching the spectacle of the president's entourage assembling. In the soggy August heat that clung to the Jersey shore, Mrs. Graham did not look like the rich, socially prominent boss of a large corporation. Her graying brown hair, crumpled by the humidity and unattended for several days, lay limp beneath a bandana; she was stockingless and her suitcase was full of dirty clothes. And suddenly Lyndon Johnson stood in front of her, asking her to join him for a weekend at his Texas ranch. She suspected the invitation was merely a polite gesture. "Don't think he ever does something he doesn't mean to do," presidential aide Bill Moyers assured her as they flew south. After all, she was the widow of Johnson's close friend and unofficial counselor, Phil Graham; moreover, she was the publisher of the *Washington Post* and *Newsweek,* whose millions of readers were important to the president's ambitions.

Earlier that month, the *Post* had given unquestioning endorsement to Johnson's giant step that ratcheted up the scale of war in Southeast Asia. The attack by North Vietnamese PT boats on two American destroyers in the Gulf of Tonkin was viewed in Washington as the gravest incident in the war to that time. The White House regarded the incident as though it were Pearl Harbor or the sinking of the Maine. Within a few days Congress speedily adopted a resolution which had been secretly formulated in advance by the White House for presentation at a moment of fortuitous crisis. Authorizing the president "to take all necessary measures to repel any armed attack against the forces of the United States and to prevent further aggression," the declaration was virtually uncontested.

One of the two votes in the Senate against the resolution was cast by Wayne Morse, a maverick Oregon Democrat. The *Post* upbraided Morse for his "reckless and querulous dissent" in calling the United States the provocateur in the naval firefight. The other Senate dissenter to the Tonkin Gulf Resolution was Senator Ernest Gruening, Democrat of Alaska. Gruening and Morse were mavericks who were used to swimming against the popular tide. In late winter the elderly Gruening, who once edited the liberal *Nation* magazine, had urged the United States to withdraw from Vietnam, a rather presumptuous and lonely viewpoint at that stage of history. Neither the *Post* nor the *New York Times* reported Gruening's remarks. "The conventional newsroom wisdom was that no one paid attention to Gruening or to Wayne Morse, as if that relieved us of an obligation to give the public the opportunity to pay attention, should it care to," Morton Mintz, a veteran *Post* reporter, later reflected. On the editorial page was the declaration, "There is no substance in Senator Morse's charge that the resolution amounts to a 'predated declaration of war.' " But that is what it was. Undersecretary of State Nicholas Katzenbach, who one day would become a director of the Washington Post Company, testified later that the resolution was "the functional equivalent of a declaration of war." It was a lawyer-bureaucrat's artifice, but it meant exactly what Senator Morse suspected. The secret Pentagon Papers, which the *Post* was widely praised for publishing in 1971, confirmed what Morse had intuited and the *Post* had discounted: For six months before the Tonkin Gulf incident American forces were staging clandestine attacks on North Vietnam and joining in provocative South Vietnamese commando raids on islands in the North's waters. But in the summer of 1964 there was no general uncertainty about the United State's position in the country or its press.

After Atlantic City the president would not infrequently phone Kay Graham to explain some action he was taking, and he would include her in the the White House social activities. Then, abruptly, the relationship ceased. There was still a trace of hurt years later in Mrs. Graham's remembrance of the Johnson freeze: "He stopped speaking to me, literally, for a while, and even if I saw him in a big group he would not speak to me. I mean he wouldn't say 'hello.' I didn't even get asked to tea for two thousand at the White House, so I began to get the message." Johnson apparently was piqued at a report that she had told her editors that the president was "trying to buy me with dinners." She wrote to Johnson that the story was untrue. The relationship bobbed up and down at LBJ's whim.

After a time she was again invited to the White House; then came another long chill after *Newsweek* reported that the Vatican resented Johnson's apparent attempt to gain political advantage by making a quick visit to Pope Paul in Rome. Mrs. Graham was skiing in Sun Valley when Secretary of State Dean Rusk phoned to complain that the story was baseless. *Newsweek* was her magazine; in Johnson's mind responsibility for the offending story, ergo, was hers.

It was odd. Katharine Graham's considerable news organization was a friend of Johnson's foreign and domestic policies, and he was giving her the cold shoulder over minutiae. But his attitude was symptomatic of his thin skin, colossal ego, and conception of a free press as one, in Mrs. Graham's assessment, that "prints what he wants printed." He also detested those influential columnists and correspondents who had been close to his predecessor, John Kennedy. The "Georgetown set," he labeled them. Many of them were the friends of Mrs. Graham, whose newspaper carried their writing, and who also were on most occasions endorsers of Johnson's aims. She thought there was some truth in his feeling that they were intellectual and social snobs. When Richard Nixon and Spiro Agnew came to power they played Johnson's tune louder, and in public.

Johnson was convinced that his identity with the South constituted a chasm between him and a prestigious bloc of the press. He worked harder than most presidents at wooing the press without much expectation of the results. "You play ball with me and I'll make big men of you," he told several press regulars soon after he succeeded Kennedy. It was like the Hollywood producer's seduction of a starlet and the reporters resented it because it made them look like they could be bought. (The Kennedy style was far more successful in seducing the press.) In April 1964, after a small dinner party in Georgetown with several editors Johnson offered to drop Georgia-born Eugene Patterson at his hotel. The president told Patterson, who became managing editor of the *Washington Post* in 1968, that he was not deluding himself that the press would ever come to like him. "They are going to be fair to you," Patterson interrupted. Johnson didn't believe it. Patterson felt that the president's suspicion of the press was self-defeating but he also decided as time passed that "the press, especially that group that formed what came to be called the Kennedy cult during the Johnson years, was unkind and needlessly cutting toward him."

At Johnson's request Patterson joined a group of observers of the American-inspired elections in 1967 in South Vietnam, which were designed to prove popular support for the government. Patterson, who supported the war, accepted on condition that the president also appoint an editor who opposed the conflict; John S. Knight of the Knight newspaper chain was picked. After ten days in Vietnam, the observers assembled in the Cabinet Room at the White House to give their assessment to Johnson. "But instead of creating an atmosphere where we could talk frankly," Patterson remembered, "he called in a pool of reporters, and it was more or less a love feast he staged. He called on his friends, like Governor Hughes of New Jersey or Archbishop Lucey of San Antonio who were predictably going to praise the effort in Vietnam and find no criticism. It was in such a situation that had you raised a criticism, you would have been guilty of letting the side down, so he was cutting himself off from what could have been some valuable reports." Crusty John Knight, when his turn to comment came, said he would give his observations in private. Patterson struck the only disharmonious chord in the president's orchestration. The elections, he said, were a valuable exercise flawed because the government barred some popular candidates from running. "When I put the sour note into it, he [Johnson] looked quickly from his pad and glared at me with obvious anger as if I were doing an unfair thing," said Patterson. "He did not take kindly to being told things he didn't want to hear."

On Christmas Day 1966 the front page of the *New York Times* carried the first of several stories about the severe residential damage and civilian casualties caused by the American bombing of Hanoi.

Written from North Vietnam, correspondent Harrison E. Salisbury's articles contradicted the official American statements that no air raids were authorized on the densely populated city and its environs. The *Washington Post* argued that the attacks were "the most restrained bombing of modern war," as was evident by the fact that the United States possessed the means to flatten Hanoi, if it so willed. The editorial piously cautioned against bombing civilians. Unknown then to the American public the CIA had estimated that the air war casualties in North Vietnam in 1965–66 totaled thirty-six-thousand persons, about 80 percent of them civilians, certainly not the rarity the administration claimed.

On New Year's Day 1967, the *Post*'s Pentagon reporter George C. Wilson wrote that Salisbury's casualty figures were "identical to those in a communist propaganda leaflet." Another *Post* reporter, Chalmers Roberts, labeled Salisbury "Ho's chosen instrument" to stop the bombing. Defense Department spokesmen took to calling Salisbury's paper "The Hanoi Times." The *Post* echoed the government line in a frontal assault on Salisbury, the first correspondent for a major American news organization to report from North Vietnam since the war began. Salisbury, the paper declared, was a reliable reporter, who was being used by the North "to convey an impression that serves its cause very well." This cause, in the administration's eyes, was to persuade the United States to halt the attacks, which Washington conjectured were hurting the North and, hence, might bring the enemy to the bargaining table. On January 19 the Associated Press moved a series by William C. Baggs, editor of the *Miami News,* who had reached Hanoi after Salisbury. Baggs affirmed Salisbury's account of civilian damage. Though the *Post* carried the Baggs story, his reference to Salisbury did not appear. Within a few days the *Post* and other papers ran the government's terse acknowledgement that the bombing, indeed, had hit civilian areas.

The heightened fighting and rising civilian casualties were to have an impact at home on the most compelling figure in the civil rights movement. The intensification of the war in Vietnam coincided with the social explosions in one after another black ghetto across the country. Martin Luther King's abhorrence of the war had been welling up, restrained in public expression only because of a well-founded belief among civil rights leaders that such opposition would antagonize Lyndon Johnson, the chief political champion of their cause.

On the night of April 4, 1967, Dr. King took the pulpit of Riverside Church on New York's Upper West Side to fervently preach against the war with a force and vision no other national figure had mustered. "I knew that I could never again raise my voice against the violence of the oppressed in the ghettos without having first spoken clearly to the greatest purveyor of violence in the world today, my own government," the minister declared. "Somehow this madness must cease. We must stop now. . . . I speak for the poor of America who are paying the double price of smashed hopes at home and death and corruption in Vietnam." King urged massive conscientious objection to the war. The three thousand persons who overflowed the church gave him a long ovation.

Shock waves rolled out from Riverside Church. Martin Luther King's indictment of the war as a moral sham provoked rebuttal from liberals who feared his angry words would divide the civil rights camp and alienate its awesome friend in the White House. Rumors traveled that pediatrician Benjamin Spock and Dr. King might run against Johnson as "peace" candidates in the 1968 presidential election.

Powerful press voices were raised against the minister. The *New York Times* pronounced, "The moral issues in Vietnam are less clear-cut than [Dr. King] suggests; the political strategy of uniting the peace movement and the civil rights movement could very well be disastrous for both causes." Andrew Young, a close associate of King, later testified that the clergyman wept over the *New York Times* editorial.

The *Post* was harsher on Dr. King than the *Times*. "A Tragedy," the *Post* headed its lead editorial which denounced King's allegations about the effects of the war. Chastising the black leader for his attack on an administration that had labored for his cause, the *Post* concluded: "Dr. King has done a grave injury to those who are his natural allies in a great struggle to remove ancient abuses from our public life; and he has done an even greater injury to himself. Many who have listened to him with respect will never again accord him the same confidence. He has diminished his usefulness to his cause, to the country and to his people. And that is a great tragedy." From 1963 until his murder in 1968, the FBI waged an unremitting covert campaign to discredit King, first as a civil rights leader, then as an opponent of the war. Agents surreptitiously circulated to members of congress and the press allegations that he was an adulterer and linked to communists. It is possible that the fetid seeds planted over the years by the Bureau, with White House acquiescence, came to bitter flower in such editorial attacks as these.

The *Post* with good reason numbered itself among the persistent advocates of equal justice and opportunity for blacks. But the paper was blind to the truth of Martin Luther King's message that Johnson's war on poverty was being ground under by the treasury-draining war in Asia. When a young black reporter named Leon Dash, who was still in college, wrote an account of how this was happening, assistant managing editor Ben Gilbert killed it saying, "Leon doesn't know enough to write such a piece." It was left to the deity of American journalism, Walter Lippmann, to write the epitaph for Johnson's noblest domestic aims. In the Sunday opinion section under a page-wide headline "The Negro's Hopes Are a War Casualty" Lippmann wrote: ". . . Once the president chose to believe that he had to prevail in a war of attrition on the Asian mainland, the Great Society lost its momentum and its soul and became nothing more than a complex series of political handouts to the poor. The hope of Negro participation in the creation of a new American social order was lost."

Another black reporter, Robert Maynard, shared King's passionate outrage. In September 1962, when Vietnam had hardly dented the consciousness of America, the *Gazette and Daily* of York, Pennsylvania, a progressive paper, predicted that the dispatch then of more American military advisers was the first step toward a tragic entanglement in Asia; moreover, the United States could not win a war there, but if by chance it did, it would not be worth the victory. The prescient editorial impressed Maynard, a *Gazette* reporter. Maynard came to Washington in the spring of 1966 with a group of journalists who met with Ben Bradlee, the managing editor of the *Post*. Maynard told Bradlee he thought the paper read like a press release for the State Department because of its stand on the war. Bradlee replied that he didn't write the editorials and he thought the news coverage was fair. Bradlee later hired Maynard with the instruction, "Do whatever you're big enough to do."

On Christmas Eve 1968, Maynard was assigned to cover the White House. As he crossed the spacious lawn and through the West Wing, he felt repulsed by the peace motif when outside the iron gates the land was in torment. Maynard hurried back to the *Post* and told his impressions to his editors. They enthusiastically budgeted his mood story for Page One. Terrified by their expectations, Maynard struggled to write what he felt so strongly. "God, kid, get it out of the typewriter," Bradlee impatiently cracked.

There was a surrealistic quality about the stories on the front page on Christmas Day, as though laid out by Salvador Dali. Three astronauts had just circled the moon. South Vietnam Buddhists and Catholics alike were celebrating Christmas, taking advantage of a twenty-four-hour truce; the twin-spired Saigon cathedral was aglow with colored lights. Maynard reported that the president alluded to "peace without calling the name of Vietnam." He found "a somber concern that the guns of a ruinous war—a war that had as much as anything to do with this being the last Johnson Christmas in Washington—would soon be silent."

Vietnam, though, was still the big story and many reporters were eager to make their reputations there. Maynard was offered the assignment. He turned it down. "I didn't think I could get my arms around it," Maynard explained. "I didn't want to have anything to do with it. I didn't know that watching all that brutality would permit me to retain the detachment of a journalist."

Alan Barth, a gentle man whose editorials on civil liberties and racial justice had helped earn for the *Post* its liberal reputation, had known Lyndon Johnson from his days as a congressman from Texas. Barth went to see Johnson at the White House in 1967 with a single message. "I said to him," Barth recalled, "that he had the greatest opportunity since Lincoln to bind up the nation's wounds, but it was all being lost because of Vietnam." Johnson reacted impatiently. Barth's perception of the war as a disaster, however, was not reflected in the *Post*'s editorial columns.

The editorial page was the province of J. Russell Wiggins. He appeared to be a contradictory character. To some reporters who watched him pad along the aisles of the *Post* newsroom Wiggins seemed rigid and aloof, a short heavyset fellow with a nervous laugh at unpredictable moments. "The establishment pays your salary," Wiggins once snapped at a young editor who urged him to take an anti-establishment editorial position. His colleagues on the editorial page spoke of him as a warm and considerate boss who could espouse his case forcefully yet still tolerate dissent. But dissent as it swelled around him failed to persuade him to change course on Vietnam.

As executive editor Wiggins ran the editorial page and commanded the news side too. But his first love was the editorial pulpit where he could employ his puissant style to condemn or laud what caught his attention. Wiggins was a native son of the American prairie, born in the rural southwestern corner of Minnesota where it borders South Dakota and Iowa. He acquired a scholarly, but orthodox, mind without attending college. At eighteen he began reporting for his hometown weekly and became its editor and publisher. Wiggins had climbed through various newspaper jobs, including assistant to the publisher of the *New York Times,* before coming to the *Post.* He was a mover in journalism societies who vigorously championed freedom of the press. In his sixties Wiggins would go back to publishing a small town weekly, the *Ellsworth American,* on the Maine coast.

"The editorial policies of a great paper stand in the shadow of previous days," Wiggins once said. For him the challenge in Vietnam ran much deeper than the Cold War. From his dedicated study of American history he drew an analogy to Vietnam. The thirteen colonies had been aided by a foreign power in their struggle for independence; so the United States should assist South Vietnam's fight for freedom, Wiggins reasoned. "Russ was an inveterate collective security man," said Alan Barth. "He believed that Germany should have been resisted when it reoccupied the Rhineland and intervened in the war in Spain; that at every step when one let the Nazis push ahead without opposing them we drove more deeply into the ground a peg which we would have to pull out with our teeth one day. He saw Vietnam in those terms, not as a civil war. If the free world didn't stand up, it would be a folly leading to another world war."

This analogy to the democracies' failure in the 1930s to unitedly resist early aggression was a recurrent refrain of American administrations seeking to explain their commitments in Vietnam. Munich had stamped its fateful lesson indelibly on the minds of Wiggins's generation. The analogy applied to Vietnam was counterfeit, but repetition and American ignorance of that country's history and society obscured its flaws.

As the war expanded in intensity with its end seemingly no closer, most of the *Post* editorialists lost their stomachs for the paper's support of the administration's strategies. Barth, Selig Harrison, Merlo Pusey, and Stephen S. Rosenfeld tried to persuade Wiggins that the views he treasured belonged to the other side. They argued that Johnson's policy wasn't working and, furthermore, was damaging our own society. Wiggins brushed them off. Rosenfeld, a specialist on the Soviet Union and then the youngest member of the editorial staff, years later contrasted Wiggins's tenacity with the disposition of such presidential counselors as McGeorge Bundy and Secretary of Defense Robert S. McNamara. "Bundy and McNamara had nothing of Russ's principles," he said. "They were taking steps in the name of ideas they didn't have faith in, or only a passing faith. They became tactically nervous when things went wrong. Russ's attachment was ideological. The idea that you should abandon a principle was repulsive to him."

Wiggins wasn't looking for a consensus on what he deemed a matter of first principle. "Winner writes" was his rule. No one ever had to write an editorial contrary to his own beliefs, and so Wiggins was left alone to express the paper's views on the most divisive American issue in a century. "He became almost isolated; everyone else was virtually hostile, but he was a man not easily turned around," said Barth. In his own office Barth hung a photograph of a South Vietnamese armored vehicle dragging the body of a dead Vietcong soldier. It was his silent, anguished protest of the war.

Wiggins would go to the White House to hear from the president's lips his appraisal of the war situation and his plans for assuring its successful end. The editor arrived with his questions written out in advance. Johnson called it Wiggins's "shopping list." The president's principle foreign policy advisers and the chairman of the Joint Chiefs of Staff also briefed Wiggins, and he'd hurry back to his typewriter fired up to write an editorial supporting them. Wiggins enjoyed having the confidence of powerful men; to be well received in such prestigious sanctums of the establishment as the Century Club in New York was important to him. His colleagues who disagreed most adamantly with him over Vietnam remained convinced that he had arrived at his views as honestly as they had theirs. But some who observed him in this period said that the editor was seduced by the flattery of intimacies with the president and his chief ministers, that his vanity cost the *Post* its virtue.

Lyndon Johnson attempted to ride the tricky trough between two contrary waves of opinion: The judgment that the full might of American arms had to be unleashed in order to bring a victorious end to the war, and the view that the realistic solution lay in pulling out. Wiggins sailed this same course. The *Post* sprang to support McNamara against Senate hardliners who denounced him for having "shackled" the air attack. Over drinks at the end of the day Johnson would tell skeptical Senate doves, "The air force can't bomb a shit house in North Vietnam without my approval." Vietnam, the hawks on the Armed Services Committee declared, was "a major war"; the *Post* called it "a limited war." In one interview in 1967 Johnson told Wiggins that Ho Chi Minh was counting on the president's declining public support and his possible defeat for re-election the following year to ultimately yield North Vietnam its triumph. Johnson doubted that more military pressure would break Ho's fighting will; offers of bombing halts and negotiations only confirmed the North's belief that the United States was irresolute. But the bombing, Johnson told Wiggins, at least kept part of Ho's forces tied up in repair work so it was worth continuing. "Not all international differences are negotiable," the president concluded. The position was doomed to deepening frustration, however, and this frustration was the seedbed for new rounds of bombing that hardened the other side's resistance to negotiations, which was answered by still more bombing.

Johnson for most of his presidency could wake up in the morning and read the *New York Times* and the *Washington Post* and feel comforted that these ramparts of elitist opinion were still with him. "He didn't have to go to Phoenix or Indianapolis to find a paper that agreed with him," said Rosenfeld. In fact the *Post*'s editorial stance was at one with the prevailing sentiments of both the country and its political leaders. "We were typically American in finally coming to the view that the war was a bummer," Rosenfeld commented. "We followed the curve, but we were in such large company." A distinguished journalist who was extremely close to the high command of the *Post* believed that if the president had early on encountered contrary views in these papers his Vietnam decisions might have gone differently. It is a very large 'if.'

There was more to the *Post* than the editorial columns. The president read the news pages, too. He observed acridly that he found "propaganda" on the front page, which meant accounts of the war that ran contrary to his. "Our reporting," said a senior editor of his friend Wiggins, "was the enemy of the views he expressed on the editorial page." Despite the steady backing the *Post* gave to the government on Vietnam, however, it was mid-1964, when the war heated up, before the *Post* took on a correspondent in Saigon. Until then the prosperous paper covered the war largely through the wire services. Alfred Friendly, then the *Post*'s managing editor, later explained, "My news judgment was what was wrong rather than political dishonesty. I can be kicked in the ass for it," he said. "But my orientation was toward the West and Europe. Southeast Asia was like Latin America to me; I didn't know anything about it."

Ward Just was one of the bright young journalists who Ben Bradlee recruited to the *Post* after succeeding Friendly in 1965. Just, a balding, bespectacled Harvard graduate whose family owned the newspaper in

Waukegan, Illinois, spent nineteen months reporting from Vietnam. "If you're interested in primary passions, war's one good place to explore them," he told a friend after he left the *Post* and became a successful novelist. "Some people survive, souls intact, and others are destroyed by it. It's one reason I admire professional soldiers." Just filed an account of the unsuccessful attempts by officers to persuade a terrified GI to board a combat-bound chopper. Bradlee, who had fought in World War II, lauded the piece. Just had caught the essence of fear, Bradlee told other reporters. "One lives," Just wrote of the Vietnamese, "with the war as one lives with incurable cancer, accommodating oneself to its pain and trying to reduce the uncertainty to a manageable level. Eyes turn inward and the war is viewed in the sweep of four thousand years of history. Will summer come now that the Americans are here?" Just, back home from one stint in Vietnam, and Wiggins, who had never been there, spent an hour "[each] trying to tell the other the war he saw," Chalmers Robert wrote. "They were ships passing in the night."

Midway through 1967 the news reports and analyses in the *Post* reflected the rising skepticism about the government's version of the war. Richard Harwood reported: "The summer's events in Vietnam have generated a major conflict between the American government and the press. It is a conflict of judgment over the course of the war. A substantial majority of the correspondents in Vietnam believe and are reporting that the war is going badly, that no victory is in sight, that the effort to pacify the peasantry has been unproductive." In June, Ward Just wrote, "This war is not being won. . . . It may not be winnable."

The war crept into the lives of *Post* people. Bradlee's wife marched in anti-war demonstrations; so did Harwood's. "We had one photographer," Bradlee related, "who covered an anti-war protest for us, then joined the protest herself."

A triumvirate consisting of the executive, managing, and city editors controlled the hiring of local reporters; any one of the three editors could veto a prospective hire. The arrangement mainly protected the local editor from being saddled with a reporter he didn't want but whose work he would be held responsible for. City editor Stephen Isaacs had a promising young reporter named Steve Zorn whom he wanted for his staff. In an interview with Bradlee, Zorn said that he would rather go to jail than fight in Vietnam. This didn't bother Isaacs, who opposed the war and had turned down a preferred assignment to Saigon on the grounds that he was an editor, not a reporter. Zorn's remark infuriated Bradlee, however, who had been a navy officer. He vetoed Zorn. The next morning, Bradlee called a still-angry Isaacs into his office. Bradlee said he was troubled by his decision and had stayed up most of the night talking about it with an old friend, Paul Moore, Jr., the Episcopal bishop of Washington. Moore had been badly wounded and decorated for bravery with the Marines in World War II. He didn't think much of the Vietnam war and thought that Bradlee was wrong on Zorn. We're going to hire him, Bradlee told Isaacs, if Wiggins agrees. Wiggins said he didn't think much of Zorn but he would go along. Isaacs telephoned Zorn that he was hired. But Zorn replied that he didn't want to work for a paper that would put him through such a trial. Within a year, Zorn was covering the Statehouse for the *Boston Globe.*

Philip Foisie, who as foreign editor directed coverage of Vietnam, bore a special cross. Foisie was married to Dean Rusk's sister. Rusk once told a group of reporters who had been zeroing in on his defense of the Vietnam policy: "There gets to be a point when the question is, whose side are you on? Now I'm the secretary of state and I'm on our side." The Rusks and Foisies would dine together once a month or so, but any talk of the *Post*'s coverage of the war was averted. The war came home in still another way to the Foisies: their nineteen-year-old son fled to Canada to avoid being drafted.

The war reached Katharine Graham too. In the summer of 1966, after graduating magna cum laude from Harvard, Donald Graham was drafted. He was the oldest of her three sons. It was the expectation of his grandfather, Eugene Meyer, and his mother that Donnie would one day take over the Washington Post Company, assuring the dynasty for a third generation and perhaps beyond. War, with its shameless caprice, put this expectation at risk.

She believed in authority; responsible people knew best how to deal with the complexities of war and global relationships. These confident, articulate, and forceful diviners and managers of policy were her friends. Walter Lippmann had once counseled her, "Don't get too far from the establishment." Until the establishment shifted on Vietnam, Mrs. Graham held firm, too. An old, intimate friend of hers observed that "Tycoons are generally belligerent; they tend to feel comfortable with the aggressive approach to things. The persons she really listened to were this way. Kay Graham is a tycoon." And this friend who esteemed Katharine Graham went on: "She had no gounding in foreign policy. As intelligent as she was it would have appeared arrogant and presumptuous for her to take on her editor, the president, her friends. All the people she looked up to were hawks. She was surrounded by them." When, as success seemed further from their grasp, some of them began slipping away from the hard line in Vietnam, Katharine Graham grew disillusioned.

She had no clear idea of what should be done except to turn the burners down rather than up, as was happening. The noble principles that impelled Russ Wiggins influenced her, but not conclusively. In the end she was a pragmatist: What was being done wasn't working. And there was Donnie.

In his senior year at Harvard Donald Graham read everything he could put his hands on about the conflict in Southeast Asia. "I had thought it over and I couldn't honestly tell myself I was in favor of pulling the entire American military presence out of Vietnam," he said of his opinion then. He moved between two poles that year as he tried to plumb the meaning of the war. "Coming from Cambridge to Washington was like coming to another world," he recalled. "In Cambridge the war was all wrong; in Washington it was all right. People had lost track of what others were thinking."

He graduated and was drafted. One evening in early June 1967 Donald Graham, on orders to Vietnam, his bride of five months, and his mother dined at the Georgetown home of *Post* columnist Joe Alsop, a dear friend of Katharine and Phil Graham. Mrs. Graham was worried when her son told her his intention to marry Mary Wissler, a Chicago physician's daughter who had worked with him on the *Harvard Crim-son* when he was editor. Her concern was a loving mother's response to the wartime marriage of a young couple, but she kept her fears a private matter.

The dinner company that night would have awed a general, let alone a lowly GI. But Don was at ease; they were his mother's friends and, therefore, his. Alsop was a cousin of both Eleanor and Franklin Roosevelt and a widely syndicated columnist. He was like an uncle to Don. Among Alsop's other guests were Richard Helms, director of the CIA, and Robert McNamara, who by then had lost heart for the war. A month earlier McNamara counseled the president to be open to accepting a coalition government in Saigon, including the Vietcong. Johnson reacted like he had been snakebit. "McNamara has gone dovish on me," Johnson complained and soon packed off the man he once thought was the best invention since the telephone to run the World Bank. McGeorge Bundy, formerly national security adviser to Presidents Kennedy and Johnson, was at Alsop's, down from New York and his new job as head of the Ford Foundation. In May, "Mac" Bundy had counseled the president to veto requests for increased troops and heavier bombing. In his White House job, Bundy had broken off discussions of the war with Alsop in early 1965 because of the columnist's espousal of a gospel more hawkish than the president's. But Bundy was an old friend, and when he left Washington Alsop gave a big dinner dance in his honor. The *Post* paid half the expenses after Alsop explained that as its columnist (and since he doesn't dance) he was able to spend his time lining up interviews with the government officials who attended.

Through dinner, the De Venoge champagne, and a nineteen-year-old brandy the talk at Alsop's that June night was of the war and the disputed administration policy. Soon afterwards Graham was in Vietnam doing public information work for the First Cavalry Division. "After I was in Vietnam for a week, I concluded the war was futile," he said later. "It was very different from what I had expected. I think most of the reasons people thought it was a lousy war were good reasons." Yet he remained ambivalent for years about Vietnam.

Alsop fervently argued that Vietnam was a proper war that was being feebly fought by a president who misguidedly was prepared to accept an avoidable defeat. Vietnam, for Alsop, was simply further bloody evidence of communism's subversive design, a swathe of the same fabric as the overthrow of Chiang Kai-shek, whose cause he had espoused earlier. The presidential campaign of 1964 emotionally and physically depressed him. Candidate Johnson had promised, "We are not about to send American boys nine to ten thousand miles to do what Asian boys ought to be doing for themselves." Alsop went off to take the waters in Montecantini, Italy. He returned still dispirited. When later Johnson did strike harder in Indochina it was not hard enough for Alsop. The absence of an American crusade in Asia, where he had served in World War II, to which he could devote his ardor left him feeling worn and isolated. "He's a very passionate man, Alsop, and really not fitted in a sense to be a journalist, because he takes things so seriously and passionately that everything becomes a crise de coeur," remarked historian Barbara Tuchman. Stories of Alsop's "grandee" manner abound. Writer Tom Kelly told this one:

When Joe was once in Israel he had an audience with the prime minister, Golda Meir. Thick black coffee was served. Joe regarded the cup with the faint distaste of the well bred and asked if it was Turkish. He was told that it was. He asked if it had sugar in it. Mrs. Meir sipped her cup and confirmed that it did. He said in an aggrieved tone that he did not take sugar.

"Get Mr. Alsop another cup," the prime minister said peremptorily to an aide.

The coffee was delivered. Joe dropped some saccharine tablets into it, looked searchingly for some minutes, and then took off his glasses and stirred the coffee with the earpiece. Mrs. Meir rose to the occasion.

"Get Mr. Alsop another pair of glasses," she said to an aide.

Alsop was an authority on the art and archaeology of Asia Minor and China, which provided him with aesthetic pleasure and a long view of the rise and fall of empires. As the war was ending he continued to insist that the real tragedy of Vietnam lay ahead. "Until very recently," he said after he ceased writing his column in 1974, "I've seen our country in a period of true greatness. I never had any doubt that the greatness would continue indefinitely and would embrace the lifetimes of the next generation and the generation after that. But it seems to me that there's some sort of loss of will now in America that jeopardizes the whole future, and it makes me very sad." Without any smile he told an interviewer, "Every night when I go to bed I pray to God that I am crazy." Alsop's friends remained his friends, solicitous of his well-being, grateful for his elegance and grace. But his persistent advocacy of tougher and tougher devices in Vietnam caused his column to be discounted. The *Post* continued to carry it as long as it did out of his lasting friendship with the publisher, some believed.

Katharine Graham changed on the war, Russ Wiggins did not. She occasionally would sit in on the editorial conferences, skeptical about his judgment but not challenging it either. Eugene Meyer had dismissed his editor in 1940 for disagreeing with him over the war in Europe. His daughter had neither the appetite nor the self-assurance to confront her strong-willed editor head-on, perhaps fire him. Wiggins had helped navigate the *Post* through her husband's mental disarray, when Phil had been like a loose cannon on a ship's deck. She was grateful for that. Nor did she have a reasonable alternative for Vietnam or the eloquence to overcome him in debate. Wiggins, she knew, planned to retire at the end of 1968. She was not so pliable, however, as to be willing to wait for the calendar to solve her dilemma. She began looking in 1966 for a successor to Wiggins, someone who could begin weaning the *Post* from Johnson's war policies even before Wiggins's departure. With the counsel of Walter Lippmann and others, she and managing editor Ben Bradlee began the search.

Philip Laussat Geyelin was a forty-three-year-old writer on the *Wall Street Journal,* a Yale graduate, and a Main Line Philadelphian. He and Bradlee had been friends since they were correspondents in Europe. In 1962 when Phil Graham was clashing bitterly with Wiggins, he tried to hire Geyelin to write editorials on foreign affairs. Graham sent Bradlee, who was then with *Newsweek,* to try to entice Geyelin. "If you take this job," Bradlee counseled, "you'll be the next editor of the *Washington Post.* " Geyelin suspected that Graham wanted him to be the publisher's "man" on the editorial page, more responsive to him than to Wiggins. Geyelin foresaw a minefield and turned Graham down.

Katharine Graham invited Geyelin to her summer home on Martha's Vineyard. They took long walks together on the beach, discussing their values and perceptions of issues and how they would work out any disagreements. But she kept coming back to the grinding matter of Vietnam. How could they move the paper "off the wicket?" she persisted. Geyelin was in tune with the Council on Foreign Relations, an ultimate Eastern establishment institution of considerable influence. The council had concluded that the war no longer was winnable, though it did not say it so bluntly. A long-held editorial page position was like a massive ship requiring many miles in which to turn around. Editorials perpetuate past editorials. The *Post*'s editorial course on Vietnam would be altered, but not abruptly. The position would shift incrementally, the way the country had sunk into the war. The job of assuring the change was Geyelin's, if he wanted it. But first he wanted an oracle's counsel. He went to see Lippmann at the columnist's retreat in Maine. Lippmann urged Geyelin to go to the *Post.* The old man had already concluded that Vietnam was disastrous, that it was totally vain to believe that America's safety depended on setting the world in order everywhere no matter what the price. Geyelin thought the same way; his editorials would buttress Lippmann's views.

Wiggins was still the editor, but he was becoming the journalistic counterpart of Lyndon Johnson isolated in the Oval Office. During 1967 *Life,* the *Miami Herald,* the *Los Angeles Times,* even the conservative *Richmond Times-Dispatch* turned doubtful on Vietnam. In May the *Washington Star* called for a bombing halt. A breath of slight unease crept into the *Post.* "Bombing should be restricted to military interdiction away from civilian population." "The president's speech and other administration pronouncements," said another editorial, "are beginning to be colored by a fixity and rigidity that does not encourage belief that the strategy and tactics of diminishing the scale of the efforts always get full attention." The modest words were Geyelin's.

Geyelin was the counterweight to Wiggins. Wiggins, as Mrs. Graham described him, was "a righteous indignation editor." Geyelin's style was polished and skeptical. He was the only one of the editorial staff who had been to Vietnam. On one trip there Geyelin, who was a Marine lieutenant in World War II, was told by a Marine general, "If we had a million men and ten to fifteen years we could win." "It was going to be their new Honduras," Geyelin thought. "It would assure the future of the corps for years." The other editorial writers knew that he bore Mrs. Graham's cachet, that he was being groomed to take over the page. Still, Geyelin had to earn his spurs. Geyelin, twenty years Wiggins's junior, was a formidable challenger. The divisiveness over Vietnam that was becoming a national pathology was poisonously reflected at the eleven o'clock editorial conferences. Sometimes the debate would erupt into a shouting match and either Wiggins or Geyelin, his cool lost for the moment, would stomp out. Some of the watchers sensed that Geyelin regarded Wiggins as an old farm boy, and that Wiggins looked on Geyelin as a bit of a Social Register snob. Lyndon Johnson is supposed to have said that Wiggins was worth two American divisions. When Geyelin heard that, he smiled, "I must be worth a battalion of V.C."

Wiggins's view of the war was confirmed by the president and those at his right hand. Geyelin talked to young, middle-echelon foreign policy operators who could afford to be pessimistic because their prestige and futures weren't at stake. He also listened to George Ball, the undersecretary of state and the whispered critic of the war. "Ball could disagree with LBJ in private if he upheld him in public," said Geyelin. "The game would have been over if Ball tried to talk to Wiggins and convince him of the futility of Vietnam."

At dinner one evening in early 1968 at the home of Adalbert de Segonzac, the *France-Soir*, correspondent Geyelin got into an argument over the war with Walt Rostow, Johnson's national security advisor. Rostow was saying that he had captured documents showing the weakness of the enemy; a dubious Geyelin retorted, "Well, why don't you leak them to all of us instead of just Joe Alsop?" In his columns on Vietnam Alsop liked to quote from enemy reports provided to him by United States officers. His reliance on the documents had become a joke among journalists. Rostow angrily slammed his foot down on his host's coffee table and crushed it. Rostow took up the challenge and the next day Geyelin and reporters Ward Just and Murrey Marder arrived in the windowless "situation room" in the White House basement to interview Rostow. The staff in the room where cable traffic from Vietnam was monitored seemed agitated. The cause, the three visitors soon learned, was the first account of a big communist drive. Ultimately the Tet offensive was beaten back. Wiggins read the campaign as a military victory. For Geyelin, the vigor of the enemy was a portent of worse to come. Tet and the further opposition to the war that it kindled led Lyndon Johnson not to run for re-election.

Johnson was a hero to Max Ascoli, who ran the *Reporter,* a liberal magazine with two hundred thousand subscribers. But Ascoli shut it down in 1968 rather than accomodate his views to the changing mood over American intervention in Indochina. Geyelin admired the work of the *Reporter*'s Washington editor, Meg Greenfield, and wanted to hire her. "She looks like a little girl, but writes like a stiletto," a correspondent remarked. Geyelin sent her in to talk with Wiggins. After a while Wiggins bounded out of his office, beaming, "She's on my side." She was hired. Meg Greenfield, though, was committed to consensus causes, and the consensus had passed Wiggins by.

Some years later a young editor asked Ben Bradlee what he would do when the excitement of running the newspaper might fade. Bradlee replied circumspectly, telling how he would pass Russ Wiggins's office in the afternoon and see him asleep at his desk. Bradlee said he would unobtrusively close the door, discretely shielding the older man's nap. "I don't want to fall asleep here," Bradlee said. In the autumn of 1968, with the Johnson administration in its final months, Wiggins accepted the president's offer to be ambassador to the United Nations. He retired from the *Post* two months early and some of his associates sighed with relief that the thrashing about over the paper's Vietnam policy was over. It was a plum from Johnson to a loyalist. There was really nothing significant that Wiggins could do at the U. N. as a diplomatic novice representing a lame duck president. But Wiggins long afterwards relished being addressed, 'Ambassador.'

Soon after Wiggins left, Steve Rosenfeld phoned him in New York and offered to work for the new diplomat. "That's how loyal to him and a bit guilty I felt," recalled Rosenfeld, who had occasionally thought of quitting in protest to Wiggins's stand on the war. Wiggins was gratified, but he told the young writer that it made no sense to quit the *Post* for just a few months at the U. N. and that it would probably end his career at the paper. Rosenfeld, still ambivalent about his ex-boss, was glad he made the offer and glad Wiggins turned it down.

After Vietnam the United States labored fitfully to sift from the ashes of that traumatic experience some understanding of what its role was to be in a still-dangerous world. Under Geyelin and Greenfield, who became his deputy in 1970 and successor in 1979, the *Post*'s pronouncements on foreign affairs were pragmatically calibrated to a cool sizing up of America's interests and a conservative assessment of its resources to fulfill them. The country, though, owed a great debt, on which it appeared to be welshing, to the veterans of the war. In a stream of editorials and articles the *Post* led the press in campaigning for better benefits for the ex-servicemen. It seemed like a penance for being wrong so long on the war.

THREE

Mrs. Graham Takes Charge

Katharine Graham resents being labeled the most powerful woman in publishing. "That's a sexist term, and I really dislike it," she says. Still, what else is there to call her?
—*Time*, FEBRUARY 7, 1977

THE SKY PROMISED A THUNDERSTORM to break the heat of that August afternoon in 1963 as the mourners slipped into the pews of the National Cathedral that towers above a promontory in northwest Washington. They gathered to memorialize the publisher of the *Washington Post*, Philip Leslie Graham, dead at his own hand in midpassage of a luminous, but grievously flawed, life. Copyboys and publishers—Otis Chandler, for example, of the *Los Angeles Times;* diplomats and a contingent of black schoolchildren; cabinet members and in a wheelchair, retired Justice Felix Frankfurter, for whom Graham had once clerked. His friend, President John F, Kennedy, entered just before the service began. Kennedy had been cruising off Cape Cod when word of Graham's death was radioed to him. In the nave facing the choir sat Katharine Graham and her children: Elizabeth, twenty; Donald, eighteen; William, fifteen; and Stephen, eleven.

Under the terms of a 1948 trust established by her parents, Eugene and Agnes Meyer, Phil and Kay Graham owned all of the voting stock of the Washington Post Company. Phil's death left her in absolute financial control of the corporation. She was forty-six years old. Before the funeral she met with the board of directors and the chief editorial and business executives who had served her husband and now would be expected to serve her as his legatee. She had been terrified of facing these men, repeating over and over again on her way to the meeting the brief remarks composed with the help of *New York Times* columnist James Reston. In this corporate analog to the royal rite of succession, Katharine Graham reassured them that the company would continue without change. "This is a family business and it will remain so," she declared. "After all, there is a new generation coming along." Donald Graham was fifteen years away from becoming publisher of the *Post.* His mother's obligatory words sounded confident enough, although she felt herself to be anything but steady. She immediately left the board room.

"Vultures and hawks," Kay Graham later called them—the newspaper titans like Otis Chandler and Sam Newhouse, who were eager to pay a fortune for her money machine. But tough old Agnes Meyer insisted that Eugene Meyer had not breathed life into the comatose *Post* so that Kay could sell the now-thriving paper. Hadn't her father declared that the paper was a public trust? An extremely close newspaper friend of Mrs. Graham told her: "You can hire brilliant people off the trees; to be great, the paper needs great character, you can provide that. You'll be a constitutional monarch; no one will be able to push you around." The years would prove his counsel wise and his prediction accurate. Agnes and others fortified Kay's own resolve to not sell what her father and husband had built. The birds of prey stopped circling.

But inside the company there were problems which soon nullified her pledge to leave unaltered the cast of leading men she inherited. The executives mostly behaved as though they were still in the *Post's* hand-to-mouth days. "The company was too conservative, not growth-minded," she recalled. "The editorial people thought there was something wrong about being good at business." She felt patronized, coddled as though she had no business playing a man's game. "There were some empires within the company that were not anxious to help me learn; they didn't take to a woman." "Mama," some of the men called her, but not to her face. In that ante-liberation age she told an interviewer for a trade journal she would try to conduct herself at business so that her managers would not think of her as a woman. "I made a mistake, didn't I?" she conceded to an admirer who chided her for the remark.

One could run a big company effectively as a family enterprise if the management stayed up to date and aggressive. Mrs. Graham had the good fortune to take over a newspaper that was already dominant in Washington. This gave her a wide margin of security over the *Post*'s principal competitor, the *Star*. But she ran all the harder to stay ahead, all the while disdaining the *Star*'s owners. In the 1950s the century-old *Star* carried more advertising than any other Washington paper. The principal advertisers and the proprietors of the *Star*—the Kauffmans, Noyeses, and Adamses—dined together at the city's exclusive clubs and golfed together at the Chevy Chase Club. When the *Post,* having absorbed the *Times-Herald,* was beginning to surge ahead, the *Star* was in feeble hands at the moment when it was most vulnerable. Samuel H. Kauffman headed the company. But he was old and in frail health; medication for a lung ailment had left him deaf, and at board meetings information was transmitted to him with a magic marker board. At least a dozen descendants of the founding families had held key business or editorial jobs at one time. "The three families at the *Star* used it not only as a livelihood, but as an occupation for too many members of the families," Katharine Graham said. Nepotism blocked professional managers and journalists from the top jobs. "The people who ran the *Star* were coupon clippers," said James Bellows, a former executive editor of the paper. "One of them said there was no point in promoting the paper with Sunday afternoon radio commercials because everyone was then out playing polo."

Kay Graham wasn't the first woman to run a major newspaper. Cissy Patterson forcefully directed the *Washington Times-Herald;* her temperamental cousin, Alicia Patterson, developed *Newsday* into a successful Long Island daily; Dorothy Schiff owned and edited the *New York Post* for thirty-seven years; Oveta Culp Hobby, the first secretary of Health, Education and Labor, was editor and chairman of the board of the *Houston Post;* and Helen Copley took charge of the Copley newspapers in California and Illinois after her husband died. But the wealth, influence, and prominence of the Graham enterprises exceeded by many times anything those organizations possessed.

The newspaper business was overwhelmingly a male preserve. Two sisters might control 34 percent of the stock of the *Wall Street Journal*'s parent company, Dow-Jones, but holding even such large blocks of stock was different from running a paper. Men were the publishers and editors; men were the business managers and production captains. At one newspaper industry meeting, the presiding publisher went around the room asking for the opinions of the other participants on a pressing issue. Mrs. Graham sat waiting her turn, constructing in her mind what she would respond when he got to her. And when her turn came, the chairman simply skipped past her to the man on her right. She was flabbergasted, but concealed her surprise and disappointment. In time Katharine Graham would be elected treasurer of the American Newspaper Publishers Association and become a force in the publishers' club. The publishers had sniggered at her company for being "soft" on labor. Later they canonized her as a savior of the industry after the *Post* broke the grip of powerful unions on the paper's production.

She had an independent mind. In the middle of the Depression, Katharine Meyer, tall, a bit awkward, and pretty, went off to Vassar College, not far from her family's baronial estate, Seven Springs Farm at Mount Kisco, New York. But all-girl Vassar was too cloistered for her. After two years she transferred to the University of Chicago, an intellectually more vibrant and politically liberal incubator for her New Deal sympathies. She arrived the year drugstore magnate Charles R. Walgreen withdrew his niece to protect her, he said, from communist influences. "Kay was one of the few kids on campus with money," recalled George Reedy, who worked his way through Chicago washing dishes and playing trombone. (Reedy became President Johnson's press secretary.)

To be liberal in those days was to be pro-labor. Heiress Kay leafletted against sweatshops for the International Ladies Garment Workers. Labor, armed with friendly New Deal laws, was organizing aggressively. When thousands of strikers and their families paraded toward the hold-out Republic Steel's South Chicago works on Memorial Day

1937, Chicago police viciously attacked, killing ten marchers and wounding ninety. Kay Meyer and her young friends rushed to the scene of the carnage to pass out coffee to the strikers and join in the tribute to "our fallen heroes." A generation later, in the pressmen's strike at the *Post,* she would be called "a union buster."

Eugene Meyer's *Post* editorialized that the Chicago strikers had "only themselves to blame" for the tragedy because they had a strong legal basis for collective bargaining but not for closing the plant or inciting violence. A subsequent Senate investigation blamed the police.

Eugene Meyer tolerated, even encouraged, his Kate's sowing of ideological wild oats. "There will be time enough for her to become conservative," Meyer presciently observed. After her graduation—Eugene and Agnes Meyer sent word they were too busy to attend the ceremony and Kay wept—she worked for a while on the *San Francisco News* covering crime and the longshoremen's fight to unionize the waterfront. She learned how to drink boilermakers, a glass of beer and a shot of whiskey, with union leaders in bars along the Embarcadero. San Francisco was marvelous, but her father wanted her to come home. Meyer's request was understandable. He was sixty-three years old. His only son, Bill, wanted to be a doctor; his three other daughters had no interest in the *Post* as a career. Kay had apprenticed as a reporter; Gene Meyer could count on her to keep the *Post* in the family. Kay came back to the *Post* to edit the letters-to-the-editor. When she married Phil Graham and he later became publisher, Meyer considered himself wise and fortunate.

Now Phil was gone and the company was Kay's to run; first, however, she had to learn how the engine worked. She sat in on the daily news and editorial conferences at the *Post* and the management meetings at her Washington radio and television stations. Each week she flew to New York to spend two days at *Newsweek.*

When Graham bought the newsweekly two years before his death, he persuaded Frederick S. Beebe, a tall, dark-haired, cigar-smoking corporate lawyer to leave Cravath, Swaine & Moore, a New York legal powerhouse, and become chairman of the Washington Post Company.

Beebe was seven months older than Graham and became Phil's partner in running the growing enterprise. Beebe was Eugene Meyer's discovery; he counseled on the crucial purchase of the *Times-Herald* and lawyered the *Newsweek* acquisition. "One of the smartest things Phil Graham did was to get Beebe to come in," a *Newsweek* executive said.* Beebe was crucial in the corporate life of the *Post* company for another decade until his death in 1973. "This company grew like Topsy," Kay Graham said later. "I was new and Fritz was new. He and I had a marvelous relationship. He was so decent, so wise; he had a brilliant corporate mind . . . he saved us." Beebe shrewdly negotiated Phil Graham's business intuitions and impulses into immense advantages for the company. He was instrumental in keeping the whole show from coming totally unglued during Graham's long, mercurial illness. Beebe had a substantial personal stake in the company. Until 1971 when he sold about half his shares, he owned more than 10 percent of the stock.

In time Kay Graham grew more self-assured. She discovered how to manipulate the levers of command, and she overturned the executive suite. Sometimes the deposed were men whom her father and husband had hired and trusted. Other times she fired men whom she had hired. All left with handsome severance purses. Some of them went badly scalded by Kay's tongue. She could be brutal and profane in criticizing them, either directly and in front of others or out of the victim's presence. And she could be incredibly shy. Before at least one crowded reception she hesitated at the door, wondering if her dress was suitable for the affair.

The change of most far-reaching consequences for the modern *Post*

---

*Though Beebe left Cravath, Swain, Cravath, Swain didn't leave the Post Company. Other lawyers came from the firm to the *Post*'s upper corporate echelon and Cravath partner George J. Gillespie, III, became a company director and a trustee who voted a large share of *Post* stock. Editor Ben Bradlee's great-grandfather was a founding partner of Cravath. The firm represented the Post Company on such things as securities and acquisitions. In 1978 a couple of stockholders asked if Cravath's representation of *Time*, also, posed a conflict of interest in view of *Time*'s rivalry with Newsweek and Time, Inc.'s purchase of the *Washington Star*. The Post Company's official reply was that there was no conflict because Cravath does not work for *Newsweek* or the *Washington Post* as such. This answer, however, left the issue nebulous because of the obvious links between the persona involved in the publications, the corporations, and the law firm. One wag asked if the frequent similarity in the covers of *Time* and *Newsweek* resulted from the Cravath connection.

came two years after Kay Graham's ascendancy. Her friends, Walter Lippmann and James Reston, the doyens of American journalism, told Kay that the *Post* was erratic in the quality of its reporting and predictable in the treatment of stories. They confirmed her own impressions. "For years Kay had heard all the talk about imminent progress in the paper," one close spectator noted. "Well, nothing happened, and she's not the sort of woman who sits around and waits. She's really dedicated to this paper, and she quite deliberately chose to make it her life after Phil died. You must realize that she could have walked away from it and lived very comfortably anywhere in the world." Fritz Beebe had a simple rule for handling the news side of the company: "You ought to be able to know when you have a good editor, but once you have one, you shouldn't tell him what to do. You should leave him alone." Mrs. Graham concluded that she didn't have the managing editor to match her ambitions for the *Post,* so she set about replacing him, not tidily, but effectively.

Alfred Friendly was more than the *Post*'s managing editor. He and Kay were almost like brother and sister. He regarded her father, Eugene Meyer, as "my spiritual godfather." Friendly wholeheartedly shared Meyer's and Phil Graham's internationalism and progressive politics. Graham had made him managing editor as well as a very wealthy man as his *Post* stock surged in value. Executives such as Friendly who took advantage of a stock-option plan that the *Post* started in 1952 watched a share rocket in value from $47.50 that year to $1,173 by 1970. With several stock splits that single share increased in value to $5,520 by 1979! Friendly lived a few blocks from the Grahams; he and Phil drove to work together. During the ragged days that followed Phil's death, Friendly stood at Kay's side.

Swiveling in his office chair, Friendly, who had lived through the *Post*'s lean years, would brush aside criticism of the newspaper's quality by citing the rising circulation figures. "We must be doing something right," Friendly would say, and the discussion was over. Of course, one of the things the *Post* had done right was to buy out the morning opposition, the *Times-Herald.* That was simply shrewd business, rather than impressive journalism. Later on when the new guard came to edit the *Post*, there was an inclination among some of them to demean the Friendly era. There were serious journalistic flaws in that period. But Friendly was responsible for the *Post*'s questioning coverage of Joe McCarthy's repeated, unsubstantiated charges of communist subversion in government—at a time when most of the press printed his allegations without challenge. Friendly, an undisguised liberal Democrat, stimulated the paper's intensive and perceptive reporting of the early civil rights movement before racial injustice was on many editors' agendas. He also laid the foundation for the *Post*'s foreign service.

Friendly wanted to improve the *Post*'s flaccid coverage of economic affairs. The financial page was "a comfort station for businessmen," said one of the paper's staff. Friendly hired Bernard Nossiter, a solid reporter with a Harvard degree in economics. This was in the late 1950s when liberal Senators Estes Kefauver and Paul Douglas were starting to examine the lack of real price competition in basic industries. Nossiter explained to readers how the practice of administered prices nullified the price benefits of a free market. No editor interfered with his reporting of the general subject until Kefauver seemed to hit pay dirt in specific drug firms. Friendly quickly pulled Nossiter off the story. "He's coming on too strong"; the hearings were getting too much "play" in the paper, Friendly complained.

"[Phil] Graham, then cementing the paper's relationship with big advertisers after the *Times-Herald* purchase, was leery of Nossiter's incisive probing into hitherto journalistically taboo areas," Chalmers Roberts wrote in his authorized history of the *Post*. Nossiter was reliably told that Graham was persuaded by his friend, John O'Connor, that the charges of price-rigging in drugs were baseless, although this was what drug company executives subsequently were convicted of. O'Connor was president of a large drug corporation. Nossiter looked back at the episode simply as confirmation of the economic kinship between publishers and other businessmen.

Habits from leaner times hung like a shroud over the paper's bright young local reporters. One of them, Daniel Greenberg, recalled: "They kept expenses down. They would get someone with a master's degree and send him out to the county for a few years where he'd work very hard before discovering he wasn't going to cover the State Department and leave, to be replaced by another." It was the ritual dance of the newsroom. Coveted assignments like the White House and Congress were literally a few minutes away, but light-years distant as far as the younger reporters were concerned. "Do you know there are people who've been working here for thirty years and they don't cover the federal government," city editor Ben Gilbert chastened a local reporter. The Kingdom of Heaven seemed more reachable.

The older reporters who comprised the small national staff were possessed of a great faith in the political institutions they covered. Edward Folliard reported the White House. An editor from that period recalled: "Folliard's rule was, 'Write what the man said.' He had covered presidents from Coolidge on, and had a reverence and awe not just for the office, but for the men."

There was one name that kept coming up as Katharine Graham took soundings on how to improve her paper: Benjamin Crowninshield Bradlee. He was already in the *Post* family. He was chief of *Newsweek*'s Washington bureau, the most prestigious job on the magazine outside the editorial high command in New York. Ben Bradlee had gone to Phil Graham late one night in 1962 to tell him the magazine was for sale and why Graham should buy it. Graham did, and it eventually became a gold mine. Bradlee was on *Newsweek*'s up escalator, bound for glory, surely. But that meant moving to New York, a prospect that had no appeal for him or his family. He was still feeling deeply the death of his friend, John Kennedy, and restless with the absence of a challenge that would productively consume his tremendous creative energy. "I was mostly thinking up ideas for my superb staff," Bradlee recalled. The deployed correspondents of the newsweeklies fed their editors in New York long, raw files on the news; these the editors constructed into articles often with little resemblance to the correspondents' work. For the reporters it could be unsatisfying and aggravating.

Bradlee had been a reporter on the *Post* from 1948 to 1951, when the paper was still in third place in circulation of the city's four papers. He loved working the "gangbusters beat," covering police and the courts. He often showed up wearing a rakish salt-and-pepper suit handed down from his father-in-law. (A lawyer who knew Bradlee encountered him on the street in the 1960s in a flashy plaid suit and stopped to talk for a moment. "Who the hell was that?" the attorney's out-of-town client asked.

"He's the editor of the *Post.*"

"Jesus," said the client, "I thought it was your bookie.")

The used suit was a mark of class rather than deprivation. The suit was like his Boston family: old, comfortable, memorable. The Bradlees went back to early Massachusetts—a family of merchants, lawyers, politicians and, occasionally, ne'er-do-wells. The depression of the thirties had hurt Ben Bradlee's family, but not enough to make life harsh or prevent his going to St. Marks, one of the most exclusive of the New England prep schools. While there young Bradlee suffered a severe attack of polio; one of his classmates died from the disease. Then he went on to Harvard, the college of Bradlee men. He hurried through the university in three years to join the navy and marry Jean Saltonstall of an illustrious Massachusetts family in the shaky wartime summer of 1942; then he sailed on a destroyer for the far Pacific.

While covering the courts Bradlee missed some important testimony in one case and city editor Ben Gilbert raked him for the sin. Bradlee's response was to learn speedwriting. And with Bradlee panache he found a spectacular occasion to apply his new skill. A would-be suicide hovered on the parapet of the Willard Hotel fourteen floors above the street. Bradlee climbed out on the ledge to record the dialogue verbatim between the policemen and the distraught man.

Bradlee was thirty in 1951 and his zeal for cops and robbers had thinned. Josephine Bradlee had made sure that her son, Ben, learned French as a boy, and he spoke it fluently. Frustrated with his prospects at the *Post,* Bradlee quit and became a press attaché in the American Embassy in Paris where the patrician David K. E. Bruce was ambassador. But Bradlee said that he wasn't happy feeding the company line to reporters who were lazy and too ready to accept the government's story without challenge. An American wire service bureau chief who was certain that Bradlee had lied to him about an important Embassy action refused to speak to him for years over the incident. Divorced and restless again, Bradlee joined *Newsweek* as chief European correspondent. Bradlee took a new wife, Antoinette Pinchot, a lovely blonde. Her father, Amos Pinchot, was a radical lawyer and a pacifist who had helped organize the Bull Moose Progressive Party for Teddy Roosevelt. Her uncle, Gifford Pinchot, was one of America's great conservationists and twice a governor of Pennsylvania.

In the spring of 1965 Kay Graham phoned to take Ben Bradlee to lunch to talk about the *Post.* He had recruited a string of bright young reporters and enabled them to flower in his Washington bureau. Bradlee's experience abroad would be an asset for the *Post* which was expanding its foreign coverage. He knew all the powerful men in town and how political Washington worked. He carried the blessing of Walter Lippmann, an old friend of Bradlee's parents, which Kay Graham valued.

Bradlee was eager to come to the *Post.* He craved the immediacy of daily "newspapering" with its vitality that the magazine didn't provide him. If Friendly's job ever became open he wanted it, Bradlee told Mrs. Graham. "I'd give my left one for it," Bradlee told her straight out, a line that afterwards was etched deeply in *Post* lore. Of course, the job would be open one day, though neither Friendly, Kay Graham, nor Bradlee realized how soon. Kay and Ben talked more. He told her the paper needed rejuvenation. There also was a problem, he told her, in the warp of the news treatment. A survey of Washington correspondents published that year showed that most of them read the *Post,* but they judged the *New York Times,* the *Star,* and several other papers to be more fair and reliable than the *Post.* Russell Wiggins as executive editor ruled over both the editorial and news pages, but he left Friendly a large hand in running the news end. Still there was a danger in this arrangement of reinforcing an editorial policy in the news pages. Bradlee thought it was more than a possibility in the *Post.* "You knew what the *Post* policy was going to be by reading the news column," he told Mrs. Graham. (A few years later when Bradlee succeeded Wiggins as executive editor, he told Katharine Graham he wanted no part of the editorial page. For several years he continued to edit the Op-Ed page which carried the columnists. He finally turned it over to editorial-page editor Phil Geyelin because "it was a basket of crabs. I knew all those people and you couldn't change a comma without their getting mad.")

Many of those who knew what she was considering did not believe she would bring Bradlee into the paper. During the terrible clash between Phil and Kay Graham, in the depths of his mental unbalance when he was threatening to take the newspaper away from her and marry an Australian woman who worked at *Newsweek*, their friends chose sides. Phil's runaway love affair was no secret in Washington. Bradlee was heard to criticize Kay; a divorce, Ben told people, was what Phil needed. Kay never forgot that, but she eventually forgave him. In August she brought Bradlee to the *Post* as Friendly's deputy.

Bradlee was forty-four; Al Friendly was ten years older. Friendly planned to remain managing editor for a few more years until he could become president of the American Society of Newspaper Editors as a deserved climax to his career. But Bradlee was pushing hard. "Look, buster, don't be in a hurry," Friendly cautioned. "Sorry, but that's my metabolism," smiled Bradlee. Bradlee practically lived at the paper trying to learn everything about its operation, and this commitment tore at his marriage. He fell in love with the *Post*.

"If my mother had had more experience, she would never have hired Bradlee," Donald Graham once speculated. She ran against the conventional wisdom. Bradlee had only a few years of newspaper experience. Some thought that Mrs. Graham should find her managing editor among that little band of men who had risen to the upper ranks of a few distinguished newspapers; such a man would bring his mantle of eminence to the *Post*. But Kay wanted something else. Exuberance, irreverence, freshness, audacity.

Katharine Graham didn't want to be the one to break the news to Friendly. So Walter Lippmann, friend to Kay and Al and Ben, asked Friendly over lunch, "Wouldn't you like to go back to writing?" Friendly got the message. "I would have rather heard it from you," Friendly told Kay that afternoon. Bradlee became managing editor in November, three months after he walked in the door, and Friendly went to Europe and the Middle East as a correspondent, his real journalistic strength. In 1967 he won a Pulitzer Prize for his coverage of the Arab-Israeli war, a professional triumph greater really than the missed presidency of the editors' society. It all turned out well, as Kay Graham had planned.

Bradlee charmed her and told her she was crazy when he thought she was off base. His manner, but more important, his professional success kept her effectively out of the news operation, leaving him virtually autonomous. On one occasion Bradlee did not tell her he had switched the city and foreign editors. Kay came across the city room under full sail, anger like a thunderhead darkening her face, and entered Bradlee's office. Thirty minutes later, the door opened and she emerged, turning back to say to Bradlee, "Maybe you're right." "Bradlee had a charismatic effect on her," said a former senior editor who had closely watched Bradlee take over. She told people he reminded her of Phil.

Ben, like Phil, was tough at business. In the mid-1960s the company, having already outgrown a recently expanded building, began planning a new building. The top managers wanted a handsome structure that would stand out from Washington's rather undistinguished contemporary architecture, some of which was being raked by the *Post*'s respected critic Wolf von Eckardt. Even general manager John Sweeterman, a diligent nickle-shaver, was swept up in the edifice complex. Mrs. Graham, whose daughter then was married to an architect, was enthusiastic about an aesthetically exciting new home for the company. She commissioned superstar I. M. Pei to design it. As Pei studied the way the *Post* hive worked, he conceived of the newsroom as the "beating heart" of the place; he would place it in an atrium for dramatic impact.

Pei drew plans for a building that would cost, he estimated, $50 million; he was $20 million over what the company had in mind. Things were out of hand. Bradlee moved in. He played the coldly calculating, hard-nosed businessman—the role that was expected of Sweeterman. What happens if the $50 million estimate ends up at $60 million? Bradlee pressed Sweeterman. Can we afford it? Should we be paying all that interest to Prudential Life (which was going to finance the building) when you're telling me to hold down the budget for the news department? Bradlee flattened Sweeterman; it happened again on other matters. Before long Mrs. Graham dismissed Pei, paying him nearly $2 million for his trouble. Sweeterman soon retired, earlier than he had planned. In 1972 the company moved into its new $25 million, architecturally unmemorable building. As it turned out, the three-story-high pressroom seen from the lobby through a huge window was the centerpiece—a beating heart that abruptly failed three years later during a bitter strike.

Katharine Graham and Bradlee fulfilled each other. He gave her, eventually, the most interesting newspaper in the country, possibly the world. She paid the rent. But much, much more than that, she encouraged and sustained the *Post*'s drive for independence and excellence. It was an extraordinary relationship for an editor and an owner.

Ben Bradlee looked out over the city room, one of his new reporters beside him. "All that deadwood has to go," he asserted. His friend, Secretary of Defense Robert McNamara, confided Bradlee, had recommended a strategy for improving the staff: hire new talent but don't fire anyone, at least for a while. This would be more expensive, but the *Post* was rich enough and it certainly would be less painful for everyone than a purge. He had no great plan for changing the paper but he began shaking up the place.

He was a sudden breath of fresh air, asking reporters for their ideas about the paper. One day he took a dozen of the younger staffers to lunch. He questioned them about the social circles they moved in. He wanted to know who they knew; from his own prominent connections he was aware that social relationships often yielded the inside stories of what was happening in Washington. Dan Morgan was a young local reporter who thought that his prospects on the *Post* were terribly gray. He was looking for another job, but decided to stay, infected by Bradlee's enthusiasm. In two years Bradlee assigned him to Europe. Morgan felt like the bit player whose name suddenly went up on the theater marquee.

The newsroom budget in Friendly's last year was about $4 million. By 1969 Bradlee had doubled spending, most of the money going for salaries as he expanded the staff and opened new bureaus abroad. The paper could easily afford it; the *Post* was coining money. Phil Graham knew that the *Post* would not be the great newspaper he wanted until it placed its own reporters in the other major capitals—reporters on whom the editors could depend and who saw the world by and large the way the editors did. Occasionally an experienced reporter working abroad for several publications was put on contract. On a trip through Africa in 1959 Friendly stopped in Accra to sign on Russell Warren Howe, a thirty-three-year-old British reporter. The old European colonies were rushing toward independence. American press coverage of Africa consisted of AP and UP bureaus in Cairo and Johannesburg and the *New York Times*'s Thomas Brady. "Do everything the *Times* does," Friendly instructed Howe—an inevitably expensive mandate for a single correspondent whose beat was two and a half times the size of the United States. During the year that Howe covered the civil war in the Congo, his cable bill ran more than $100,000. The editors winced but they did not tighten his budget. Howe sensed that Friendly's interest in Africa related to the editor's concern with the mounting civil rights movement at home. When Howe tried to offset his own personal abhorrence of apartheid by filing a balanced article on South Africa's racial policies, he got a note from Friendly that he had been too fair.

After Graham bought *Newsweek* in 1961, he proposed that the *Post* and the magazine share their foreign correspondents to save money. Howe and others who reported for the *Post* and *Newsweek* tried serving both publications for a while, before the arrangement was dropped. Fritz Beebe, chairman of the Post Company, conceded that such sharing proved "a fallacy and false economy. The newspaper and the magazine each has its working rhythms." Besides deadline differences, newspaper correspondents felt themselves far more independent than magazine staffers in choosing what to cover.

Building the *Post*'s foreign reporting was not to be the thirty-day wonder Graham once had heroically contemplated. The *New York*

Times with its sophisticated, internationalist readership maintained a large corps of correspondents abroad. Like most papers, however, Graham's relied mainly on the Associated Press and United Press. Reuter, the British press wire, was kept out of the *Post* for years because one editor dismissed it as "that limey news service." Step by step over a generation Graham's dream was fashioned into reality so that by 1979 the *Post* would have sixteen of its own correspondents and scores of part-time "stringers" stationed around the world. This tremendously enhanced the *Post*'s independence and stature.

This foreign network was presided over by Seattle-born Philip Foisie. He was an artillery officer in China during World War II, stayed in Shanghai for a while as an editor on an English-language newspaper, and married a Russian émigré. Foisie always looked worn, as though he had gone without sleep for a month. He had a priestly devotion to the editor's craft. "Phil is the only guy I know who stands at the urinal and reads copy," one colleague said. "He has that thousand-yard stare and in his rumpled suit he looks like a pudding and talks like a pudding, but he is a pro." He was possessed by a near-religious fealty to the *Post*, which counted a great deal with the managers. Bradlee had wanted to fire or reassign him. "I'm too scholarly and he's too pop," Foisie was heard to say with a wan smile. "But he lets me do my thing." He assigned his correspondents imaginatively and, in the face of rampant inflation and a declining dollar, nimbly juggled budgets and currency exchange rates to enable them to roam widely.

"Persistent," Katharine Graham called him. Foisie argued for twelve years before he won his case for a separate copy desk to handle foreign stories. Nine assistants worked for him editing and writing headlines; among them they could speak nine different foreign languages; each knew well some patch of the foreign world. Often a newspaper copy desk was the place to lodge staffers whose legs and exuberance had played out; the work was restrictive, demanding, and unsung. But some newspaper people spent their entire careers at desk work; they were a special breed. "Talking a reporter into becoming a desk editor is like persuading a woman to become an RN instead of a doctor," lamented Foisie. "Desk people don't go to parties, they don't get to have lunch with Mrs. Graham when a foreign dignitary is in to see her. They are 'below the salt.' They are usually regarded as hacks who couldn't make it elsewhere on the paper and they sometimes vent their animosity on a reporter's copy. It is all part of the class system in the newsroom." "On *Le Monde,*" said Foisie of the renowned French newspaper, "the copy editors who do the final editing are called 'niggers.'"

There was a time when to be a foreign correspondent was to be virtually at the pinnacle of journalism. Foreign correspondents in Burberry trenchcoats dashed about covering wars and rumors of wars and the rise and fall of nations. The romantic model of Ernest Hemingway was alluring. "We used to be the grand dukes of the profession," mused a newspaperman who had reported from Europe for many years. "Americans," he said, "identified with such wrenching events as Haile Selassie's defense of Abyssinia and the Spanish Civil War in the 1930s, the fate of Britain in 1940, and the Budapest uprising against the Russians to a large degree because they identified with the people who were reporting from those places—radio journalists like Edward R. Murrow and H. V. Kaltenborn. . . . With that great sense of the dramatic, they had a tremendous impact on the public's consciousness," he said. "Now nobody gives a shit about Ethiopia. . . . There is no visible enemy, no clear-cut rights and wrongs and this, too, has led to a de-dramatizing of news from abroad. At home, the issues are more clear-cut, there is a public identification with sides and this has a subtle impact on the key people in the news media." For most thoughtful reporters conditioned by more than a decade of social and political turmoil and swift economic crises, the action was here. Affluence, too, colored their ambitions. "Many of them are no longer lured by overseas travel," said a *Post* editor. "Many of them go to Europe every year on vacation."

Foreign news, nevertheless, remained important to Americans who knew that distant, murky events can quite abruptly and harshly touch their own lives. And the lesson of Vietnam where the *Post* failed to assign a reporter to cover the early years of America's war was stamped indelibly on the paper's managers.

Bradlee had covered Europe for *Newsweek*. During the Algerian civil war in 1956 he had slipped through the French lines to try to reach the rebel headquarters in the Kabylia Mountains, but a winter storm had shut the pass. He believed that a gutsy, intelligent generalist—someone like himself—could hit the tarmac anywhere, spot the story, and quickly file a respectable account of events. A good reporter, Bradlee contended, need not be deeply steeped in the history and culture of a country to accomplish this. While Foisie worried about superficiality in a correspondent's copy, fresh eyes were what the editors wanted most; a competent reporter with as few preconceptions as possible about the assignment. Bernard Nossiter went to India for the *Post* in the early 1960s when the liberal myths still dominated American perceptions of the subcontinent. "I began filing stories that portrayed India not as the world's largest democracy," Nossiter recalled. "Perhaps I wrote myself out of the job." The New Delhi bureau was closed for several years after Nossiter's stay when Bradlee concluded, "the Western world's fate didn't depend on anything that happened in India."

No single path led to a foreign assignment. There were times when a reporter who covered the suburbs one week was dispatched the next to war-battered Beirut or some other cataclysm. The big jets made it relatively easy to cover a big story in a remote part of the world from Washington if necessary. The "Dulles Bureau," the staff labeled it, after the international airport outside Washington. Foisie didn't think a reporter could responsibly do much more than report revolutions or earthquakes this way. His kind of correspondent was more like Jay Matthews, who had edited the *Harvard Crimson* and spoke and read Chinese. Matthews worked for a while as a local reporter so the editors could size him up, but his assignment in 1977 to cover China was written in the stars. The scramble to prepare for an overseas bureau was itself demanding work. Before Karen DeYoung took the Latin America beat, she had to immerse herself in a crash Spanish course while cramming everything she could learn about twenty countries.

Kevin Klose was surprised when Phil Foisie asked if he wanted to cover the Soviet Union. Klose was turned down the first time he applied to the *Post.* Two years later Richard Rovere, a Washington correspondent and old friend of the Klose family, recommended that another old friend, Ben Bradlee, interview Klose, a Harvard graduate. In his eight years on the paper he had never been farther than Chicago on assignment. And he didn't speak Russian. "It will be a grand opportunity for you and your family," Bradlee counseled Klose. "Moscow is the *only* other major capital." Bradlee reassured the thirty-five-year-old staffer that his career wouldn't suffer if he turned down the Moscow assignment. As Klose started out of Bradlee's office, the editor called, "Oh, you know Bradlee's rule, don't you? 'You can only say no three times.' "

Klose started language training and a cram course in Soviet studies. Klose also was finishing a book; to Foisie's dismay he fell behind in preparing for Moscow. But the assignment occurred as scheduled because it was a key element of a newsroom shift that in execution resembled a three-cushion billiards shot. Klose was replacing Peter Osnos, who was returning to succeed Ron Koven, Foisie's assistant. In turn Koven would open a full-time bureau in Paris. Another consideration made this recasting even more felicitous: Klose's successor as District editor would be Herbert Denton. Denton was black. In a city that was 75 percent black it seemed a fair and prudent move.

Some days Bradlee spent more time being a chaplain than editing the paper. There were nearly four hundred men and women working for him. He held in his hands people's careers, which many of them took to be their lives. This made him more than a father confessor. He told a reporter who was hitting the bottle that he once had retrieved his brother from the Bellevue Hospital alcoholic ward and the episode both saddened and bored him. Drunks were dull, Bradlee said; boredom was an abomination to him. No one who bored the editor could profit. The reporter understood this central fact and stopped drinking. Another reporter was struggling through a crumbling marriage and his work slipped miserably. Bradlee sent him to Vietnam, thinking the move would help him regain his reportorial edge. When that didn't work, Bradlee tried the man on other assignments with no more luck and, finally, put him on the police beat, square one for neophytes and

Siberia for burnt-out cases. The reporter quit.

The newsroom was a fiercely competitive place. Reporters and editors frequently vied more intensely with one another for prominence for their stories than with their opposition, the *New York Times* or the *Star.* Part of the explanation for this was a kind of first law of newspaper dynamics: There is always more copy than space. The second law is that better stories drive out good stories. Also there was Bradlee's modus operandi. Richard Harwood, a *Post* editor, described Bradlee's management style: "He got the best horses he could find and threw them into the pit and said, 'sink or swim.'" The mangled metaphor fit. "Everyone in the newsroom knows of people—white and black, male and female—who were talented and promising, but who failed because the *Post* is a big, busy and impersonal place," a staff committee told Bradlee in 1972. "It's a sink or swim operation, and some awfully good people have sunk." The *Post*'s reputation didn't repel applicants; it attracted them. One young reporter exhilaratedly phoned his wife to tell her that the *Post* had just hired him. "It's just like a national park of journalists," he said.

The genius of an editor lies not so much in smelling a great story when only a fragment of it appears; genius is in hiring well—the most important management decision. Bradlee thought this was his great strength, for he had brought very good people onto the paper. Most of the time it was, but not always.

After Russ Wiggins retired as executive editor in 1968 and Bradlee succeeded him, Bradlee's job as managing editor was open. Bradlee and Mrs. Graham passed over several prospects on the staff and picked an outsider, Eugene Patterson. M. E. Patterson possessed impressive newspaper credentials, better really than Bradlee's. He had won a Pulitzer prize for his progressive editorials on the race question in the *Atlanta Constitution.* He had served on President Johnson's Civil Rights Commission, was a war hero, and had an honorary degree from Harvard. He looked a little like E.G. Marshall. Some observers thought the arrival of Patterson, a University of Georgia graduate, was designed to leaven the newspaper with a strain of middle-Americanism. Others believed that Patterson was hired to foreclose the promotion of Ben

Gilbert, the deputy managing editor who often was at odds with Bradlee. Gilbert had been on the paper for twenty-seven years; to Bradlee
he represented the old guard whose time had passed. Patterson was told
by an old friend, a prominent editor in another city, that he was making
a mistake to take Bradlee's offer even though he was job hunting. "The
Post is a snake pit," the friend warned.

Patterson was a professional, decent, and gracious man; those qualities, however, were not enough on the *Post.* He seemed to lack a facile
grasp of Washington's political gears, a honed sense of where the real
centers of power were. This was an egregious flaw for an editor in a
company town where the company's product was politics and power
was an all-consuming, full-time fascination. The *Post* itself, of course,
was a base of power in Washington and its editors knew it. Ben
Bagdikian, a senior editor, was in Patterson's office when the Georgian
got a phone call saying Ron Ziegler, President Nixon's press secretary,
wanted to see him at the White House. Patterson said he would be
right over. "Gene, you're the managing editor of the *Washington
Post,*" Bagdikian said exasperatedly. "Call back and say, 'Have Mr.
Ziegler call me if it's urgent. If it isn't, tell him to come over for lunch
some time.'"

Normally, the managing editor made the final decisions on the play
of major stories. In the daily news conferences "you could see them
sticking it to Patterson," one of the participants recalled. "They just
put him through a very small hole; they were making ravioli out of
him." . . . "Vince Lombardi was their hero; you had to show visible
toughness," said Bagdikian. Bradlee admired physical courage. He once
ordered a large photo of an airline pilot who foiled a hijacking: "That
guy has balls," Bradlee declared. Patterson, who had been one of
George Patton's tank commanders in Europe, simply was outgunned
by his rivals. Bradlee did not discourage the bruising contest; he frequently ended up deciding the front page.

"Bradlee can be heartless, but he is never thoughtless," observed
one of his colleagues. Patterson finally had enough and resigned in
1971. At a small good-bye luncheon with other editors Bradlee said he
was sorry to see Patterson go because he was "the best Irish tenor we

ever had here." After that Patterson quickly left the building. Much later Bradlee said of Patterson's travail: "Gene was born to run something. I wouldn't let him be managing editor. He ended up by doing the scut work."* "Bradlee needs a managing editor like a boar needs tits," Patterson remarked. The quip amused Bradlee. "This is a very fast track, savage, savage, savage and swift," said an editor who had watched the whole bloody affair.

It was 1966 and Phil Graham had been dead for more than three years. Katharine Graham was working hard at running the Post Company and her friend Truman Capote thought his sometime neighbor in Manhattan's swank United Nations Plaza co-op apartments needed a bit of fun. A few days after Thanksgiving the writer gave "a little masked ball" for 540 friends in her honor. "The guests, as spectacular a group as has ever been assembled for a private party in New York, were an international Who's Who of notables," the *New York Times* rhapsodized. They included the crowned heads of communications empires such as William S. Paley of CBS, Samuel I. Newhouse, Sr., of the Newhouse chain, and John Hay ("Jock") Whitney, with whom Mrs. Graham had just closed an important newspaper deal; Henry Ford, II; Undersecretary of State Nicholas deB. Katzenbach; and Secretary of Defense Robert S. McNamara, who was there on a night away from the Pentagon where a possible Christmas-to-New Year's cease-fire in Vietnam was under debate.

Frank Sinatra and his wife, Mia Farrow, twisted to Peter Duchin's orchestra in the candle-lit, white-and-gold ballroom of the Plaza Hotel. Millionaire author Capote laid on four hundred bottles of chilled vintage Taittinger champagne to wash down twelve thousand dollars worth of food. Through that shimmering evening Kay Graham smiled in her white Balmain gown, a matching, bejeweled mask clamped to her thin nose. Some of the masks reputedly cost as much as six hundred dollars; even the Secret Service men guarding the president's daughter, Lynda Bird Johnson, were masked in the hope of being unobtrusive.

---

*Patterson later became editor of the *St. Petersburg Times*, a fine newspaper, and president of the American Society of Newspaper Editors.

More than 150 cameramen, who photographed the luminaries, puzzled over the guest of honor, who was a stranger to them. "What they saw was a tall, well-tended matron, now fifty, with gray Kenneth hair, a scooped-up nose, a chilly little mouth that escalates from C minus to A plus when she smiles, and eyes that Capote artfully describes as 'the color of sherry held to the light' but which are really just plain brown," Judith Viorst wrote. "Nobody could ever call her pretty —handsome is as far as one could go—but the figure, courtesy of tennis and the Canadian Air Force exercises—is admirable. Her voice, though excessively well bred and too redolent of expensive private schools, nevertheless comes off great because it is throaty and mellow and can convey enormous warmth. The laugh—and she has a ready, responsive laugh—often winds up in an inelegant but somehow appealing snort. It seems fair to say that Katharine Graham is not the type to cause large crowds to gather. Having few delusions about herself, Mrs. Graham would agree." Kay Graham remembered that night as "an odd, overaged and gray coming-out party." It was a foretaste of the celebrity that lay ahead for her and the *Post.*

The deal between Kay Graham and "Jock" Whitney involved the *Paris Herald Tribune.* The Washington Post Company was expanding its reach for new places to invest its wealth. Kay Graham's self-confidence at the game of big business had expanded, too, from the time of her tremulous and untutored succession. She was ready to take her first real corporate leap with the counsel of Fritz Beebe, "a negotiator par excellence," as she called him. The significance of the venture involved more than its promise of financial gain; it was another big step for the company—the first was Phil's creation of the Los Angeles Times–Washington Post News Service—toward becoming a global communications giant.

The Paris newspaper had a romantic and exciting past. James Gordon Bennett, Jr., the brash, obstinate, and inventive son of the founder of the *New York Herald Tribune,* established the English-language paper in Paris in 1887 for the American colony. Young Bennett introduced the linotype, the process of photoengraving, and the comic strip to Europe's newspapers. During the German attack on Paris in World

War I, the *Trib* kept publishing after all of the other papers in the city halted their presses; it was the last newspaper in the kiosks when the Nazis marched into Paris in June 1940.

The *Trib* passed into the hands of John Hay "Jock" Whitney, Eisenhower's ambassador to England, when he bought the parent *New York Herald Tribune* in 1958 from the Reid family. The Reids sold because they were losing to their morning competitor, the *New York Times.* Emboldened by that success, the *Times* in 1960 launched a Paris edition to battle the *Trib* for the growing market for an American-oriented daily in Europe. Circulation of the Paris edition of the *Times* lagged behind the *Trib,* which for a while was hawked by pretty American girls wearing yellow T-shirts imprinted with "Herald Trib-une." With the parent *Times'* resources, though, it seemed the new paper would remain a serious challenger, an eventual winner perhaps. By January 1964, however, the *Times* had lost a pot of money on an unsuccessful California-based edition and was losing more than $1 million a year in Paris. Still the *Times* seemed ready to hold on in Europe, no doubt expecting to undo the *Trib* there as it was doing in New York. Success seemed close.

The *New York Herald Tribune* was awash with red ink, and Whit-ney, whose wealth *Fortune* magazine estimated at between $100 and $200 million, folded the paper on April 25, 1966; the Paris edition, which had lost money for many years, looked certain for the same fate. The *Trib,* which depended for much of its editorial copy on the stateside *Tribune* now needed another news base. Whitney turned to the *Wall Street Journal*'s publishers to help strengthen the *Trib* against the *Times,* but Dow-Jones didn't see "room in Europe for two Ameri-can newspapers"—a correct appraisal.

The wobbly prospects facing the *Trib* came up at Art Buchwald's home where his dinner guests included Katharine Graham and Walter N. Thayer, president of Whitney's corporation. Buchwald had worked on the *Trib* for years in Paris until he settled in Washington in 1962; his humor column ran in the *Post.* It was not her first exposure to the possibility of getting hold of the *Trib.* Phil Graham's relations with the *New York Herald Tribune* had been rancorous; with big contracts he had lured prized columnists Walter Lippmann and the Alsop brothers away from the *Tribune.* Graham and wealthy diplomat David K. E. Bruce had talked about bidding together for the European *Tribune.*

Kay Graham was ready to shore up the *Trib* with a generous amount of cash and the daily news file from the *Post;* in return she wanted 50 percent of the embattled paper. She settled for 45 percent, with the option to acquire another 5 percent on Whitney's death. The sixty-two-year-old Whitney remained in control. In October 1966 she and Ben Bradlee flew to Paris for a cocktail party at the chic Lancaster Hotel to christen the new *International Herald Tribune.* For Bradlee, who had lived and worked in Paris for years, it was homecoming weekend. "I still remember," wrote *Tribune* staffer James O. Goldsborough, "Kay Graham at the party shattering one of the yellow T-shirt set who fancied herself a Paris correspondent by blurting, 'Gawd, how young you all are around here.' "

Seven months later, confronting a greatly reinforced, front-running *Tribune* and the continuing drain of its capital, the *Times* closed its European edition. In return for this act of hara-kiri, the *Times* was able to buy into the *Trib* with Whitney and Mrs. Graham. The *Post*'s share of the *Trib* dropped to 30 percent but the gains from elimination of a competitor were worth it. In 1966 when the *Post* and Whitney sealed their bargain, the European *Tribune* reportedly was worth about $4 million; in 1974, the estimated worth was $20 million, and the paper's circulation had doubled. The *Tribune* was directed by a troika of Whitney, Mrs. Graham and Arthur Ochs Sulzberger, publisher of the *New York Times.*

Both Eugene Meyer and Phil Graham had been enthusiastic backers in this country of the European Common Market, which as it turned out was a crucial, albeit unforeseen, factor in the growth of the revitalized *Tribune.* The Common Market, which was the outgrowth of the economic recovery effort, proved a powerful magnet for American capital. Between 1958 and 1967, United States corporations invested $10 billion in Western Europe, according to French politician-journalist Jean-Jacques Servan-Schreiber; half of the six thousand new businesses started overseas by Americans during that period were in

Europe. From 1965 to 1966, American investment rose by 17 percent in the rest of the world, and 40 percent in the Common Market countries. Just as those national borders were becoming a little more than colored lines in atlases to global business managers, the *Trib* was reaching out beyond its traditional base in France. No longer was the paper aimed mainly at American tourists and expatriates. The "Golden Girls" no longer peddled the *Tribune*—they didn't fit the paper's new image as a profit center for three corporations.

Amazing changes in technology have altered the possibilities for continent-hopping specialized daily newspapers. Facsimilies of the *Trib*'s pages edited in Paris are transmitted over leased telephone lines to printing plants in Zurich and near London's Heathrow Airport, from where copies are flown to Scandinavia. The *Trib* is printed at night and many readers have it by breakfast, as fresh as newly picked fruit.

The paper claimed that its subscribers were the elite of the corporate world: 73 percent, executives; at least one in four readers on the board of directors of a major company. In the *Trib* these subscribers got news from the *Post* and the *Times*, as well as editorials from the two papers. "Our appeal is to the advertiser who wants to talk directly to the most important, wealthiest people in Europe," said a *Trib* executive. The *Trib*'s ad rates based on the number of subscribers made it "the most expensive print medium in the world—seven times more expensive than the *New York Times*, six times more than *Le Monde*," *Advertising Age* reported. By the end of 1979 the *Trib* was close to publishing an Asian edition in Hong Kong.

Katharine Graham's maiden voyage in an international business had gone well, indeed. She found time, too, for other global ventures.

Katharine Graham pushed open the heavy glass doors leading from her office suite and walked briskly through the reception room with its black leather and chrome seats and a large Jack Best painting of yellow, blue, red, and green fragments. Behind her the secretaries buzzed worriedly: A chill rain was falling that afternoon in early April 1978 and Mrs. Graham, in a blue dress, was coatless; she'd get wet going from the entrance of the *Post* building to her waiting, chauffeured Mercedes. As she started through the duplicate glass doors leading to the elevator, she slightly turned her head and without breaking stride called back, "I'll want the Brandt report."

They were initially self-styled, neither immodestly nor inaccurately, the Commission of Notables on Third World Development. Former West German chancellor Willy Brandt presided over the unofficial council of luminaries which was the brainchild of Robert S. McNamara, the president of the World Bank. Since leaving the Pentagon in 1967, McNamara had used the Bank's majestic, chandeliered, and wood-paneled offices as a pulpit from which he preached an old gospel that the rich should help the poor. Friends and critics alike interpreted this as McNamara's way of overcoming his possible sense of guilt for his role in the Vietnam war. McNamara charged the Brandt commission in November 1977 with seeking ways to reconcile the potentially explosive differences between the wealthy, industrialized societies and the poorer countries. Besides Brandt the group included Edward Heath, Pierre Mendes-France, Olaf Palme, and Eduardo Frei, once the prime ministers or presidents of Great Britain, France, Sweden, and Chile respectively. Another commissioner was the president of the Washington Post Company, Katharine Graham, probably the richest and most influential among the seventeen notables, and one of the two female members.

For several reasons Mrs. Graham was receptive to McNamara's request that she serve on the commission. When she was attempting to modernize her company, she turned for counsel to McNamara who once ran the Ford Motor Company. When she sought a new president for the Post Company, McNamara recommended that she hire Paul Ignatius, who had been a high-level administrator in the Pentagon. That hadn't worked out, and she let Ignatius go. But her respect and friendship for Bob McNamara held fast. The McNamaras and Mrs. Graham had summer houses on Martha's Vineyard. Her father had been the first president of the World Bank, which was another link between Kay and McNamara. Mrs. Graham had a journalist's intense curiosity, a working knowledge of international finance, and personally knew many leading foreign political figures. Then, too, population control and women's rights, subjects of concern to her, were on the Brandt agenda. The depth of the Graham-McNamara friendship was well known. Such relationships counted far more in the American establishment than business ties; they were subtle and almost always private. This led others to quickly conclude that someone like McNamara was shielded from hard scrutiny from the *Post* by virtue of his bond with the publisher.

By 1975 the World Bank's principal borrowers, the less-affluent countries, were suffering from the sharply rising costs of imported oil. That summer Hobart Rowen, the *Post's* economics editor, spent several weeks investigating reports that McNamara was unwilling or afraid to confront the foreign oil cartel on its actions which were strangling the very development the Bank was supposed to nurture. McNamara, his critics told Rowen, sought to stay in the good graces of the Arab oil states because they had become a major source of the Bank's capital. Rowen, a thorough journalist, also probed allegations that the Bank, in "tilting" toward the Arabs, discriminated against its Jewish employees by yielding to the Saudis' requirement that only Bank personnel with baptismal certificates could enter that country. Rowen also discovered that a few months earlier McNamara had participated in a private meeting called by Secretary of State Henry Kissinger aimed at increasing the pressure on Israel to come to terms on a Mideast peace agreement. The gathering of the so-called "Wise Men" included such former high government officials as Dean Rusk, William P. Rogers, McGeorge Bundy, Cyrus Vance, George Ball, Peter Peterson, and banker David Rockefeller. McNamara, Rowen learned, violated his organization's own rules against such political activity by participating in the meeting.

His digging virtually done, Rowen asked McNamara for an interview. McNamara later would explain to Rowen that he always tried to keep divisive matters "unemotional, rational and in the privacy of the board room." But there in his elegant office, McNamara exploded in outrage. How could Rowen possibly entertain the thought that the Bank or McNamara himself could be anti-semitic. McNamara ranted on, refusing to answer any questions. Rowen got up and walked out.

"In thirty years of reporting, I hadn't been subjected to that kind of abuse," he recalled. The next day McNamara invited Rowen back to his office. He also asked Rowen to submit a list of written questions to him in advance of this second meeting, which the editor did. McNamara expressed what Rowen took to be an apology. But he still refused to answer any substantive questions on the record, saying it was "inappropriate."

Meanwhile McNamara's press officer, and perhaps McNamara himself, complained to Mrs. Graham about Rowen. She asked Rowen about his reporting which involved, tangentially, other friends of hers —such as Kissinger and Rogers, who at one time was the *Post*'s lawyer. She also asked the *Post*'s ombudsman to check into it. Dozens of people complain every day to one person or another in authority at the *Post* about some story. But this was Mac, a dear friend and counselor of Katharine Graham. She was upset that her friend was upset and she wondered why all of this had to be dragged out.

This vignette ends with Rowen's articles running without delay just as he wrote them, two of them on the front page. They were quite blunt about McNamara's administration of the Bank. In their own way they were an eloquent measure of the *Post*'s independence even when its best friends' interests were at stake. More than anything else this journalistic autonomy was Katharine Graham's most significant contribution to the *Post*.

Kay Graham took her work on the Brandt commission seriously, though the severity and complexity of the problems that the group addressed could produce little but humanitarian exhortations. Mrs. Graham on her own could do far more. Before flying to commission meetings in Mali, Lausanne, or India, she carefully interviewed her reporters and editors who had experience in the pending subjects. One of the editors, Peter Osnos, saw the condition of the underdeveloped countries as a major uncovered story. Osnos sounded out McNamara on a series and found him enthusiastic. The stories written by a team of reporters were displayed prominently on the front page. The series, as Mrs. Graham put it, "raised consciousness" about the Third World. In Washington that meant they had political impact.

She took a direct hand in raising consciousness at the *Post* and *Newsweek* on another subject, Asia's "boat people." While traveling in the Far East she went to the Malaysia coast where twenty-six thousand Vietnamese refugees huddled pitifully in a wretched camp with sixteen toilets. She was appalled. She told her editors that they had missed the refugee story. (Henry Kamm of the *New York Times* won a Pulitzer prize in 1977 for his coverage of the mass exodus of Vietnamese and Cambodians.) After that, as the tide of refugees increased, the *Post* and *Newsweek* gave it much heavier attention.

On another occasion Mrs. Graham went to Morocco for a ninety-minute discussion with King Hassan II, an important actor on the African stage, in his Moorish palace. When the Rumanian government got wind that she was going to be abroad, word was sent that President Nicholae Ceausescu would welcome a visit from her. She said that she accepted because "it's the kind of place where the *Times* and the *Post* only go to cover earthquakes, then leave." She wanted to know better the most westernized of the Communist bloc countries. In the Philippines the ruling Marcos family paid her court. They all wanted something from the American government: Hassan, more arms; Ceausescu, most-favored-nation trade status; Marcos, foreign and military aid despite his human rights abuses. They all hoped that Katharine Graham's influence on Washington opinions would work in their favor.

In 1976 the *Post* supported Jimmy Carter for president. After Carter won, his talent scouts asked Mrs. Graham if she would be interested in an ambassadorship? The offer was not intended as a political reward; the editorial endorsement was rather lukewarm and a patronage plum was certainly not what she sought or needed. Graciously she told Carter's emissaries that she wasn't interested. She was far too diplomatic to tell them that there was more real influence in the pages of the *Post* than any ambassador could dream of possessing.

FOUR

Spin

The news of the day as it reaches the newspaper office is an incredible medley of fact, propaganda, rumor, suspicion, clues, hopes and fears. . . . The power to determine each day what shall seem important and what shall be neglected is a power unlike any that has been excercised since the Pope lost his hold on the secular mind.

—WALTER LIPPMANN, 1920

WHEN THE CHICAGO POLICE savaged the young war protesters at the Democratic National Convention in August 1968, they also took a few hard licks at newsmen within reach of their nightsticks. Frank Sullivan, the police public relations man, explained why: "This unruly group of revolutionaries is bent on destruction of our system of government. They represent a pitiful handful, but, by golly, they get the cooperation of the news media." (The protesters were not all moved by ideology; some only wanted to slug cops and the *Post* coined a label for them—"fuzzophobes.")

A press badge provided no immunity from the angry cops and anyone who displayed "media swagger," as Nicholas von Hoffman put it, was a target. The photographers got it the worst. When they pointed their cameras, it was like thumbing their noses at the police, and, of course, their film bore the proof of the blue power rampage. Stephen Northrup of the *Post* was clubbed to his knees twice in fifteen minutes as he tried to photograph the police chasing and beating demonstrators; television camera crews and journalists were assaulted—twenty-one were hurt in one night—by Mayor Daley's finest. The *Post,* though, hired a police chaplain with a flasher-equipped car to get its reporters and, on one occasion, Katharine Graham, around town safely. Von Hoffman, who was one of radical Saul Alinsky's political organizers in Chicago from 1954 to 1963, told the younger *Post* reporters they were there to report, not get hurt or tossed in the slammer.

Mrs. Graham and other media executives wired Mayor Daley to protest the beatings of the newsmen. Daley was unmoved. He felt in his belly what the news moguls with their sophisticated antennae supposedly tuned to public moods were missing, which was that public sympathy was running for the police and against the dissenters and the press. The moguls were astonished: "It was not only the humiliation of discovering that they had been wrong; there was also the alarm at the discovery of their new unpopularity," wrote British journalist Godfrey Hodgson.

The cause of the rising hostility toward the press was not hard to finger. Other institutions that formed the fabric of American society —government, the church, schools, even the family—were being rocked by an earthquake of dissension and skepticism. It was the press, however, unlike the other institutions, that constantly reminded people that their world could be an exceedingly ugly and treacherous place: pollution, crime, poverty, city riots, spaced-out kids, hunger, a war without hint of conclusion. People were offended and frightened by these daily reminders. They yearned for a respite and there was none. They blamed the press for creating the problems that it reported. Shakespeare well understood the problem: "Yet the first bringer of unwelcome news/Hath but a losing office," he wrote in *Henry IV.* But it all was a king's feast for journalists; they were nourished by disasters, strife, and scandal. They were neither inhumane nor morbid, at least no more than anyone else; it was simply that they were rewarded most often by how graphically and quickly they could convey bad news.

The times were made for stereotypes: the streets were filled with them and they made great copy. The "flower children," for example. Newspaper and television photos of long-haired demonstrators inserting flowers into the barrels of GIs' rifles captured the symbolic contest between making love and making war; the *Post,* however, caught on early that dope and peace were not synonymous. Some journalists filed lyrical tales of the greening of America on the hilly sidewalks of San Francisco. Nicholas von Hoffman didn't believe them. In 1967, in "the summer of love," not long after he came to the *Post* from the *Chicago Daily News,* he spent three months burrowing into the Haight-Ashbury demimonde. He'd frequently phone his editors to tell them bizarre bits, and they'd ask if he had become a hippie. There was all that marvelous von Hoffman conversation but no copy.

Ben Bradlee was intrigued. "Finally, I had to go out there and see for myself. I saw drugs, kids bedding down in crash pads, the whole scene. I was convinced." A bunch of bad people were making, dealing, and consuming bad chemicals and it had nothing to do with love. Bradlee was stunned by the poisonous freak show. He came back assured that the counterculture was a dramatic and important story. Von Hoffman's sixteen-part series, "The Acid Affair," declared: "There never were any flower children. It was the biggest fraud ever perpetrated on the American public, and it's your fault, you the mass media. . . . This community is based on dope, not love." This swing-from-the-heels, against-the-grain kind of reporting was precisely what Bradlee wanted. The *Post* was to be surprising; some on the paper criticized it as erratic. This character and tone matched the unpredictability of the turbulent period.

"There has been no more traumatic clash of cultures than that which marked the confrontation between the arriving Nixon administration and the awaiting resident press since Pizarro first dropped in on the Incas," Meg Greenfield wrote in the *Post* soon after the new president entered the White House.

The great Nixon-press war which broke out a year later was an assault on certain wholesalers of news—the major television networks based in Manhattan with their huge national audiences for the nightly news, and the two newspapers that profoundly influenced the news judgments of those networks and other strategic journalistic outlets. The two papers, the *Washington Post* and the *New York Times,* also operated world-wide news services that reached hundreds of other papers. This greatly broadened their impact on the public. At long last these purveyors had turned sour on the Vietnam War, which persisted though Nixon had claimed during the campaign that he had a secret plan to end it. They were liberal on civil rights, favoring an aggressive national commitment to erase racial injustices. Indeed, their intense coverage and emphasis had played a crucial role in the social revolution of the sixties. The irony was that the heavy press attention to the upheaval strengthened the appeal of Nixon to those that feared its consequences. Nixon's constituency wanted government to restrain social change, or at least slow it. Nixon had felt misused by the Eastern wing of the press in his previous political incarnations; he knew that it would be a thorn in his side. A Kennedy or a Johnson by nature could easily stroke the powerful egos that controlled these news organizations; Nixon, constitutionally, could not.

The men closest to the president, H. R. Haldeman and John D. Ehrlichman, were like their liege from the Pacific slope and shared his virulent distrust of the New York–Washington news media axis. Ehrlichman, the president's domestic counselor, Attorney General John Mitchell, and other Nixon associates ventured into what they regarded as the enemy camp several times with complaints about the *Post*'s treatment of their leader. On one occasion over lunch at the paper, the editors met Ehrlichman's indictments of their coverage of the Nixon government with well-reasoned explanations. Ehrlichman curtly dismissed their rebuttal saying, "You're all from New York, anyway." "None of them happened to be from New York," recalled Ben Bagdikian, one of the editors present. "But it was true that two of them were Jews, which in WASP suburbia is often synonymous with 'New York.'"

Nixon believed that much of the liberal press's antagonism to him stemmed from his investigation of Alger Hiss in the late 1940s. The *Post* initially stoutly defended Hiss against the allegations that he supplied State Department secrets to the Russians. But publisher Phil Graham, having decided that Hiss might not be innocent and that the *Post* was being hurt by accusations that it read like *Pravda,* reversed the editorial position.

There was always Herbert Block to convince Nixon that the *Post* truly hated him. Herblock editorial-page cartoons portrayed Nixon sometimes as a simpleton, sometimes reeking of malevolence. Herblock could be a thousand times more devastating than any editorial writer. The cartoons were prominent and aimed at Nixon the politician; there were also little, personal things like reporter Judith Martin's article about Tricia Nixon: "A twenty-four-year-old woman dressed like an ice cream cone who can give neatness and cleanliness a bad name." The White House barred thirty-two-year-old Martin from covering Tricia's wedding.

The *Post* was no cauldron of hatred of Nixon, though during Watergate that became a widely held perception. In the first year of his administration, casualties and violence in Vietnam declined as Nixon sought to negotiate an end to the war. David Broder was one of the rising stars that Bradlee had attracted to the *Post*. In a column that was widely quoted, Broder supported Nixon's efforts. "It is becoming more obvious every day," he warned, "that the men and the movement that broke Lyndon B. Johnson's authority in 1968 are out to break Richard M. Nixon in 1969. The likelihood is that they will succeed again. . . . But when you have broken the president, you have broken the one man who can negotiate the peace." In other articles Broder commended Nixon as an efficient manager of the Rube Goldberg bureaucratic apparatus.

Bradlee once attempted to illustrate to conservative publisher William Rusher the fairness of the paper toward the president. "Richard Nixon happens to be one of the most unphotogenic men," Bradlee said, so his editors continually tried to find "the one untypical picture that represents him in a halfway decent light." "I am touched," replied Rusher, publisher of William Buckley's *National Review,* "by the image of Ben Bradlee sitting there night after night looking, looking anywhere for a single picture of Richard Nixon. . . . it's enough to bring tears to the eyes of a brass Buddha."

In November 1969 Richard Nixon dispatched his surrogate, Vice President Spiro Agnew to Middle America to attack the Eastern media, which was, like "Middle America," an ideological rather than a geographical term. In Des Moines, Agnew criticized "a tiny and closed fraternity of privileged men" in control of the television networks and holding unprecedented power over American public opinion. A week later in Montgomery, Alabama, Agnew—whose vice-presidential nomination a *Post* editorial had called "the most eccentric political appointment since the Roman emperor Caligula named his horse a consul"— opposed "censorship of television or the press in any form. I don't care whether censorship is imposed by government or it results from management in the choice and presentation of the news by a little fraternity having similar social and political views." Interestingly, Nicholas Johnson, a maverick liberal Democrat who spoke with some authority from his seat on the Federal Communications Commission, commented: "Vice President Agnew simply did publicly . . . what corporate and government officials have been doing for years in the privacy of their luncheon clubs and paneled offices. They cajoled and threatened publishers and broadcasters in an effort to manage news and mold images."

Agnew sounded like a twice-born Populist. But there was, not surprisingly given the animus that propelled the White House, a more sinister and hidden aspect to this war on the enemy press. Several weeks earlier Jeb Magruder sent a memorandum to his boss, Bob Haldeman, detailing plans for the assault. Magruder counseled that the Internal Revenue Service, the Justice Department, and the Federal Bureau of Investigation be ordered secretly to harass critical journalists and their publications, and that the Federal Communications Commission secretly apply its regulatory powers to complicate life for unfriendly broadcasters. Before Agnew's speeches, which Nixon himself had edited and toughened, the White House began what Ben Bagdikian called "the greatest assault against the press since the Alien and Sedition Acts of 1798." Nixon had turned press criticism into "Mein Kampf." But it was a narrowly targeted war: Most newspapers backed Nixon for president in 1968; more would again in 1972, even after Watergate broke.

Agnew challenged the unslackening "trend toward the monopolization of the great public information vehicles and the concentration of

more and more power over public opinion in fewer and fewer hands."*
There was, for example, Agnew said, "a single company, in the nation's
capital, [which] holds control of the largest newspaper in Washington,
D.C., and one of the four major television stations, and an all-news
radio station, and one of the three major national news magazines—
all grinding out the same editorial line. . . . these four voices hearken
to the same master." Mistress, not master, Katharine Graham denied
the accusation. Her stations, *Newsweek,* and the *Washington Post*
"disagree on many issues," she retorted, and "they compete vigorously
with one another." The editorial disagreements, when they occurred,
were not about fundamentals; her publications and stations all saw the
world from the same, socially concerned, strongly centrist, capitalist
position.

Nixon wasn't creating public disaffection with the press; rather, he
was feeding on it. Half a century before Nixon was elected president,
no less an observer than Walter Lippmann saw "everywhere angry
disillusionment about the press, a growing sense of being baffled and
misled, and wise publishers will not pooh-pooh these omens. . . ."
Pollster George Gallup, who had been sampling public opinion for
nearly four decades, was saying, "Never in my time has journalism
. . . been held in such low esteem." Louis Harris, another pollster,
reported: "A high seventy-two percent of the most educated people are
the most distrustful of news out of Washington. . . . Scarcely more than
a third of the public agrees with the proposition that the way Washington is covered is a free press operating at its best. . . ." The month of
the Agnew salvos, Nixon's popularity reached a new high of sixty-eight
—up twelve points in one month as the press was sinking in public
regard.

Mrs. Graham complained that her business friends were convinced
that the treatment of the news was distorted. "People in suburban
Prince George's County felt this wasn't their newspaper," an editor
recalled. "P. G. County" in the city room shorthand was blue collar,

*Agnew was hypocritical in his attack on press monopolies. Giant chains like Newhouse and
Hearst—among the good guys in Agnew's press lord pantheon—escaped his ire. They were
powerful proponents of the Newspaper Preservation Act, which legalized per se violations of the
antitrust acts. The *Post* opposed passage of this law.

silent majority, George Wallace territory.

Phil Foisie, a veteran editor, thought that he had a way to defuse at least that part of the attack that was not politically inspired. Foisie proposed to Bradlee that the *Post* hire someone to monitor the *Post*'s treatment of the news. This full-time critic would be chosen by a panel that would represent the various patches of the Washington social quilt, including, for example, a militant black and an erstwhile government official. The critic idea had not seriously been tried by any American newspaper. Probably that was one reason why Ben Bradlee liked it. He saw it this way: "The press is not understood; like most businesses, its initial instinct is to cover up and not tell the truth. If the *Post*'s business is reporting the powerful institutions, we might as well start with ourselves."

In some eyes editors were the country's last autocrats, tightly controlling what went into their papers and, save for the supremacy of their publishers, untrammeled except by their own consciences and tastes. Bradlee thought that was romantic nonsense. The last autocratic editor, he said, was the man who could read his newspaper from beginning to end before going to bed. The *Post* was far too huge, hundreds of thousands of words every day, for him to get through it all.

Bradlee had no intention of surrendering to a full-time critic any of his authority to decide the quality and character of the *Post*. He would, though, welcome the help of someone charged specifically with assessing the completeness, balance, and fairness of the paper's reporting and writing about the *Post*'s performance; someone, though, who was an insider. Bradlee picked national editor Richard Harwood for the job. Harwood had his personal misgivings about the Age of Aquarius with its flower children, draft resisters, and hostile blacks. He was reared in the small towns of the Midwest where his father had been a preacher. Knowing the foibles and prejudices of the press from inside, Harwood sympathized somewhat with what the Agnews were carping about. He was not alone at the *Post*.

In the newsroom, "Spin," as it was called, meant a perceptible bias in a story that distorted reality. But like beauty, spin lay in the eye of the beholder. A reader's own political prism determined how one viewed a particular news story. A group of politically conservative press critics called Accuracy in Media once pressed Katharine Graham to tell them whether anyone on the *Post* was as ideologically right-wing as Ronald Reagan. These critics and others were convinced by their own admittedly biased examination of the news columns that the editors' handling of the news reflected their own left-of-center politics. Mrs. Graham answered that she neither knew nor believed she should know the political persuasions of the staff of nearly four hundred. She then named two men whom she thought might be sympathetic to Reagan —one a correspondent, the other a senior editor—though one could not confirm it by their work, which was what the debate was supposed to be all about.

Emotional times made for emotional copy, and managing editor Eugene Patterson worried about the inclination towards "spin" in the *Post*'s reporting of the rising anti-war movement in the late 1960s. Personally, he supported the war, but he wanted the newspaper's coverage to be balanced and fair. As reporter Haynes Johnson was leaving the newsroom to cover an anti-war procession, Patterson urged him to look for the "other side" of the story. Each of the hundreds of marchers carried a placard with the name of a dead GI. Jonson spotted one with the name Homer Ruple. He reported the anguish of the teen-ager who carried the sign; then he tracked down Ruple's mother in Michigan and reported her grief that the protestors would use the name of her dead boy who had been proud to go to war. Johnson almost won a Pulitzer Prize for the story.

While dismantling some stereotypes, like the hippies, the Post clung to other one-dimensional images until those, too, were excised. Bill Greider, who grew up in Ohio and went to Princeton, came back from an extensive reporting assignment feeling the *Post* suffered from an incredible opacity about the rest of America. He wrote to Harwood:

Anyone who grew up west of the Appalachian range understands, down deep, that what Agnew says about the eastern bias (and what Goldwater and Wallace said before him) is right. Agnew describes it as liberal, which suits his political purpose, but it is really cultural. It turns up in the news columns of the *Post, Times* and other members of the media axis. The core of it is the unspoken assumption that the rest of the country is filled with boobs, simple folk who look eastward for their model of the nobler goals, but can be expected to do the wrong thing. . . . Even the occasional "Visit to Main Street" stories, which admittedly are attempts to overcome this bias, often wind up confirming that Babbitt still lives just over the mountain.

Harwood relished any chance to puncture some widely held belief, especially if it carried the liberal seal of approval. A slight smile would form on his lips as he made his point. He was hardest on his own craft, convinced that the press was far off base in its perceptions of that mist-shrouded object of endless journalistic scrutiny, the "body politic." Richard Scammon, one of the foremost political demographers and a Democrat, had been talking to Harwood and confirmed his doubts. In the spring of 1970, Scammon said, a Gallup survey showed "Nixon's strongest support in the country was among people under thirty and that his least support was among people over fifty. I suggest you would never have guessed that if all you had been reading was the *Washington Post.* . . . I do think that by limiting yourselves to happenings you may be creating a very false picture of this country today. You have even gotten into the habit of using the words 'student' and 'youth' interchangeably, as if the Harvard radical and the Italian boy in the White Castle kitchen are the same guy. They aren't."

The *Post* gave the campus upheaval heavy play. Over lunch at the *Post,* Alexander Heard, the chancellor of Vanderbilt University, justified this emphasis. He had just been appointed Nixon's special adviser on campus sentiments. It was more important for the president to listen to seven million college students, Dr. Heard said, than to heed ten million Wallace voters because the students are "more important —they will run the country one day." The elitist rationale that Heard put straightaway to the editors may well have been subliminally shaping their news judgments about college dissension for several years.

Daniel Patrick Moynihan, newly out of the Nixon Cabinet, attempted to put a scholarly sheen on the White House attack on the news media. "One's impression," Moynihan wrote in the March 1971 *Commentary,* "is that twenty years and more ago the preponderance of the 'working press' (as it liked to call itself) was surprisingly close in origins and attitudes to working people generally. They were not Ivy Leaguers. They now are or soon will be. Journalism has become, if not an elite profession, a profession attractive to elites. . . ."

Ben Bradlee at times agreed that the *Post* news staff was "too Eastern, too Ivy League, too elitist." Occasionally, he would make a stab at offsetting this tilt. "Go get me a Boy Scout from Texas," he told the committee which each year picked news interns from more than a thousand applicants. "And they got me a Boy Scout from Texas with a brush cut," Bradlee recalled, "and he turned out to be radically left." "I doubt we're susceptible to being Middle American," Bradlee concluded.

Measured by income and education, journalists on the *Post* are an elite. Most reporters with at least four years' experience make more than \$30,000 a year; many on the staff earn considerably more. Only five percent of American families have annual incomes of more than \$32,000. Almost all of the reporters and editors have college diplomas and many have graduate degrees, while only about one in seven adult Americans have completed four years of college. (The Washington area was far ahead of the rest of the country by these income and schooling measures, too.) One could conclude from such numbers almost anything to match one's predisposition about the biases of journalists. Such interpretations tended, on close challenge, toward squishiness as far as providing any insight into behavior.

Still there was a kind of gene pool from which many reporters were drawn. "All—*all,* not some—they're all idealistic," said Steven D. Isaacs, who as city editor had directed many of the young reporters on the *Post.*

They all believe in change in the status quo. They come not because they're good writers, not because they have printer's ink in their veins, it's only because they want to change the world. They're all, or vitually all, Democrats because that's been the party of change. It explains the clash between the Young Turks in the newsroom and the older guys who've come to terms with the world, who know how difficult it is to change anything. Agnew was right. A particular type of person, a little bit crazy, a little bit immature, a little bit foolish to be that idealistic.

Isaacs was overdrawing. Many saw reporting as a front-row seat on the world rather than a way to change it.

His reporters, Bradlee said proudly in a reprise about Watergate, were "more activist, more impatient" than those of an earlier generation. But Bradlee was wary of world-savers in his newsroom. Some reporters had their own agendas for social reform, though it would have been heresy and worse, professional suicide, to admit it. "We don't wear our political hearts on our sleeves," he'd say, regarding himself as properly apolitical for his job. This predisposition dated back to before he became a journalist. After getting out of the navy in 1945, Bradlee needed a job and he turned to a friend from Boston, Roger Baldwin, who ran the American Civil Liberties Union, an organization dedicated to defending the Bill of Rights. Baldwin hired Bradlee for three months at thirty dollars a week to catalogue the A.C.L.U.'s library. "Roger thought I'd read the books, which I did, and be influenced by them. I did it to eat, not for the politics," Bradlee recalled.

Nick Kotz came to the *Post* with a Pulitzer prize for investigating abuses in the meat packing industry in Iowa. He had been writing about economic and racial injustices since 1961 and was dedicated to using journalism to end these social evils. In 1973 Kotz and Bill Greider wrote a series that ran almost fifty thousand words which described inequalities that persisted despite the wave of Great Society laws. Dick Harwood, who had assigned the series, twitted the two that their final piece read like a Marxist essay, which it wasn't, of course. But they had corroborated their conclusions, and it ran. Kotz reported the impact on small farmers and consumers of the massive spread of corporate farming. Tenneco, an agribusiness giant, pulled its ads out of *Newsweek* to punish the Washington Post Company for Kotz's articles. Bradlee told Kotz it was nothing to worry about. A reporter who could back up his assertions and write an interesting article could get a story on virtually any subject, no matter how controversial, into the paper.

Bradlee wanted stories that deftly explained how the economic engine worked, though his eyes would glaze over at lengthy discussions of economics. He wanted someone, for example, to dig into the stock market, but there were few daily journalists around who could deliver such reporting. He wanted the paper to be out in front of events, but a profound reality of most popular journalism is that it is the servant of events. "We're always writing about the sunsets," he complained. "I want someone to write about the sunrises."

Philip M. Stern, a wealthy liberal Democrat, was an old friend of Bradlee. Ben called him "Pepe." Stern had written a first-rate book that exposed inequities in the federal tax laws. He was going through a painful divorce and was looking for a way to restore some order to his life. He asked Bradlee for a reporting job. To strengthen his case, Stern prepared a list of more than a dozen stories he proposed to pursue, including Nixon's politicizing of the Internal Revenue Service, the conduct of the regulatory agencies, and several consumer issues. Just before Christmas 1973, Stern was asked to lunch with managing editor Howard Simons, Harwood, and economics columnist Hobart Rowen. "This is just Ralph Nader stuff," Simons said as he leafed quickly through Stern's seven-page list. "Nader had learned how to use the press to get his voice heard; he was a genius at it," Simons observed on another occasion. (Simons later ruled that the term "public interest" as a descriptive for Nader-like organizations be dropped or preceded by the conditional "self-styled" because where the "public interest" lay was under unending debate.) Stern, it was true, got most of his story possibilities from friends in consumer action organizations, but he argued, correctly, that Nader had been doing the press's work in probing and reporting consumer abuses.

The luncheon ended with Stern convinced that he had struck out. Harwood, however, soon wrote to Stern about his own sense that the country was entering a period "when such issues as the distribution of wealth and the social responsibility of corporations will be on the agenda later or soon." Harwood continued: "It would be enormously helpful, in any case, to have someone on the staff who understands real life economics—the corporate mind, marketing imperatives, multinational operations, profits and losses, the banking system and its relation to the corporate system, the workings of money markets, Wall Street . . . the nature of the economic machine." Harwood's proposal awed Stern. "It was like the mythical Harvard test question: 'Explain the universe and give two examples'," Stern recalled. Harwood saw a need for a latter day Ida Tarbell, the writer who tore the wrappings off the innermost unscrupulous workings of Standard Oil with her penetrating journalism at the turn of the century.

Stern came to work on a six-month trial. He produced a few lengthy dissections of the insurance industry, an enterprise that affects everyone's purse and is barely covered by newspapers. The subject was complex; the articles were not light going. His copy would sit for days on national editor Harry Rosenfeld's desk waiting to be read. Finally Rosenfeld would pick up the manuscript, turn to the last page and groan, "Jeez, how long is this?" Two months after Stern joined the *Post* and a few of his stories were on the front page, he saw his old friend, Katharine Graham, at a party. "Are you in the city room?" she asked with genuine surprise when he told her what he was doing. "Wasn't the publisher reading her newspaper?" Stern asked himself. Then he had a darker thought: His articles were landing with a thud rather than a bang.

When the six months were up, Rosenfeld told Stern, "There is no slot for you." Stern tried to explore with Bradlee what went wrong and what leads for other reporters to follow he could leave behind. The editor was preoccupied. Bradlee talked mostly about the time he was having to devote to his accountants because of all the money he was making on his memoir of John Kennedy.

While there are common standards for fair and responsible reporting and editing, much about these processes is amorphous, vulnerable to distortion, and amazingly fragile. Howard Simons, the *Post* managing editor, had no doubts that bias shaped the way the news was reported and edited. But the bias was an amalgam of "differing metabolisms, skills, inculcations, and educations, not to mention whether they slept well the night before," as Simons put it, rather than partisanship or ideology.

By the time of the 1972 election campaign, Nixon's war against the press had largely succeeded. The news system inherently operates as an instrument of the presidency. A White House incumbent dominates the national political news and commands massive attention by virtue of the office. "Any sort of bullshit will be given a seriousness and authenticity because it is from the White House," said Bill Greider. "We give them substance because they are presidential words when we know presidential broadsides don't have much substance." "Tympanies and trumpets," Greider called these presidential outpourings. Richard Nixon, no less and probably more than any other modern president, capitalized on this reality of journalism. Nixon remained aloof from the campaign hustings. Instead he issued statements from the sanctum of the White House, which were subjected to little critical reporting.

The opposite was the case with Nixon's challenger. Through September and into October George McGovern was intensely covered by the press as he stumped the country while Nixon played the working president too busy for politics. Bill Greider was covering McGovern for the *Post* and complained to his editors that Nixon was getting "a free ride" from the press. Watergate had broken in June and, mainly because of the *Post*'s probing, the links to the Nixon campaign committee and the White House were known. Safe in the Oval Office, however, Nixon escaped any direct press questioning. Greider's editors told him he was soft on McGovern from having traveled with the senator so long. Greider's reporting was sensitive but honest and not protective of McGovern when he fumbled, as in the Eagleton fiasco. "McGovern didn't get overscrutinized," said Richard Harwood. "Nixon got underscrutinized." The press was aced out by Nixon.

Like Mr. Dooley's Supreme Court, editors also read the " 'lection returns." As the Nixon re-election landslide was crushing the Democrats, the two newspapers that were the prime targets of the White House attack went shopping for conservative commentators for their opinion pages. Philip Geyelin, editor of the *Post* editorial page, offered William Safire, a Nixon publicist and speech writer, a column in the newspaper and *Newsweek* and a broadcast slot on the *Post*'s stations in Washington. The *New York Times* also cast its net for Safire and outbid the *Post.*

Geyelin said later that the *Post* was looking for "a genuine philosophical Tory and not a house Republican apologist." It found him in George Will, a thirty-one-year-old Princeton Ph.D. who had worked for a conservative Republican senator and was literary editor of the right-wing *National Review.* Will, however, was unshakably faithful to the Constitution. He condemned the sacking of the great charter under Nixon. Will wrote in early 1974 that the impeachment process in motion against Nixon was first among the constitutional "securities to liberty and republicanism" and, therefore, "Conservatives should not flinch" from supporting impeachment.

Liberation. If any one word characterized the past decade and a half in America, it was liberation—from a hundred real and imagined oppressions, from foul air, from college grades, from marriage, sometimes from reality. Social conventions were being rapidly overturned. These tidal changes in long-held proprieties washed into the newsroom.

In late October 1969 Richard Cohen, a young reporter, handed in a story about a controversy in Maryland over the showing of the Swedish movie, *I Am Curious (Yellow),* the hottest pornographic film around then. Speaking to four hundred librarians, Attorney General Francis Burch, the state's highest legal officer, defended censorship of the movie. Cohen reported Burch's fatherly worry, "I don't want my daughter to go out and watch *I Am Curious (Yellow)* in an open-air theatre and go out and get laid after that." Hank Burchard, who was Maryland editor that Friday, left intact Burch's unambiguous statement. The copy editors blanched when they saw it and were debating its removal with Burchard as Ben Bradlee walked in. Bradlee quickly penciled out the words "and get laid" and put parentheses around "go out," assuming most readers could supply the term needed to make sense of the sentence. After the story ran, Burchard, a huge fellow with curly red hair, angrily wrote a memo to Bradlee with copies to others including Katharine Graham. Burchard titled his epistle, "I Am Curious Why We Are So Yellow." The thirty-year-old staffer questioned the extent to which editors should arrogate to themselves the protection of their readers' feelings. Editors on most days dealt with the question in one form or another. But the memo, as Burchard soon realized, was incredibly smart-ass and self-defeating.

On Monday Bradlee replied with a note that played back Burchard's inflammatory indictments. "There's a long answer to your latest pop-off and I'd be happy to give it to you if you give a shit," Bradlee said. "But there's a much shorter answer. If I worked for an organization and for people who were 'yellow,' 'outrageous,' 'unworthy,' 'pitiful,' 'laughable,' and had committed a 'perversion of the public trust,' wild horses couldn't keep me on the premises. What's keeping you?" Burchard apologized.

In part the episode was generational. Older journalists tended to be more protective of their readers' sensibilities. "This is a family newspaper," they'd say. A reporter would then know that the word or phrase in dispute would be excised or transmuted into an elision, a euphemism, or paraphrase so that the story could be seen by anyone in the household. Editors were careful about letting "Christ" as an expletive or "Goddamn" into the *Post* lest deeply religious readers take offense. Younger editors and reporters wanted stories to appropriately reflect at least a touch of the sexual explicitness that had become common in the language of the young and the hip. Many younger staffers were readers of the underground press, the tabloid anti-establishment newspapers that proliferated in the counterculture of the sixties; some reporters on straight newspapers had worked on alternative papers where obscene language was frequently used to shock and ridicule authority. (When the *Washington Free Press* got in trouble with the law for running a crude drawing of a local judge masturbating, the *Post* defended the weekly. "Its purpose was to arouse political, not sexual, excitement," a *Post* editoral said. "It lampoons a judge. That may be scurrility but it is not obscenity.") *Newsweek* in 1969 estimated that these papers had a total circulation of two million, and some said the figure was much higher.

Sometimes an editor would slip a phrase or sexually vivid treatment into the paper simply to test the "family newspaper" tolerances. The Sunday morning dawned when Style carried Tom Huth's fictionalized portrait of his passing love affair. "She spread her legs out rather lavishly," he wrote of the woman he met on the Mall. Later in her bedroom, Huth continued, "she rose up on her knees and gaily flung off her nightie. She fell back on the pillow and fluffed out her hair, in

B-grade imitation. 'Yes,' she whispered, 'let's.' . . . I came quickly."
Judy Bachrach wrote a long Style section article about a young woman
who was killed by her lover, a hairdresser. He inserted a .375 magnum
revolver in her mouth as they lay nude with two other women with
whom they had just had sex, and fired a single shot, Bachrach reported.

The *Post*, perhaps, wasn't deliberately appealing to prurient tastes.
But it had not escaped the paper's managers that the fastest growing
segment of the Washington area's population was the eighteen- to
thirty-five-year-olds—between seven and eight hundred thousand of
them, the baby boom of the forties. They tended to be well-educated;
a large share of the married couples were childless. They spent freely
on clothes, records, books, and leisure. They were a generation that
read *Playboy, Penthouse* and *Rolling Stone,* publications with enormous advertising profits.

Ads that were sexual in nature raised questions for the *Post* and
other newspapers. The *Los Angeles Times* banned sexually explicit
movie ads and the *Post* considered following suit. Robert McCormick,
the *Post*'s vice-president for advertising and a graduate of Jesuit
Georgetown University, agreed personally with the *Times*'s decision.
On his office shelf were blue and black binders entitled "Standards of
Acceptance," the guidelines for handling questionable ads. The *Post*
decided to accept ads for abortion clinics, which were not licensed,
based on whether a physician was associated with the services; it ran
ads for condoms, too. The paper vetoed massage parlor notices. "I took
the calls from the massage parlor operators," McCormick recalled.
" 'There's no reason not to believe that they're all whorehouses,' I told
them. 'That's not your problem,' they answered. They didn't argue
with me about my conclusion, just my denial of the ad space." The
Post decided finally to continue running ads for sexually provocative
films—the annual revenue from which totalled "six figures," according
to McCormick—because people "can go or not go, it's voluntary,
there's no physical harm."

Homosexuality was a subject that had long been avoided by the
press, except in the most roundabout phrases. In the closing weeks of

the 1964 presidential campaign, Walter Jenkins, one of President Johnson's closest aides, was arrested for a homosexual encounter in the YMCA men's room near the White House. The *Washington Star* killed the story after a hurried entreaty from Abe Fortas and Clark Clifford, two of Johnson's most trusted confidants. They also urged editors at the *Post* to suppress the story, which they knew would embarrass the president and perhaps threaten his election. The editors were sympathetic because of the political climate. There was an interest in protecting Johnson, who was trying to reknit a nation and a government terribly shaken by the murder of John Kennedy and who was being challenged for the presidency by a reactionary. Earlier in the year *Post* reporters covering the corruption investigation involving Bobby Baker, a Lyndon Johnson Senate protégé, witnessed their editors' uneasiness over the political harm that disclosures might do LBJ. "We don't shit on the president of the United States," one senior editor declared during a discussion of how to handle an article about the Baker scandal recalled Laurence Stern, one of the reporters on the story. The sluice gates opened on the Walter Jenkins incident when the wire services reported the arrest. The *Post* and other papers then carried the news.

But homosexuals, encouraged by the gains of the civil rights and women's liberation movements, organized, demonstrated, lobbied, and litigated their way into the news. "By discussing the issue in terms of conflicting public views, of opinion polls and votes, the press shattered the taboo against visibility, and homosexuality suddenly found for itself a place on the political map," Ken Ross wrote in the *Nation.*

The vestiges of taboos, however, have a way of lingering. Post reporter Karlyn Barker turned in an assigned story on the problems in the women's political movement, including the schism between gays and straights. The story obviously troubled the editor handling it. For several days he repeatedly asked Barker for more attribution from official spokespersons and specific numbers of movement members. The movement in 1971 was loosely structured, had no official voices, and above all, inherently distrusted the press for its frequently cavalier reporting of the subject. Finally, the editor told Barker, who was new on the *Post,* "I find lesbianism personally offensive." She complained to District editor Barry Sussman. He put the story in the paper with the reference to lesbianism in the first paragraph.

By the mid-seventies the *Post* regularly covered the emergence of homosexuality from the closet. Style ran a detailed account of the "marriage" and domestic life of two young gays, illustrated with pictures of their hairy hands with matching silver wedding rings. A measure of the gays' political power in Washington—there were roughly fifty thousand ¹omosexuals in the city—was the prohibition against barring homosexual teachers from District schools, the country's first such ordinance. They were news that couldn't be ignored.

For all of the criticism that the news spin of the *Post* favored the dissenters in the streets, the long-standing bias of the paper and others in the press was toward established authority. The relationship between the press and the FBI, for instance, was particularly close.

Many reporters were sympathetic to the FBI, believed it was incorruptible, and relied on it as a sole source for certain stories. These factors mingled with a fear of what the agency could do to those in its disfavor. A bare handful of journalists in the fifties like I. F. Stone, James Wechsler, and Fred Cook criticized the Bureau for its abuses against the political left. "But one would search the *New York Times* and *Washington Post, Time* and *Newsweek* of the 1950s in vain for the exposure and disapproval such journals lavished on Hoover twenty years later when it at last became safe to take on the FBI," observes Arthur M. Schlesinger. In March 1954 the lead article in *Harper's* questioned the effectiveness of the FBI's vacuum cleaner kind of collection of information about government employees. The byline was that of Alan Barth of the *Post.* Publisher Philip Graham had refused to run the piece, contending that the *Post* was taking on enough enemies in its fight against Joe McCarthy without going to war with the FBI. Barth, a gentle man of tough principles, rejected Graham's request not to give it to the magazine. In an FBI-prepared Senate speech the next month, Barry Goldwater indirectly linked Barth to a supposed plot to smear the bureau.

In 1964, when the FBI was still virtually unassailable, Ben Bradlee, then Newsweek's Washington bureau chief, was privy to two political abuses by the FBI involving LBJ. On the night of August 14, Bradlee interviewed Johnson for a little more than three hours in the White House for a *Newsweek* cover story on the approaching Democratic presidential convention. Johnson was brimful with confidence about the November election: A stack of polls was on a table next to him and they all showed him steamrollering Barry Goldwater, the Republican nominee. Bradlee asked Johnson if anything surprised or shocked him since he had been in office. "By God, I'll tell you something that shocked and surprised me," Johnson blurted. Bradlee in his memo to *Newsweek*'s editors in New York recounted, in his words, "this incredible tale—here somewhat cleaned up in the interests of propriety and taste":

It appears that one night during the Republican convention, LBJ was lying in bed reading the FBI report of that whorehouse. . . . It was supposed to be Bobby Baker's whorehouse, but it wasn't. (You'll remember back about two months ago Whispering Willie Williams of Delaware announced that a prostitute in nearby Maryland had turned over to Prince Georges County authorities a list of more than one thousand customers in a card index file, including 'several' members of Congress and some ball players. We all looked into the case, and since it stood on the single testimony of a convicted prostitute, everyone dropped it. Not LBJ, nor apparently the FBI. The story continues in LBJ's priceless words.)*

I'm damned if this Republican member of Congress didn't call up this whorehouse and announce that he wanted to get hisself some blank. He didn't know that four FBI agents heard him ask for such and such a girl. So he went out there and knocked himself off blank blank, and he even came downstairs and put his arm around the girl and told her how good it was, and all the time the FBI is under the stairs getting it all. And then so help me God just then I look up at the television and here is this same feller pounding the podium out in San Francisco talking about Bobby Baker. (We have the entire staff working on this, fellows. Be patient).

LBJ at this moment was leaning forward, right hand on his knee, elbow akimbo, grinning from ear to ear.

*Bobby Baker was Johnson's chief aide when LBJ was the Senate majority leader. In 1964 the Justice Department was investigating Baker's questionable relations with lobbyists, including allegations involving call girls. Baker later was convicted for tax evasion and fraud. Senator John J. Williams, a Delaware Republican, was one of Baker's most vocal critics.

Furthermore, he went on, there was an eighty-three-year-old former Republican senator who went out there regularly to blank blank blank.

Quite obviously the FBI was wiretapping or bugging the premises, perhaps as part of its legitimate probe of corruption, and passing the juicier morsels to the President of the United States for whatever amusement or political gain he could derive. Johnson's political misuse of the FBI was disclosed almost ten years later through a Senate investigation of intelligence agency abuses. Johnson, according to William Sullivan, a former assistant FBI director, also used FBI-gathered derogatory information against his opponents within the Democratic Party by leaking it to friendly Republicans. The *Newsweek* story on Johnson, written by the staff in New York, omitted any suggestion of questionable practices by the FBI. Could so sharp and responsible a journalist as Bradlee, whose memo included the number of times Lyndon Johnson belched during the long interview, have missed them? What *Newsweek* did say was that any opponents who tried in the campaign to tie Johnson to anything shady would be "taking certain risks themselves. Lyndon Johnson knows where many a political body is buried and he plays to win." The opponents probably got the warning.

Three months later Bradlee was preparing another *Newsweek* cover article, this one on J. Edgar Hoover. Bradlee interviewed the FBI director at bureau headquarters. After he left Hoover's office, Cartha DeLoach, the director's assistant, made the journalist a rather startling offer. According to Bradlee, DeLoach had a transcript of what was purported to be an adulterous sexual encounter between the civil rights champion Martin Luther King and a woman in a hotel room. The transcript patently was the product of FBI or police bugging of Dr. King's hotel room. Much later the public learned that from December 1963 until his murder in 1968, Dr. King was the target of an intensive campaign by the FBI to destroy his effectiveness as a civil rights leader. "No holds were barred," said William Sullivan, who ran the FBI's clandestine effort against the black minister. "We have used similar techniques against Soviet agents," Sullivan testified before a special senate committee investigating abuses of intelligence agencies. Spurred on by Hoover, who despised King, the bureau tried to destroy his reputation as a moral exemplar with government officials, churches, universities, and the press.

Bradlee refused to accept or examine the transcript that DeLoach proferred. He told Attorney General Nicholas DeB. Katzenbach about DeLoach's offer. The period was extremely touchy for the civil rights movement and Katzenbach realized the FBI was playing with political dynamite. Three days later Katzenbach and Burke Marshall, head of Justice's Civil Rights Division, flew to the LBJ Ranch in Texas to inform the president. Hoover's enormous power, solidified over a tenure of almost half a century, was measured by the fact that his statutory boss, the attorney general, had to implore the president to control the director rather than attempt it himself. About this time a reporter asked Katzenbach why he didn't fire Hoover. "Of course, I can fire Hoover," Katzenbach smiled, "but who would be the attorney general the next morning?" Hoover's license was such that he could cavalierly ignore attorneys general and deal unilaterally with presidents and a few key allies in Congress.

Katzenbach later said that at the LBJ Ranch he and Marshall "expressed in very strong terms our view that this (the King tapes) was shocking conduct and politically extremely dangerous to the presidency. I told the president my view that it should be stopped immediately and that he should personally contact Mr. Hoover. I received the impression that President Johnson took the matter very seriously and that he would do as I recommended." Marshall testified that Johnson was "shocked" and that the "conversation was in the context of it being very important and a very nasty piece of business that had to be stopped." The two officials, however, left the ranch without knowing the president's precise intentions.

What happened, it was revealed by a senate investigation in 1976, more than ten years after the events, was this: Johnson's assistant, Bill Moyers, advised DeLoach that the president had learned that Bradlee was telling others in Washington about the incident. Speaking for Johnson, Moyers, according to a DeLoach memorandum, attributed to Bradlee the statement that, "If the FBI will do this to Martin Luther

King, they will undoubtedly do it to anyone for personal reasons." DeLoach's memo went on: "Moyers stated the president wanted to get this word to us so we would know not to trust [the newsman]. Moyers also stated that the president felt that [the newsman] lacked integrity and was certainly no lover of the Johnson administration or the FBI. . . ." Moyers later did not refute the conclusion that Johnson took offense at Bradlee's comments rather than at the FBI's violation of King's constitutional rights.

Back in Washington from Texas, Katzenbach heard from one or two other reporters of similar offers from DeLoach a week earlier. He recalled that he asked at least one of the reporters if he "would join me in confronting the bureau on this issue. [He] declined to do so."

"Bradlee was very courageous to do what he did, to warn the attorney general . . . ," said Washington journalist David Wise, a specialist on the intelligence bureaucracy. "The press," Wise recalled, "was used to living with these agencies and feeding off them and relating to them and using them as sources, and it would have been like pushing a self-destruct button for a reporter to have done it [expose the FBI]." Wise also reasoned that there was the practical deterrent that a reporter would have to describe to some extent the nature of the King tape's contents in order to clearly tell the story. "I was outraged by it, but it was a private thing," Bradlee explained later. He had acted as citizen Bradlee, not journalist Bradlee.

During the height of the civil rights and anti-war movements, reporters frequently were told that the government was secretly and illegally trying to destroy political dissent. "We were hearing from the crazies in the street about spying and provocateurs, but we were disbelieving in conspiracies," *Post* reporter Bill Greider remembered. "Despite their supposed cynicism reporters' political consciousness could not accept, wouldn't recognize the hypocrisy and mischief of these police and intelligence agencies. There was a romantic, conventional faith in the government."

Then came the documents. Papers stamped "secret" that could be laid on a reporter's desk and studied as tangible evidence of what the crazies were alleging. A glimpse into a police state sewer. On June 13,

1971, the same Sunday that the *New York Times* disclosed the secret Pentagon Papers, the *Post* had a story on Page One that presented more undeniable evidence of the government's paranoia and indecency. The story was based on documents stolen from the FBI's office in Media, Pennsylvania, and widely circulated to the press. The Media papers revealed that the FBI, among other abuses, had conducted an elaborately planned clandestine campaign of harrassment against American organizations and individuals whose political views were perceived by the bureau to be a threat to the country's tranquility. Ed Guthman, the national editor of the *Los Angeles Times,* put the story on the front page of his paper, too. Guthman had been Attorney General Robert Kennedy's press secretary; he understood the importance of the Media papers. They were, in their way, the domestic version of the Pentagon Papers, revealing government abuses of its citizens.

Out of the social upheaval and protest politics of the sixties there arose a new and revolutionary attitude toward government and authority in general within important segments of the press. This attitude took firm root at the *Post.*

FIVE

Awash in Lies

"You think we lie to you," Lord Tyrell, permanent undersecretary of state of the British Foreign Office, once told a correspondent. "But we don't lie, really we don't. However, when you discover that, you make an even greater error. You think we tell you the truth."

"The lies. The lies."

They had been pouring out of the government for years, Ben Bradlee was saying, and the press had printed what the government said without hard challenge, as though reporters actually were part of the steno pool. And then "the rules changed," said Bradlee. "They changed over Vietnam. The lies people were told. All that promise at the end of the tunnel. Richard Nixon had the misfortune to run up against those new rules." "It was almost inevitable," said Carl Bernstein.

It was too simple a formulation to entirely explain the *Post*'s extraordinarily aggressive reporting of Watergate, though the war undoubtedly was part of the reason. The Pentagon Papers; the military's attempted cover-up of the My Lai massacre; the secret, sustained bombing of Cambodia ("The people who were being bombed knew it, the godless Commies knew it, only the American people didn't," Bradlee recalled angrily): the official, studied, deception, once peeled away, consumed public confidence like a cancer. Bradlee once tried to explain how the limitations of the daily news business often made the press a party to this mendacity: "We don't print the truth. We print what we know, what people tell us. So we print lies." And Richard Nixon loved that confession and quoted Bradlee in his memoirs. In his eyes, Bradlee unintentionally had vindicated him and proved that he was right all along to believe that the *Post* hated him.

The press long embraced what Nixon's transient head of the FBI, L. Patrick Gray, called "that presumption of regularity" about the government. Watergate broke in a period when more, but certainly not all, journalists were questioning authority and challenging assumptions about news that were long taken for granted; namely, that news, in effect, meant "quote the cops," or other "authorities," as the providers of the "facts." Reporters tended to accept the word of experts, and the government had most of the experts; slowly the journalists learned that the experts' information and judgments might be seriously flawed. This challenge of authority was the "most profound change" in the press in recent times, in the opinion of Howard Simons, the *Post* managing editor. "We had been too slavish in our respect for authority," said Stephen Rosenfeld, a *Post* editorial writer. "It was like a coiled spring was loosed by Watergate, a way to undo the shame of the sixties for our excessive respect of authority." Bradlee believed that the publication of the secret Pentagon Papers the year before Watergate marked the end of journalistic innocence; there was a realization that the Emperor might not have on any clothes.

The Pentagon Papers case was the most colossal breach of security in the nation's history. At least it seemed so in the beginning. Thousands of pages of highly classified Defense Department and White House documents concerning Vietnam were handed over surreptitiously, first to the *New York Times* and later to the *Washington Post*, by Daniel Ellsberg in the spring of 1971.

Ellsberg was a former defense analyst who had served in Vietnam and worked on compiling the top secret documents. He had lost his prior zeal for the policies the papers chronicled and had tried to prompt congressional hearings on the papers, a copy of which he had pirated. After that didn't work, Ellsberg leaked them to the press in the hope that the disclosures would stir increased opposition to the war. The

Times began publishing long excerpts from the material on Sunday, June 13.

During a visit to CIA headquarters soon after the stories appeared, E. Howard Hunt, an ex-CIA officer of long experience, told the agency's deputy director, General Robert E. Cushman, Jr., that this cloudburst of classified information "electrified" the White House, where he worked. At the time President Nixon was beginning tightly shrouded and delicate negotiations with China to end a generation of hostility between the two countries. Might a leak encouraged by the Pentagon Papers example derail the sensitive talks? The Pentagon Papers documented how a succession of presidents had deceived their countrymen about the government's intentions in Vietnam. This evidence further undermined the public's sinking faith in the government and complicated Nixon's own murky notions for resolving the war. Nixon was furious over the leak of the Pentagon Papers.

His closest counselors had recruited a flying squad of erstwhile cops and intelligence operatives for special missions which the White House did not trust the FBI and the CIA to handle. The "plumbers," as they became known, among their nefarious jobs were told to plug leaks of government secrets by whatever means they could. Howard Hunt was an important member of this merry band. In September he was involved in the break-in of Daniel Ellsberg's psychiatrist's office in Los Angeles. Hunt later testified that he wanted "to plumb Dr. Ellsberg's mind. We had no idea what type of animal we were dealing with." The burglars sought derogatory information that might be used to discredit the newest hero of the antiwar movement. They did not find Ellsberg's psychiatric file. Three of the others with Hunt on this mission would also be with him ten months later in the Watergate break-in. After that event the Los Angeles break-in would be called "Watergate West."

Three days before the *Times* began running the Pentagon Papers, Philip L. Geyelin, the *Post's* editorial page editor, was discussing economic development with Robert S. McNamara, the president of the World Bank. McNamara casually mentioned that he had gotten wind that the *Times* was about to break a Vietnam story that involved him. In June 1967 McNamara's six years as secretary of defense were wan-ing. He was on the verge of a backstage break with President Johnson over LBJ's acceleration of the war. McNamara wanted to leave behind an authoritative record of the two decades of American involvement in Vietnam. Robert Kennedy, who was in the Senate and pondering his own opposition strategy, told his confidant, McNamara, the history was a good idea. Comprised of forty-seven volumes, the work was drily titled, *History of U. S. Decision-Making Process on Vietnam Policy, 1945–1967.* The memos, directives, and analyses that McNamara ordered assembled were the paper trail along which this country had slogged deeper and deeper into the Asian morass.

Curiously both the *Times* and the *Post,* which were rightly extolled for publishing the Pentagon Papers, had carried word of the documents much earlier without causing a ripple. Henry Brandon, the well-connected Washington correspondent of the *Sunday Times* of London, wrote in the November 9, 1969, *New York Times Magazine* that McNamara had ordered the preparation of the "definitive history" of the Vietnam War. Brandon said "thirty to forty volumes" were already completed. Eleven months later Lloyd Shearer's *Parade Magazine* column, which is carried by the *Post,* identified Leslie Gelb as the McNamara aide in charge of the study. "There are no plans to make it public," Shearer added. Neither the *Post* nor the *Times* apparently chased those leads. Perhaps "history" sounded too dull or self-serving to bother. Leaked secret documents on the other hand have an authenticity and aroma of mystery that makes journalists salivate. So McNamara's history was assembled. It sat ticking away like a time bomb loaded with explosive proof that the government lied, repeatedly and systematically, about Vietnam.

On Monday, the day after the *Times* coup, Richard Harwood, a *Post* editor, lamented to Ben Bradlee that he thought it reinforced "this myth that the *Times* is number one, vis-à-vis us." "We were down by three touchdowns before we even had the ball," Harwood recalled telling his fellow Redskins fan. "Our main concern was not the public's right to know, it wasn't that we ought to tell people about this dreadful war in Vietnam. We had one basic consideration, and that was here was a hell of a news story and we were getting our ass beaten." The

Post was stuck, embarrassingly, with rewriting its rival's big story. Later that day a few hundred pages of the papers that dealt with President Kennedy's Indochina decisions were mysteriously delivered to Phil Geyelin, but the *Times* printed them before the *Post*, intensifying the *Post*'s dismay.

The Nixon administration moved quickly to silence the *Times*—the first time the federal government had gone into court to try to censor a newspaper. A historic constitutional confrontation loomed starkly: could the government bar a newspaper from publishing information that this same government had stamped secret for national security reasons despite the First Amendment guarantee of freedom of the press? On Tuesday a federal district judge in New York granted the Justice Department's request for a temporary restraining order against the paper. The *Times* was barred from publishing anything more from the documents pending further judicial review. The *Times* obeyed, but appealed. There was something about the affair that caused national editor Ben Bagdikian to think of Daniel Ellsberg as the possible *Times*'s source. The papers seemed to reinforce arguments that Bagdikian had heard from an intense and troubled Ellsberg when they both were consultants for the Rand Corporation. On Wednesday Bagdikian finally reached Ellsberg on the phone and arranged to fly that night to Boston where Ellsberg was lying low. When Bagdikian, a slightly built, wiry fellow, returned to Washington the next day he was lugging two large boxes of photocopied papers.

A squad of the *Post*'s top editors and specialists in diplomatic and military affairs set to work furiously in Bradlee's home to turn the mass of papers into coherent stories for Friday's paper. Their competitive juices were at flood stage. "Beneath the surface was the notion that the *Post* was getting ever closer to its goal of being a truly 'national' newspaper, increasingly mentioned in the same breath as the *Times*," Sanford J. Unger wrote in *The Papers & the Papers*, a fine account of the conflict over the documents.

There were other people at Bradlee's that day—the Post Company lawyers. As the journalists plowed through the documents and typed, the attorneys argued against immediate publication of the articles.

They posed several legal reasons for waiting, perhaps until the *Times* case was clearer. Frederick Beebe, a seasoned corporate lawyer as well as the Post Company's chairman, spelled out a wholly different cause for prudent delay. By happenstance, the company was about to become a public corporation by offering its stock for sale outside the Meyer and Graham family and company employees. Underwriters had prepared a prospectus for the sale of Post shares through the American Stock Exchange. The underwriting agreement could be cancelled if some "catastrophic event" struck the Post Company, Beebe explained. In his opinion, an injunction or even criminal prosecution, which was not awfully remote given Richard Nixon's wrath over the security violation, might be construed as such a catastrophe. Moreover, the company's ownership of a string of lucrative broadcasting stations might be imperiled, it was suggested, because a convicted felon cannot hold a television or radio license.

Through the day Katharine Graham kept in touch by phone with Beebe and Bradlee. She assumed that once her people got their hands on the papers, the information would appear in the *Post.* Later in the day, though, as the lawyers and reporters began battling, she questioned, "Why don't we hold it up for a day? After all, the *Times* had the papers for three months before publishing." For the *Post,* however, delay was competitively risky. If the government learned that the *Post* had the classified history, it might move against the *Post* before the paper could close with the frontrunning *Times.*

By eight o'clock with the deadline for the first edition pressing closer, Bradlee discovered a staff rebellion brewing in his parlor. Bagdikian had been promised that if he produced the papers, the *Post* would print them. He now threatened to resign if the *Post* did not publish the documents story in the upcoming edition. The dean of the reporters present, Chalmers Roberts, almost sixty years old and twenty-two of them on the paper, declared that he would advance his retirement and publicly announce his reason if the articles were delayed. Finally, to break the impasse, Bradlee and Beebe phoned Mrs. Graham. Bradlee said if the *Post* didn't publish the story, the word would get out and the *Post* would look cowardly. Beebe told her that he was inclined to wait, but he wasn't adamant. "He left the door open," she remembered. "I felt I could decide. The momentum had to be maintained or the fifth floor [newsroom] would go to pieces."

"I say we print," Kay Graham ruled. Those four words were a declaration of journalistic independence.

The *Post* published its Pentagon Papers articles for two days before it, too, was restrained. The same attorneys who had so vigorously argued for delay now, lawyerlike, zealously attacked the government's restraining order and succeeded in having it lifted. But the appeals court reversed the initial decision favoring the *Post.* The *Times* and the *Post* cases were joined as one and headed for final judgment by the Supreme Court. In the midst of the legal battle, Henry Kissinger, Nixon's national security advisor, phoned his friend, Katharine Graham. "Have you heard," Kissinger quipped, "that Anatoly Dobrynin, the Russian ambassador, is saying that there is nothing more for him to do in Washington now that the *Post* has published all the country's secrets?"

The constitutional collision was made to order for the *Post*. It was the kind of momentous issue the paper loved to sink its editorial teeth into. "In the fifties it was the editorial page that earned the *Post* its journalistic reputation," observed Stephen Rosenfeld, who joined the editorial page after that era. "The Pentagon Papers case was the inheritor of that constitutional tradition," he said.

Throughout the case the government claimed that publication of the papers would pose a "grave and immediate danger to the security of the United States" and do "irreparable injury" to the national security. The newspapers were not unmindful of the risks involved. They avoided publishing the full texts of dated cables, for example, because of the possibility of compromising American codes, though this was quite remote given the sophisticated cryptographic techniques.

What quickly became evident during the *in camera* court hearings and in subsequent assessments was that there was very little that was really news in all that mountain of top-secret-stamped photocopies. The essence of the documents had appeared over the years in books and newspapers and elsewhere. What then was all the sound and fury about? An answer came later from Phil Geyelin, who four years earlier began edging the *Post* editorial page away from its stout defense of the government's Vietnam policies:

Highly classified though they were, most of what they said had been alluded to somewhere along the line; there had been hints and suggestions and you could look it up and find it all. But you couldn't find it in black headlines, and you could rarely find it on Page One because it had been said by "official sources in Saigon" or an "administration official in Washington"; but never had it been said forthrightly and for attribution by the President or the Secretary of State for they were otherwise occupied, vigorously denying that it was so.

It was their massiveness, their officialness that made the Pentagon Papers so overwhelming as an indictment against the government and against the man who had instigated them, Robert S. McNamara. Perhaps this complex man wanted it so. "I think it will be awhile before another government can move us into a major war surreptitiously," Geyelin said.

On June 30 the Supreme Court by a six-to-three vote ruled that the government had failed to prove that publication of the documents would directly harm the nation. There simply was too much speculation in the government's case, and it fell. The court held that the government restraining orders violated the First Amendment protection of freedom of the press. Justice Hugo Black, in what would be his last opinion before retirement, pronounced, ". . . Only a free and unrestrained press can effectively expose deception in government." Another ailing justice, William O. Douglas, who was laboring to hold his seat so that Nixon could not replace him with a conservative, wrote that "secrecy in government is fundamentally antidemocratic, perpetuating bureaucratic errors."

The defendants and the press were jubilant for the moment, but their victory was clouded. Some of the justices suggested that they would be sympathetic to the government possibly proceeding against the newspapers under the Espionage Act or some other law after they printed the classified papers, rather than by restraint in advance. To forbid prior government censorship was the intention of those who wrote the First Amendment. Six of the justices said in various ways that there were circumstances in which the press could be restrained from publishing. And for the first time the press had been halted, even though for a relatively brief time, by the government. That was of crucial significance. It was not to be the end of the matter. The ensuing years would bring more and more court-sanctioned restraints on the press.

Ben Gilbert spent twenty-nine years on the *Post.* Looking back to those years when he was a top editor as well as a local political operator for the paper, Gilbert said that he would bet that if Eugene Meyer or his son-in-law, Phil Graham, had been running the paper during Watergate "Nixon would not have been unseated." Gilbert concluded this, despite his loyalty and affection for the old regime of which he was a principal, from an episode involving the powerful chairman of the House of Representatives committee which controlled the District of Columbia government. Gilbert's reporters were investigating allegations that the chairman was getting free automobiles from a local Cadillac dealer. The *Post* kept running snatches of information that indicated wrongdoing.

Bored and exasperated, managing editor Al Friendly finally asked Gilbert, "Do I have to read another story about John McMillan and his automobile?" Gilbert thought the paper was close to nailing the congressman; he sensed that McMillan might resign from his chairmanship if the stories kept revealing more incriminating evidence.

"Give me another week," Gilbert proposed.

"We're not the U. S. attorney," Friendly answered.

Gilbert's investigation withered. Friendly wanted to avoid distorting the news by aggressively building it up and thus seeming to be prosecuting a case rather than reporting events. It was to be a concern of *Post* editors during much of the paper's early reporting of Watergate; especially when the White House vehemently criticized the paper's coverage and when new information ran dry.

In 1966 Gilbert hired Carl Bernstein, a harum-scarum kid who used to play with Gilbert's children and had worked on the *Washington*

Evening Star and a New Jersey paper. Bernstein hadn't rented a cap
and gown until the very morning of his high school graduation because
it was not until the eleventh hour that the school decided it was better
to let him graduate, even though he was flunking gym and chemistry,
than to keep him around for another year. Instead of being in his
afternoon classes, Bernstein amused himself in a nearby pool hall. He
dropped out of the University of Maryland, just short of graduation.
He wore his hair long. His editors exploded at him for running up
expense accounts. Bernstein was a good writer, but the editors found
him undependable on stories he either did not originate or wasn't
interested in.

"Carl alone would not have had enough credibility to convince his
editors of the reliability of his Watergate reporting," Gilbert said. "He
was ready to believe the worst."

Bernstein's father had represented many federal employees who
were accused of disloyalty to the government during the late 1940s and
through the heyday of McCarthyism. Al Bernstein won most of his
cases. "We got the bastards," Bernstein would say when the Nixon
crowd was on the ropes. Bob Woodward would speak evenly of "valid
assumptions."

Bob Woodward had a clean, solid, dependable look. He grew up in
a conservative Republican family in Wheaton, Illinois. His father was
the Chicago suburb's leading attorney and a respected local judge. "In
high school Bob ran for student council president and lost," a school
friend remembered. "He was always too smart, too good, too cute, too
everything. He never was the underdog." On graduating from Yale in
June 1965 Woodward was commissioned an ensign in the navy. He
served at sea and spent the last of his five years in the Office of the
Chief of Naval Operations in the Pentagon.

While stationed there Woodward, according to a Washington attorney, learned that the navy for years may have secretly intervened in
Puerto Rican politics with cash and by other means in favor of gover-
nors who would permit part of the island of Culebra to continue to be
used for target practice against the wishes of nearby residents. Woodward, as the attorney tells it, confided this information to a friend in

government. The friend, in turn, related it to the attorney, who was representing the Culebrans against the navy. Anxious to shore up his case with details, the lawyer twice pushed Woodward for more details. But Woodward, by then out of the service, denied knowing anything more than having seen messages from admirals who wanted to retain control of Culebra—nothing about secret political operations. "If I knew that the navy was doing what was alleged," said Woodward later, "I would have leaked it" to the press.

Long before Watergate, Woodward had grown skeptical about the honesty of government. He shared the growing disbelief in the government's brief for the Vietnam War, which, he concluded, was absurd and ridiculous. It was why he decided to look for a reporting job rather than go to Harvard Law School where he had been accepted for admission. Reporting seemed like "honest work," as opposed to being a lawyer, he decided. It was a way to seek the truth without lawyerlike hedging. Later it would be said that the notoriety of Woodward and Bernstein prompted the rush of students to journalism schools in order to emulate their Watergate heroics. Woodward was quick to note that the surge of enrollments began before Watergate for the same reasons he became a reporter.

Woodward with no reporting experience applied to the *Post.* Metropolitan editor Harry Rosenfeld sent him to a suburban weekly to cut his journalistic teeth; a year later he hired him on the *Post.* It was the week that E. Howard Hunt and Gordon Liddy flew to Los Angeles to case Daniel Ellsberg's psychiatrist's office. Woodward could be incredibly tough; yet at times he seemed almost coquettish in the way he could get people to tell him what he wanted to know. In the spring of 1978 he went on a French television talk show with John Ehrlichman. Ehrlichman, the Watergate villain turned writer, and Woodward, the Watergate hero, spent most of the day together walking the streets of Paris and talking. It might have struck one as utterly incongruous but they enjoyed each other's company.

Carl Shoffler was one of the three Washington tactical squad plainclothesmen who caught the burglars in the Watergate offices of the

Democratic National Committee. He had been an army cryptologist and did police undercover intelligence work, which brought him into contact with the CIA. Shoffler suspected that there was more to the five well-dressed, elaborately equipped and rather cocky but uncommunicative men he and his partners were booking at a district precinct station that early morning in June 1972. It was possible, he thought, that they had the kind of connections that would allow them to slip away from the law. The press might keep that from happening. Shoffler went to a payphone and called the *Post* newsroom. The final edition was gone and the place was like a tomb. But someone, Shoffler doesn't know who nor is there any record, answered his call; he gave the barest facts about the arrest and suggested a photographer be sent. He hung up when he was asked for his name.*

Several hours later Joseph A. Califano, a lawyer for the Post and the Democratic National Commitee's counsel, phoned Howard Simons, the *Post* managing editor, to alert him to the break-in. At almost the same moment another managing editor, Charles B. Seib at the *Washington Star,* also got a tip from inside. Philip C. Seib, a special assistant to Democratic national chairman Lawrence O'Brien, called his father with the suspicion that anti-Castro Cubans who were looking for information on the Democrats' relations with peace groups were responsible for the burglary. Later that day Seib again called his father with information that linked James McCord, one of the men arrested at the Watergate, with John Mitchell. Mitchell had resigned as attorney general to run the Committee to Re-Elect the President. Charlie Seib called his office from home and was told the *Star* was carrying a story

*After the arrests, Shoffler had no further police connection with the Watergate investigation. Months passed and a week before the five burglars were to stand trial, early in 1973, Shoffler got a phone call from Paul Chung, his former army lieutenant, who asked to see him. On this occasion and at a second meeting, according to Shoffler, Chung indicated that "his people" wanted Shoffler to change his testimony regarding the circumstances of the arrests in order to make it appear that the Democratic Party had contrived the burglary to embarrass the Republicans. Chung, as Shoffler, relates it, indicated that "his people" were connected to CREEP. He knew the recantation would cost Shoffler his police job, Chung said, but it was worth fifty thousand dollars to the interests he represented, the policeman related. Shoffler turned it down and later reported the incidents to his superior officers. In turn they told the Senate Watergate Committee whose staff then interviewed both Shoffler and Chung. Apparently, the staff concluded that there was no conclusive evidence of a bribery attempt; it was Shoffler's word against Chung's. There was no public hearing. The U.S. Attorney apparently wasn't told about the matter at the time.

on the break-in. But the *Star* did not chase the story with the *Post's* intensity.

The *New York Times, Time*, and the *Los Angeles Times* uncovered several major pieces of the Watergate puzzle. But the *Post* more than any other news organization kept Watergate in its jaws, like a terrier with a rat. In time the *Post* reported the flow of money from supposed GOP campaign treasuries into political espionage, the sweep of that spying and harrassment, the involvement of the president's closest aides, and the frenzied efforts to stonewall the investigations of the White House horrors.

"Watergate found Woodward and Bernstein," said Howard Simons. Local editor Barry Sussman's choice of this odd couple to be the "Watergate team" seemed utterly zany, but it worked. Metro editor Harry Rosenfeld spoke of them as "this sort of inexperienced reporter and this sort of B-minus reporter." He regarded them with wonder and admired their persistent and successful digging at the hottest story of a lifetime until it all but burned them. In contrast, journalists with far more experience were reluctant to touch it. Some of them were on the *Post.* Initially there was a sense among some staffers that the dogged pursuit of the story in the face of unequivocal White House denials of any ties to the break-in only proved the bias that Nixon and Agnew ascribed to the *Post.* In fact, the White House relied on "non-denial denials" so as not to lend any credence at all to the newspaper reports of misconduct. "The White House chose to make the issue of Watergate the conduct of the press . . . and not the conduct of the president's men," Bernstein said.

The national staff of the *Post* was regarded as the cream of the crop. Making it to this corner of the newsroom was like reaching Broadway if you were an actor or the Superbowl if you were in pro football. National reporters traveled the world with the president. They covered bigtime politics. Their stories dominated the front page and moved on the news service to hundreds of other papers.

The national desk didn't think, then or for some time after, that there was very much to the arrest of five men with bugging gear and cameras inside the Democratic National Committee offices that June

17, 1972. The national reporters' attention centered on their territory, the presidential primaries, and the impending campaign, not on what Ron Ziegler, Nixon's press secretary, dismissed as a "third-rate burglary." "There was an enormous amount of disinterest in the story . . . that . . . stemmed from a disposition to answer the questions as soon as they arose," recalled Roger Wilkins, who wrote most of the *Post*'s editorials on Watergate. "There was a clumsy break-in at the Democratic headquarters. Could [John] Mitchell have been behind it? Obviously not." "The metros wanted to stick it to the nationals who they thought were lazy and bloated, and they were partly right," said Bill Greider, a national reporter. The competition inside the *Post* newsroom was as bloody as the contest with other newspapers. Bradlee encouraged this rivalrous atmosphere. Someone had called it "controlled tension," management's way to keep a staff challenged; but that sounded rather ugly and manipulative, and somehow it became "creative tension." In the beginning Woodward and Bernstein felt the other was horning in on the Watergate story and resented it. The feeling evaporated as together they ferreted deeper into the story. The intimacy of the partnership was such that the two reporters were soon dubbed Woodstein by their editors.

Oddly enough, Woodstein's initial ignorance of the inner workings of the White House gave them an advantage over the paper's big league reporters who talked to big league politicians and officials. Woodward and Bernstein got important information from secretaries and bookkeepers. They were strangers to the powerful men around the president. "A reporter who called Henry Kissinger by his first name wasn't worth a damn on the Watergate story," said Ben Bradlee.

In Richard Nixon's 1977 television interview with David Frost, the former president remarked that "one of the reasons that the press' attitude toward me through the years has been at times not too favorable" is that "I'm not a very lovable man." There was much truth to those words. Nixon, it is not inconceivable to believe, might have escaped his fate had he been as charming as, say, his chief advisor on foreign affairs. "Many persons in the Washington news business have an institutional affinity for anyone who is funny, bright, engaging, responsive, and important," *Post* managing editor Howard Simons comments. "Henry Kissinger is a very good example and practitioner of the phenomenon. . . ." "He played the press like a glockenspiel— dazzling them with his secret missions, beguiling them with his Central European charm, fascinating them with his glamorous dinner companions," wrote Anthony Lukas of Kissinger's manner with reporters.

Between 1969 and 1971 wiretaps were placed on the phones of some of Kissinger's subordinates and reporters who were suspected of being involved in leaks of foreign policy confidences. Kissinger averred publicly, in 1973 when the taps were disclosed, that he made no direct recommendation for these interceptions. Stanford N. Sesser, a former *Wall Street Journal* reporter, interviewed "one of Washington's best-known journalists" about Kissinger. The journalist would not permit Sesser to use his name, but he related to Sesser: "When the wiretaps were being revealed, he [Kissinger] told six different things to six different reporters. He told me he didn't see J. Edgar Hoover at all to have the wiretaps put in place. Then later in the conversation I took a chance and asked, 'Henry, did you visit Hoover's office or did he come to you?' and he answered, 'I went to his office.' " The story, in view of the controversy over the wiretapping, was significant and possibly damning. But the journalist did not write it.

Woodward was told by two sources that Kissinger authorized some of the wiretaps. He phoned Kissinger, who equivocated and seemed to hint at his complicity. Woodward pressed harder. Woodstein's *All the President's Men* relates the end of the encounter:

"You aren't quoting me?" Kissinger asked.

"Sure I was," Woodward said.

"What!" Kissinger shouted. "I'm telling you what I said was for background."

Woodward said they had made no such agreement.

"I've tried to be honest and now you're going to penalize me," Kissinger said.

"No penalty intended," Woodward said, but he could not accept retroactive background.

"In five years in Washington," Kissinger said sharply, "I've never been trapped into talking like this."

Woodward wondered what kind of treatment Kissinger was accustomed to get from reporters.

Kissinger then phoned Bradlee to complain. The story was too late for the first edition and Simons decided to hold it for the next day. The delay angered Woodward, who concluded that his editors hedged because it was Kissinger. The *New York Times* beat the *Post* into print with an account of Kissinger's role in the taps.

What sent nervous chills through Bradlee and the other editors was the feeling of being so alone on much of the reporting, so far in front of the pack, especially when the president's men so confidently disparaged the allegations published in the *Post.* When Katharine Graham looked back to those months she recalled how the story simply "grew by inches. . . . You were in up to your waist having gotten yourself in gradually. I couldn't say, 'this is getting too dangerous.' Having put them [the editors] in you stuck with them." (Two *Post* editors, Philip Geyelin and Meg Greenfield of the editorial page, met regularly on off-the-record terms with special prosecutor Leon Jaworski for confidential background on his probe. The *Post* editorials, as a result, had a special authority.) It was an act of faith—and hope. The publisher had taken the same approach in deciding to print the Pentagon Papers. Watergate was far more dangerous. The stakes were the presidency of the most powerful country in the world, and the future of her own company. At moments a dreadful uncertainty gripped her. But she did not believe that Bradlee was leading the paper into quicksand, only perhaps across thin ice.

Clark Mollenhoff, a veteran Washington correspondent with a Pulitzer prize for investigative reporting, figured that no more than two dozen reporters made substantial contributions to advancing the Watergate story—a number that becomes significant in the light of Ben Bagdikian's estimate that there were 433 Washington-based reporters with freedom to cover what they chose or whose assignments made the emerging scandal their logical territory. A few columnists sympathetic to the Democrats suggested the possible larger implications of the episode. Eight days after the break-in Joseph Kraft, who had been a speechwriter for John Kennedy, wrote that unless the White House explained Watergate, "they will find that they cannot get away with keeping the president above the battle." Clayton Fritchey, who had been a counselor to Adlai Stevenson, commented on September 2 that the event was "rapidly rivaling Teapot Dome as a metaphor for scandal." Their columns ran in the *Post* which made the paper's Watergate reporting seem all the more partisan. Most commentators, however, had no appetite then for Watergate, or believed with Vermont Royster of the *Wall Street Journal* that "The hounds of the press are running with their tongues lolling." Except that there weren't very many hounds.

Most Americans had heard of Watergate by September, but 75 percent of those sampled by the Gallup Poll labeled it "mostly politics" and not uncommon. The *Christian Science Monitor* in October surveyed the nation and found no evidence "that the issue has emerged as a major one in the presidential campaign." (Despite the possibility of a White House scandal, 93 percent of the daily press supported Nixon's re-election, compared with 80 percent in 1968. This big gain may have had more to do with opposition to George McGovern than esteem for Nixon.) The exposé was being greeted with "a shrug, not a roar," as the *Minneapolis Star* headlined an editorial on the matter. The *Post*'s disclosures were getting big play in the Northeast which was not Nixon territory. Elsewhere most editors "downplayed the Watergate story and dismissed it as a vagary of the *Washington Post*," Bradlee said. In mid-October CBS ran a two-part series reporting "charges of a high-level campaign of political sabotage and espionage apparently unparallelled in American history. . . ." "The editors," said Bradlee, "began to move these stories up only after Cronkite did the two segments on Watergate—they were blessed by the great white father." Cronkite had nothing more than the *Post*, but television had an extraordinary capacity, more so than print, to convey an impression of reality and immediacy.

"Testimony Ties Top Nixon Aide to Secret Fund," read the headline on the front page of the October 25 *Post*. A column-and-a-half mug shot of H. R. Haldeman ran with the story. Woodstein reported that a witness testified before the Watergate grand jury that Haldeman, Nixon's chief of staff, was authorized to approve payments from a secret campaign fund. From these funds came disbursements for dirty tricks. The two reporters had confirmed Haldeman's role with four separate sources, all seemingly reliable, including an FBI agent and a grand jury witness.

The story was wrong. No one had given sworn testimony to the grand jury about Bob Haldeman and the slush fund. "It was the worst moment of all of this," Woodward recalled. "We were so sure of that." Immediately the White House and GOP leaders accused the paper of "character assassination." The Haldeman error was evidence, they asserted, that the *Post* was engaged in a plot of its own to "get" the Nixon administration. Richard Harwood, who ran the national staff, feared that the *Post* was going out on a limb that might be sawed off. He urged that his nationals take over because the story was too complex for Metro. Bradlee and Simons stuck with the locals, who had done the real work from the beginning.

Their Haldeman story also was right in one essential fact, Woodstein soon established. Haldeman could authorize spending from the secret kitty. Their mistake was in reporting that this was revealed to the grand jury. Watergate was now at the door to the Oval Office. But Watergate seemed to have been mined out. Bernstein and Woodward were unable to turn up anything more solid in the period before Election Day. Not for more than a month, after Nixon's landslide re-election, would Woodstein be back in the paper with another major Watergate story, followed by another long dry spell. Not for another two months would one of the Watergate intruders, James McCord, tell U. S. District Judge John J. Sirica that the defendants had committed wholesale perjury and were being paid to lie or keep silent. That, would be the moment when the White House cover-up would begin to unravel.

They were still holding out in the White House in the early spring of 1973: barricaded and confident that they could beat off the press, the special prosecutor, and the Senate investigating committee. On a Saturday night in mid-April the president, H. R. Haldeman, and John Ehrlichman put on smiles and tuxedos and attended the annual White House Correspondents' Association dinner. It could not have been a huge joy for them. The Watergate jokes told from the rostrum were mordant. That night the White House correspondents gave awards to Woodward and Bernstein for their Watergate reporting. Harry Rosenfeld, their boss, encountered Raymond Price, a Nixon speechwriter. They had worked together on the *New York Herald Tribune* and liked each other. Price said the *Post* was picking on the Nixon people because they were Republicans. "You're wrong, Ray," replied Rosenfeld. "There's a lot of stuff we're not putting in the paper because it hasn't been confirmed. Don't be confused because you're working there. We've got the goods." Price was "troubled, even shaken" by Rosenfeld's self-assurance. Price reflected that things might be worse than he had thought. They were.

Earlier in the day, Jeb Stuart Magruder, the deputy director of the Committee to Re-Elect the President and a former Haldeman assistant, started talking to the prosecutors. Fearing that he was about to be made a scapegoat for higher-ups involved in the campaign illegalities, Magruder implicated John Mitchell, the former attorney general, John Dean, the president's counsel, and others. The stonewall was crumbling to dust. But on Tuesday afternoon, before word got out that Magruder was singing, Bob Haldeman and John Ehrlichman met with the president. "You know where the Watergate story is in the *Washington Post* today? Page nineteen," said Haldeman. "And it'll be page nineteen five months from now if we handle it right," the president predicted. Nixon was wrong. Thirteen days later Haldeman, John Ehrlichman, and John Dean resigned.

As the White House sank into a bunker gloom, the siege was being lifted at the *Post* a few blocks away. "I don't think anyone who wasn't on the floor of the newsroom at that time could understand," Bradlee said. "We were dumped on every day. That can grind you down, if you let it." Bradlee noticed that one of his eyelids sagged peculiarly and he went to a doctor about it. One physician suspected an aneurysm; another mentioned a possible brain tumor. After more examinations they concluded that there was no organic cause; Watergate simply was taking a toll on Bradlee's nerves. The condition passed. There was fear in the air, too, talk of surveillance and taps on the phones of editors and reporters. Howard Simons and his wife suspected their suburban Virginia house might be bugged. They'd sit outside in their station wagon to discuss the investigation. Watergate also seemed to be inducing nervousness in investors considering the Post. The company had its best year in 1972; but the stock dropped from thirty-eight dollars in December 1972 to twenty-one dollars in May 1973, possibly out of uncertainty about the effects that Nixon's hostility would have on the company.

Many of Woodward and Bernstein's best leads and most significant information came from Republicans who resented the extreme practices of their leaders. But there was a bias in the *Post*'s treatment of the story. For a newspaper to mount and sustain a serious investigation, there must be a predisposition to believe the worst about the target. "It is easier to believe the worst about those you like least," editorial writer Steve Rosenfeld said of the *Post*'s attitude toward Nixon and the unexpected opportunity Watergate presented to spear him. Sometimes when Bradlee had uncertainties about the information the two reporters were turning up, he'd talk out his doubts with one of his closest pals. Bradlee and Edward Bennett Williams had been friends since Bradlee, as a young reporter, covered Washington's criminal courts and Williams was a young attorney. Williams became one of the leading criminal lawyers in the country. He also headed the Washington Redskins, and Bradlee was often in Williams's box at the stadium when the team played at home. Williams represented the Democrats in their suit against the Republicans for various campaign abuses. Within seventy-two hours of the Watergate break-in, Williams began gathering depositions in the case. In Bradlee's moments of doubt, Williams would reassure him that the *Post* had the story right.

Nixon thought of Williams as one with the *Post,* the heart of evil. The infamous White House tapes reveal this exchange between the President (P), Haldeman (H), and Dean (D) on September 15, 1971, well before Watergate:

P: . . . I wouldn't want to be in Edward Bennett Williams's position after this election.

* * *

H: That is a guy we've got to ruin.

* * *

P: You want to remember, too, he's an attorney for the *Washington Post.*
D: I'm well aware of that.
P: I think we are going to fix the son-of-a-bitch. Believe me. We are going to. We've got to, because he's a bad man.

* * *

P: . . . we have not used the power in this first four years, as you know.
D: That's right.
P: We have never used it. We haven't used the bureau (Federal Bureau of Investigation) and we haven't used the Justice Department, but things are going to change now. And they're going to change, and they're going to get right.
D: That's an exciting prospect.
P: It's got to be done. It's the only thing to do.

* * *

H: The *Post* [unintelligible].
P: It's going to have its problems—

* * *

P: . . . The main thing is the *Post* is going to have damnable, damnable problems out of this one. They have a television station.
D: That's right, they do.
P: Does that [federal broadcasting license] come up too? The point is, when does it come up?
D: I don't know. But the practice of non-licensees filing on top of licensees has gotten more—
P: That's right.
D: More active in the, this area.
P: And it's going to be God damn active here.
D: [Laughter] [Silence]
P: Well, the game has to be played awfully rough . . .

It was a game that Bradlee, Williams, and the *Post* were willing to play. And they ultimately won. But there were problems.

In January 1973 Florida allies of Nixon challenged the pending Federal Communications license renewal for WJXT, the Post Company's television station in Jacksonville. (In 1969 another group of

Nixon supporters unsuccessfully contested the relicensing of the Post's Miami station.) In 1970 WJXT uncovered the fact that G. Harold Carswell, a Florida jurist who Nixon nominated to the Supreme Court, had made a speech in 1949 praising racial segregation. The revelation contributed substantially to the Senate's rejection of the nomination. At the time of the Jacksonville challenge the Post was trying to buy a Hartford broadcasting property from the Travelers Insurance Company; the Post Company was reluctant to go forward while a possible legal hurricane threatened its Jacksonville station.

The stakes were bigger than Hartford and Jacksonville. Under the Federal Communications Act, if the Post Company were found unfit to operate WJXT, it also would be unable to hold the licenses for its Miami and Washington stations and would have not been permitted to take on Hartford. "That would have ruined the company," a key participant in the proceedings later said. Despite this uncertainty Travelers' president Roger C. Wilkins did not withdraw. Wilkins was a "solid, Yankee Republican who was outraged by the undisguised attempt to exact political vengeance on the Post," one of the principals in the negotiations remembered. Larry Israel, the Post Company president, repeatedly tried to calm Katharine Graham's fears that the company would be stripped of its precious broadcast licenses; the White House's loathing fueled those fears. She breathed more easily after the FCC ruled in favor of her company.

In April 1974 Richard Nixon's political career was being snuffed out by the effluvia of Watergate. Anticipating impeachment or some other convulsive resolution of the growing crisis, the *Post* started planning a twenty-four-page special supplement to chronicle "The Nixon Years." On the first Monday in August, Washington rumbled with rumors of the president's imminent resignation. The editors responsible for the supplement were frantically trying to complete their work. Only two-thirds of the copy was in type, Carl Bernstein still hadn't finished a major article. Nixon might exit at any moment and the paper's retrospective on its longtime adversary would not be ready.

On Wednesday afternoon Mrs. Graham met with the editors in

Howard Simons's office to check on progress. Some of the staff had been working for seventy-two hours straight on the supplement; some of them braced themselves with "speed" to keep functioning. As the meeting was ending, a reliable signal came through that the president would resign the following night—ironically, in perfect time for the *Post*'s deadline.

Nixon's diehard partisans, the kids in the journalism schools dreaming of emulating the new folk heroes, Bernstein and Woodward, and even some liberals who thought the press had become a rogue elephant as dangerous as a rogue president were all absolutely convinced that the news media, and particularly the *Post*, had toppled the government. The avalanche of notoriety, including a box-office smash movie with superstars Robert Redford, Dustin Hoffman, and Jason Robards playing the good-guy journalists, sustained this impression. Reality and illusion were entwined in this perception. From his Elba on the Pacific shore, Richard Nixon said he believed that he would have had more power as president of a broadcasting network or the *Washington Post* than he did as president of the United States. A president who commanded fleets of bombers to level countries had less power than a media mogul?

Katharine Graham is a realist. She knew what her paper and others had done. "I do not think the press brought down the government," she said. "I think it would be extremely unhealthy if we had. We kept alive the story they were trying to cover up." She also was wary, possibly, that a press that was, or appeared, so powerful would be reason for further attempts to control it. The Pentagon Papers experience was still fresh in her memory.

In the spring of 1974 Mrs. Graham provided an audience at Colby College in Maine these important, if forgotten, facts: "I don't mean to take away anything from the superb performance of Bob Woodward and Carl Bernstein, and the team of experienced editors who guided and checked their work during those months of hard, lonely digging. But the fact is that their work was productive only because a number of people, many inside government and mostly Republicans, were willing to talk with them—to tell them pieces of the truth, often at great peril to their jobs. And it's also worth considering that, even after their stories about secret funds and political sabotage had appeared, a great deal remained hidden. Many of the key revelations came from elsewhere—from James McCord, as a result of Judge Sirica's pressure, from John Dean, from the hearings on L. Patrick Gray's nomination to be head of the F.B.I., from the work of the Senate Committee, from lawsuits of the Democrats, Common Cause, and Ralph Nader, from the work of the special prosecution team and the grand juries. And what may have been the crucial event—the discovery that a voice-activated tape system had been installed in the White House—came not from the work of the press, but from a Senate staff question put to a man, Alexander Butterfield, who had been thought of as a peripheral figure."

Keeping the story "alive"; riveting public attention; creating the "media storm," as Nick von Hoffman called it, were crucial to the administration's fall. Those who were part of the government's investigative machinery and the White House and Republican apparachiks who were the unnamed sources of stories knew it as the scandal burgeoned. Woodward's ace source, "Deepthroat," whom he described as in "the executive branch," knew this central reality. The press fed the fire under the White House and kept the pressure on the official probers, some of whom wanted the force of public opinion to prevent their investigations from being sidetracked for political reasons. They fueled the pressure with leaks. This symbiotic relationship was essential to the press because it was the government and insiders, rather than the reporters, who were the originators of virtually all of the major investigative information.

While the special prosecutor, the Congress, and the court of public opinion proceeded against Richard Nixon, Bernstein and Woodward began writing their Watergate book. At first the book was to be a detailed account of the scandal itself. But the natural and obvious story for the two reporters to tell was how they covered what the paperback cover called "the most devastating detective story of our century." This approach made a far more exciting book and dramatic movie. It also fanned the blaze of notoriety that swept over them and the paper.

"They've got a million nuts in the bank, and they're—like it or not
—folk heroes," said Ben Bradlee. They finished the book and resumed
covering other stories together as though their byline was indivisible.
Woodstein on any story gave it infinitely more importance than it
probably deserved. The Hawthorn effect operated: "The very existence
of Woodward and Bernstein on the other end of the phone changes
the event," commented Bradlee. Harry Rosenfeld, the metropolitan
editor, initially resented that they were off writing a book, and on the
talk show and high-priced lecture circuit. "Then I decided it was really
unreasonable that they be required to do more; they deserved all the
attention." Some on the staff cautioned that the hoopla was bad for
the paper, putting reporters and editors on the stage rather than in the
audience.

The newsroom had been on a long emotional high. Bradlee and
Simons sensed the difficulties of decompression. Woodward and Bern-
stein, said Bradlee, face the problem that "there'll never be another
Watergate."

In December 1976, Carl Bernstein resigned from the *Post* to write
a book about McCarthyism's impact on Washington and the Bernstein
family. Bernstein remarried and became a father for the first time. Bob
Woodward also married again and had his first child. In the spring of
1979 Woodward became an assistant managing editor, taking the job
Harry Rosenfeld once held. Nine years had passed since Rosenfeld sent
Woodward to a suburban weekly for experience. Bernstein became an
ABC News executive.

Watergate raised the Post to the pinnacle of journalism. It was an
uneasy perch. Katharine Graham made a speech in which she both
praised investigative reporting and cautioned against its inherent tend-
ency to become extreme. Downstairs in the newsroom they paid most
attention to the second half of her remarks, trying to detect what it
signaled, if anything. When the paper reported abuses by the comptrol-
ler of the currency, financier David Rockefeller importuned her about
tearing down the credibility of banking. The possible backlash of Watergate worried the newsroom chiefs: "We at the *Post* might settle
down and not rock any boats again," Harry Rosenfeld worried. Bradlee

didn't want his editors making a news decision based on whether "it's the safe and conservative thing to do."

There was cause for Mrs. Graham's concern. Charles Seib arrived at the *Post* in 1975 to be the press critic and to monitor the day-by-day performance of the *Post.* Seib, who previously was managing editor of the *Star,* found the paper suffering from "overkill." Frequently, the lead was not supported by the balance of the article, or the mitigating circumstances were buried at the tail in order to not diminish the impact. "It was ironic because the actual Watergate stories were very carefully edited," he recalled. There was a drive, subconscious or deliberate, to pull off something big again, "to go out and cover the Arlington School Board and bring back another Watergate," Seib recalled. Bradlee and Simons were "emotionally exhausted" and the period was one of drift, Seib said. In time they got the paper back on course.

When Ben Bradlee worked for *Newsweek* in Washington, his neighbor and good friend down the street was the Democratic senator from Massachusetts, John F. Kennedy. After Kennedy became president, Tony and Ben Bradlee spent many evenings and weekends with John and Jacqueline Kennedy. No other journalist enjoyed such social intimacy with the president, and Bradlee used this remarkable access to *Newsweek*'s advantage. Bradlee was sensitive to the charge that he may have reported far less of public concern than his relationship with the president revealed. "If I was had, so be it," Bradlee wrote in his popular memoir, *Conversations with Kennedy.* The book was published in 1975, after Nixon had been strangled by what was divulged in his White House tapes. *Harper*'s magazine titled its review of the book, "The Ben Bradlee Tapes." The memoir revealed Kennedy's capacity for raw vengefulness not greatly unlike the Nixon captured on tape. This caused Taylor Branch, the reviewer, to suggest that the book may have been "an unwitting catharsis of Bradlee's illusions." "Your partner cocked me," Bradlee told a writing associate of Branch. Their paths crossed at numerous parties after that, but Bradlee never spoke to Branch.

An episode from those bright *Camelot* years came to light early in

1976 and involved Bradlee personally. In February the gossip weekly *National Enquirer* reported that Kennedy had a sexual relationship with a lovely blond artist, Mary Pinchot Meyer. They had smoked marijuana in a White House bedroom, the *Enquirer* said. Mary Meyer was Ben Bradlee's sister-in-law. Much earlier Bradlee had talked of Mary Meyer to his close friend, Larry Stern, another *Post* editor. Stern was convinced that Bradlee genuinely did not know about the affair.*

Bradlee, by then divorced from Mary's sister, Tony, was vacationing in a tropical rain forest when his editors phoned about the story. He wanted to hold up publication until he could get a clear focus on the story. Editors Howard Simons and Harry Rosenfeld argued for running it. "We're not going to treat ourselves more kindly than we treat others," Rosenfeld asserted. Bradlee's unease about the story was understandable involving, as it did, a relative and his intimate friends. Moreover, its source was his erstwhile friend, James Truitt, a former vice-president of the *Post* and close aide to Philip Graham. Truitt later was a correspondent for *Newsweek* and returned to the *Post* as an editor until 1969. Bradlee had no way to interrogate the source, as he sometimes did on extremely sensitive stories. Nor was it likely that this source would have been helpful to him. Truitt, living in Mexico, felt that the *Post* had treated him unfairly after Graham's death and that Bradlee was his enemy; his story to the *Enquirer* seemed designed somehow to embarrass Bradlee, perhaps for not reporting more about Kennedy while revealing so much about Nixon. Bradlee also knew that in 1969 a physician had certified in court that Truitt was suffering from mental illness "such as to impair his judgment and cause him to be irresponsible." It was a painful business, but Bradlee, reluctantly, okayed the story with the Truitt background included. Had the *Post* suppressed the story, which was not Bradlee's intention, word of that would have spread quickly in press circles. Rosenfeld felt that his

---

*Mary Meyer was shot to death near her Washington home on October 12, 1964, eleven months after Kennedy was assassinated in Dallas. A jury acquitted the man charged with her murder. The case was officially closed. Later it was disclosed that Mary Meyer kept a diary of her relationship with the president. After her death Bradlee's wife, Tony, found the diary. James Angleton, then a high CIA official and the trustee of her children, may have destroyed it. Mary Meyer's former husband, Cord Meyer, Jr., was a senior CIA officer.

insistence that the story be printed "did Bradlee and the *Post* a favor by preserving their credibility."

The country over an anguished decade had moved from *Camelot* when all things seemed possible, to Watergate when all things were suspect. Revelations about the CIA's clandestine use of American journalists for intelligence operations cast suspicion on the credibility of the press itself.

JOURNALISTS AND SPOOKS

In November 1973, an extraordinarily authoritative source, the director of central intelligence himself, William E. Colby, leaked to a reporter the information that "some three dozen American journalists working abroad" were on the CIA payroll. Colby was not a sudden apostate to the theology of secrecy which he had practiced for nearly thirty years. But columnist Jack Anderson reported that Seymour K. Frieden, the Hearst newspapers London bureau chief, had worked for the CIA; by his limited disclosure Colby sought to head off possibly more revealing accounts of CIA-press ties. Colby also said he ordered a sharp cutback in the use of journalists from major news organizations. Colby hoped the planted story would leave the impression there was nothing more to tell. A flurry of stories followed and then the matter faded away until Congress probed intelligence agency abuses.

Mrs. Graham asked Colby if any of the *Post*'s news staff or stringers who reported occasionally also were currently employed by the CIA. Colby assured her that no one on the staff worked for the agency. He refused to discuss stringers, apparently because the agency still regarded part-time correspondents as fair game for intelligence assignments. By oversight, she later said, Mrs. Graham did not inquire about possible past connections with the agency.

The roots of the CIA's connections and various intelligence uses of some journalists and high executives in publishing and broadcasting traced back to the early days of the Cold War. The key figure in planning and orchestrating covert operations against the communists abroad was a veteran of the wartime Office of Strategic Services, Frank

G. Wisner. He and his wife, Polly, were very dear friends of Phil and Katharine Graham. Wisner, a Mississippian, was regarded by insiders as one of the half-dozen or so most important men in Washington during his CIA prime when the agency was fighting its secret war around the world. The Cold War had a cultural and intellectual front on which East and West struggled for men's political allegiance. To win this struggle, "Wisner built an organization that he laughingly but lovingly called 'my mighty Wurlitzer,' " Stuart H. Loory wrote in the *Columbia Journalism Review.* "The press was an important instrument in Wisner's Wurlitzer." "The CIA," said *Post* editor Phil Geyelin, "regarded having dummy newspapers like having dummy corporations." The other side, naturally, played the same game.

In establishing the agency soon after World War II, Congress foresaw the dangers of an American-made Gestapo and a Goebbels propaganda machine. Neither was wanted here. By law the CIA was barred from intelligence or propaganda activities inside the United States. The *Post* was an apparently unwitting accessory on one occasion when the CIA engaged in a major domestic propaganda mission. In the fall of 1965 the *Post* and twenty-nine other newspapers began running excerpts from *The Penkovsky Papers,* a hot new book published by Doubleday. The book purported to be the testament of Oleg Penkovsky, a high Russian intelligence officer with excellent Kremlin links who spied for the British and Americans. Caught in 1962, Penkovsky was tried and executed in May 1963. The best seller told of Penkovsky's deep disillusionment with his government and his fear of nuclear war which caused him to provide the West with valuable Soviet secrets. The Soviet Embassy wrote to the *Post* to brand the book "a crude forgery cooked up two years after Penkovsky's conviction by those whom the exposed spy served."

One Western journalist—Victor Zorza who analyzed Soviet affairs for England's *Guardian* and later became the *Post*'s chief Kremlinologist—said the book was tainted goods. Zorza was fourteen years old in 1939 when the Red Army swept into Poland. His family was deported to Siberia; none of them survived. But he escaped and was sheltered by the writer, Ilya Ehrenburg. Zorza joined the Free Polish Air Force operating from Britain, and learned English by reading *Alice in Won-*

derland, a work in which things are not always what they seem.

So with *The Penkovsky Papers.* Zorza discovered inconsistent dates in the spy's chronicle and curious historical references, though much of the intelligence information was genuine. No one could locate the original Russian manuscript which Zorza asked to inspect. The *Post,* which later said it tried to authenticate the book before publishing the excerpts, finally agreed to carry Zorza's challenge as the long series ended. Zorza began: " 'Their authenticity,' says the introduction to *The Penkovsky Papers,* the memoirs of the Anglo-American spy in Russia, 'is beyond question.' It is not." "The book," he concluded, "could have been compiled only by the CIA . . . the CIA has been repeatedly provoked by the attempts of the Disinformation Department of the Soviet Intelligence organization to discredit its activities throughout the world." American intelligence, Zorza suspected, was using the Penkovksy work to revenge a KGB-sponsored book by one of their agents in the West. The CIA, denying any connection to the book, calumniated Zorza. A decade later, the Senate Intelligence Committee confirmed Zorza's allegations. The agency had engineered the book, selected writers who wittingly produced and sold the manuscript through a CIA-established trust fund to the publisher, who was unaware of the government's role, according to the committee. The book portrayed the Soviet Union in the worst possible light, leading some to suspect it may have been calculated to persuade Americans of the futility of better relations with the Russians. ("Books differ from all other propaganda media," the chief of the CIA's Covert Action Staff wrote in 1961, "primarily because one single book can significantly change the reader's attitude and action to an extent unmatched by the impact of any other single medium . . . books [are] the most important weapon of strategic [long-range] propaganda.") Intelligence agencies in democracies, Zorza warned, "suffer from the grave disadvantage that in attempting to damage their adversary they must also deceive their own public."* "Fallout in

---

*When the CIA conducted its intensive covert news media campaign to influence Chileans against President Salvador Allende starting in 1970, some of that propaganda, unlabeled as to its manufacturer, richocheted back in news dispatches to the *Post* and the *New York Times* and their readers. With good reason the agency might be suspected of also trying to sway Americans against Marxist Allende.

the United States from a foreign publication which we support is inevitable and consequently permissible," CIA executive Desmond FitzGerald stated in 1967.

The Russians retaliated against the *Post* by ousting the paper's first Moscow correspondent, Stephen S. Rosenfeld. Looking back to the episode, Rosenfeld said: "You can conclude that newspapers in the 1960s were naïve, inadequately alert to the need to challenge the uses of secret power. Our plea must be guilty as charged. Only a few of us journalists are immune to the temptations and vulnerabilities of the larger society. But which of us?"

Not all of those in the press who aided the CIA were paid for their help; some got no money for their services. Columnists Joseph and Stewart Alsop were very close to the agency. In a 1977 interview with Carl Bernstein in *Rolling Stone,* Joe Alsop said: ". . . The Founding Fathers [of the CIA] were close personal friends of ours. Dick Bissell [former CIA deputy director] was my oldest friend, from childhood. It was a social thing, my dear fellow. I never received a dollar, I never signed a secrecy agreement. I didn't have to . . . I've done things for them when I thought they were the right thing to do. I call it doing my duty as a citizen." Alsop said he went to Laos in 1952 at Frank Wisner's urging and to the Philippines the next year at Desmond FitzGerald's request. In both cases the CIA correctly assumed that Alsop's reporting of political events would help America's interests. Those interests came first for Alsop.

Some of the journalists spied; others simply volunteered information, or imparted it in the normal give-and-take between reporters and sources. Some newsmen went further. They reported stories both true and false for the agency. Sometimes they helped recruit agents, or kept tabs on foreigners of interest to the CIA. Sometimes agents used press credentials as cover; other journalists lived double lives, filing legitimately for their news organizations, while doing the CIA's bidding on other tasks. Their motives were varied. Many believed the republic and free people everywhere were in grave danger, and they took on intelligence assignments out of admirable patriotism. Their acts, however, now were being judged because they were seen by the public for the first time and against the moral backdrop of Watergate. Money, adventure, and the chance to obtain exclusive stories propelled others to the CIA.

The Watergate period was the worst of times for the CIA. It stood in the dock accused of crimes and, what probably stung worse, bungling. In the autumn of 1975, a committee chaired by Representative Otis G. Pike, a New York Democrat, began investigating the agency, including alleged connections with the press. Since the CIA does not reveal the names of assets, Pike's staff set about compiling the names of suspected newsmen-spooks. Their list ultimately had about fifty names. One of those names was supplied by John A. Bross, who had run CIA clandestine operations in Eastern Europe. Bross, then retired, said the correspondent he identified had secretly kept tabs for the CIA on Iron Curtain travelers in Western Europe. The name he furnished: Philip L. Geyelin, the editor of the *Washington Post* editorial page. Geyelin was a *Wall Street Journal* correspondent in Europe in the mid-fifties.

Aha! That explained, for the committee staff privy to Bross's little secret, those *Post* editorials criticizing the committee for the way it was handling the investigation. Geyelin directed one of the most influential editorial pages in the country. In terms that Washington understood, he was the equivalent of at least a cabinet officer or senior presidential counselor. It was no minnow the committee investigators had netted. At one point Searle Field, the committee staff director, considered going to see Geyelin about the matter, then thought better. But reporters were telling Geyelin that his name was popping up around the committee. He thought the committee was leaking his alleged tie to the CIA in order to blunt his editorial criticism.

Phil Geyelin was twenty-eight in December 1950 when he took leave from the *Wall Street Journal* to join the CIA. The Korean War was in full swing; that it might metastasize into a world war seemed dangerously probable. He went to work in the CIA's drafty, decrepit, two-story buildings between the Washington Monument and the Lincoln Memorial, writing reports about Cuba. Geyelin found the work dull and he never got out of Washington, he recalled. Eleven months later he decided to quit and to rejoin the *Journal*. His boss, Tom Braden, arranged for a farewell meeting for Geyelin with Allen Dulles, the head of the CIA. After Braden himself left the agency, he became a columnist whose work Geyelin published.

Geyelin learned that Bross had identified him to the committee. Confronted by Geyelin, Bross said, "That is what Dick Helms told me." Richard M. Helms, the CIA director from 1966 to 1973, was a friend and guide to many Washington journalists and an experienced traveler in the upper reaches of capital society.

More than Geyelin's personal integrity was now at stake. The precious credibility of the *Post,* swelled by the paper's Watergate success, also was threatened. Geyelin called for help from Joseph A. Califano, Jr., the *Post*'s attorney, an expert on the bureaucratic maze. Both men knew the curse that could be visited on someone by selective, malevolent use of a secret government dossier. They got CIA permission to examine the agency's file on the editor.

They found nothing to corroborate Bross's assertion. A reference to Geyelin as a "willing collaborator" turned out to be the agency's quaint jargon for anyone who knowingly talked to a CIA officer for any reason, including a reporter's routine practice of checking information. Cables suggested that Geyelin be recruited to spy while he was a correspondent abroad. Another document stated that Geyelin had too weak a grasp of French for him to be useful in Paris, an unkind cut for the son of a former French Line agent. A cryptonym assigned to Geyelin lent credence to the appearance of him as an intelligence asset. Geyelin's effort to have the files reflect reality led to an exchange of letters between Bross and Helms.

Bross, who married into the family that owns the *Chicago Sun-Times,* told Helms that he thought it "wholly admirable" for journalists to have served intelligence purposes, "particularly in the early fifties when many of us in Germany could practically hear Soviet tank treads churning around Berlin. What I totally fail to understand is the implication that journalists who choose to serve in this capacity are somehow morally contaminated. Phil Geyelin seems to feel that this is the way it is, however."

Helms replied from Tehran where he was then the American ambassador that he did not recall anything about Geyelin's association with the agency. But his comments revealed an interesting perception of the press-CIA issue:

It is not difficult for me to understand that an individual newspaperman's perception of this relationship might change at different points in history. . . . After all, we have been living during this past year with a sea change in the public's view of what a secret service should be permitted to do. The national attitude in 1955 was obviously significantly different from that of 1975. . . . From what you write it strikes me that Phil feels himself caught up in the same phenomenon which has caused the Intelligence Community so much trouble during the recent press revelations and Congressional hearings . . . the practice of journalism is loaded with ambivalence. For example, "The public has a right to know" is trumpeted by editorial writers when it comes to information they want to print. But the public has no right to know when it is a question of the source or origin of the information. If I am handed a glass with a clear liquid in it, I have a right to know (1) that it is water, and (2) that it comes from a poisoned well. The newspaperman, in defending this practice of concealing sources, is guilty of the worst kind of sophistry.

Ward Just, who had written for *Newsweek* and the *Post,* made Helms's point from the opposite perspective. When intelligence agencies and the press are too chummy, the loser is the reader or television viewer who "doesn't know where these sources are coming from and the result is he doesn't know whose hand is on whose leg," Just said.

The disclosures added a further burden to American reporters working abroad, particularly in the new nations of Africa or in politically volatile Latin American countries. The governments and factions in those places grew more suspicious of American correspondents. In one case, the *Post* moved quickly to disprove an erroneous rumor that one of its correspondents and an editor had furnished information to the CIA. They feared with cause that an allegation of a CIA link, though baseless, might dry up some sources and jeopardize his life. Looking for some way to get back the press's presumed good name, professional newspaper groups urged Congress to make American journalists untouchable for intelligence tasks. Phil Geyelin agreed that news people should not do anything for the government that would compromise their autonomy, from writing speeches for politicians to collecting intelligence. But "when the press asks for legislation to protect itself from exploitation in one way or another by the CIA," Geyelin commented, "what it is asking, really, is for the government to save it from itself." There were dangers in such a legislative favor far greater, perhaps, than those that had prompted the request. The truth, though, was that no law would save a journalist who was willing to sacrifice his responsibility to his readers for other purposes, however noble. Whatever the reasons for the working relationships between the press and the intelligence system, though these relationships poisoned the concept of a press free from any government control, they were between consenting adults. A reporter could always say no to the CIA; management could always refuse to compromise its news organization.

Following Colby's 1973 leak about the CIA's own "press corps," the agency had declared that it would not employ American journalists and foreigners working for American news organizations. But every savvy bureaucrat digs a loophole. The same regulation that barred recruitment of American news people concluded, "No exceptions to the policies and prohibitions stated above may be made except with the specific approval of the DCI (Director of Central Intelligence)." Journalist operatives had been quite productive in the past; their talents might be needed again, the agency reasoned. Back to Square One.

For six weeks in early 1975, the Central Intelligence Agency and nearly a dozen of the country's leading news organizations, including the *Washington Post,* willingly joined in what CIA Director William E. Colby called "the weirdest conspiracy in town . . . an American conspiracy." Colby, whose covert career dated back to wartime OSS operations against the Germans, was at the eye of the plot to prevent press disclosure of a top-secret CIA attempt to retrieve a foundered Russian submarine. At one point as Colby and his agents desperately labored to keep the conspiracy intact, he quipped to Lt. General Brent Scowcroft, a top White House national security official, that the frantic exercise reminded him of *The Perils of Pauline.*

Colby's press caper was touched off on February 7 by a fascinating story on the front page of the *Los Angeles Times,* reporting that the United States had tried to raise a sunken Soviet sub from the Atlantic Ocean floor. There were errors and holes in the account—it was the Pacific, not the Atlantic—but it said enough to alarm the CIA. In many ways the story was a local one for the *Times.* Although the paper did not have all of these details at the time, the secret project involved Howard Hughes's Summa Corporation, which operated the unique retrieval ship *Glomar Explorer* for the CIA and was based in California; the exotic vessel's home port was Long Beach. Intelligence officers ran the recovery effort, codenamed Project Jennifer, from secret offices in the San Fernando Valley and they rendezvoused in "safe houses" in Santa Monica and Long Beach.

After word of the article's appearance was flashed to CIA headquarters in a Washington suburb, the agency instructed Jennifer officers to meet with *Los Angeles Times* managing editor William Thomas. Fifteen minutes later they were in his office. They asserted that the article was "a serious compromise" of national security, and they appealed to the editor's patriotism to not pursue the clandestine operation. *Glomar Explorer*'s huge claw had reportedly snagged part of the Russian sub from its ocean grave north of Hawaii the previous summer. The CIA maintained that publicity would blow its chances to obtain more of the hulk. Convinced by his visitors and a phone call from Colby-deputy Carl Duckett that the CIA's case was legitimate, Thomas said he would have killed the story had he known the stakes sooner. But he ordered the story off the front page and buried on page 18 in the last edition in an attempt to downplay its significance. He cautioned his callers that other press organizations were working on the story. Hardly anyone else in the press, however, appeared to have taken notice of the episode.

Next morning Colby phoned an executive at the *New York Times,* whose reporter Seymour Hersh had started digging into the *Glomar Explorer* operation a year earlier. On that occasion Colby had warned the reporter that "writing or even talking" about the project "would result in a serious loss to the United States." Now with fragments of the story out, Colby was anxious to know if Hersh's paper would unwrap what he might have found before his editors dissuaded him from pursuing the investigation. "This seems to be coming out a little bit at the seams," Colby told the *Times* executive. "I would still hope we can keep it from blowing up. . . . I thought I would give a little whistle to see if a larger effort was being planned, it might be possible to cool it down a little."

"I will get right on it," the *Times* man replied.

Sy Hersh was an agressive journalist with a Pulitzer prize for reporting the My Lai massacre. Just a few months before the Russian submarine story surfaced, Hersh dropped a journalistic blockbuster on the CIA, disclosing that the agency "conducted a massive, illegal domestic intelligence operation during the Nixon administration directed against antiwar and other dissident groups. Colby flatly and repeatedly denied Hersh's report but a presidential commission and congressional committees subsequently confirmed it.

Hersh applied a variety of techniques to ferret out information: threats, shouts, cajolery, bluff. Using all of these devices Hersh phoned the CIA two days after Colby's call to the *Times*'s brass with a message for the director: "He has a choice again . . . either he delegates someone . . . to sit down with me and I will make it as good as I can. It is a positive story. Or else I am in a position of writing what I know, which is more than he thinks I know about our lady friend program [a reference to Project Jennifer]. I am not going to do anything about it tonight. It is a problem because the only professional thing I have is to protect my rear. . . ."

A half hour later, Colby rang Hersh, commending his silence on Jennifer: ". . . you have been first-class about this thing for a long time. . . . You have been damn good."

"It is not a question of being good," replied Hersh. "I am a citizen too. I don't know that God damn much about it," the reporter confessed. Hersh mentioned the upheavals within the CIA in the wake of his disclosures and the official probes, suggesting a story about the submarine retrieval would show the agency in a better light.

Colby did not tell Hersh about his Saturday call to the *Times* executive nor his follow-up phone conversation with the same person earlier that day. The newspaper which boasts at the top of its front page, "All the News That's Fit to Print," ran a wire service re-write of the *Los Angeles Times* article, but nothing of Hersh's reporting. "Obviously, you did very well, and I appreciate it," Colby told the *Times* man, who replied,

"I very gently passed on the word, and I think everyone understood."

Next morning Colby phoned the *New York Times* official again about his conversation with Hersh. "I wanted to tip you, and I will get out of it," said Colby, obviously trying to again head off Hersh.

"Good, I have it," the *Times* executive replied.

Secretary of State Henry Kissinger, at the CIA's request, also interceded with the *Times* to hush the story.

In Los Angeles Bill Thomas told a CIA officer he suspected the *Post*, which considered his paper a competitor because of its large Washington bureau despite their joint news service, had a team of reporters chasing the story. Thomas suggested that the *Post* would be as responsive as he had been to the CIA's appeal for secrecy.

On the afternoon of February 13 publisher Katharine Graham listened attentively to her diffident visitor matter-of-factly explain his problem. She'd consider his appeal for help, the publisher told William Colby. He convinced the publisher secrecy was needed to cloak another try for the submarine. ("There have been instances," Mrs. Graham said later, "in which secrets have been leaked to us which we thought were so dangerous that we went to them [the government] and told them that they had been leaked to us and did not print them. The fact is that they did get out later.")

Before dinner time that evening, having heard from managing editor Howard Simons that no one on the *Post* staff had heard anything about the deep-sea venture, Mrs. Graham phoned the CIA chief:

"This seems, as far as we can tell, to be nothing."

"Great," said Colby.

"It is all agreed with you that it is not anything we would like to get into."

"You are very kind," said Colby.

"It can be that things are starting that have not gotten here yet," Mrs. Graham said, allowing the *Post* an out if conditions changed.

"It is a great tribute to our journalists, you are very kind," Colby glowed.

"It is totally agreed with you that . . . we have no problem with not doing it," Mrs. Graham pledged.

"Good enough, I certainly appreciate it. Thank you very kindly for your time. I do not know whether it will work or not, but I want to do my damnedest if I can," Colby concluded. His overture, however, prompted the *Post* to assign reporters to the story, as he may have assumed would happen.

Meanwhile, *Los Angeles Times* reporters kept dogging the secret project in Hawaii, Texas, and elsewhere, probably using leads from the CIA's confidential briefings of Thomas and others on the staff. One agency man nervously conjectured: "Perhaps Mr. Thomas has not totally leveled and we're being set up." But Thomas was being squeezed between his partnership in the agency's plot to hush the press and his credibility as a journalist. His Washington Bureau chief, Jack Nelson, told Colby that he didn't think the plot would work because too many news organizations were pursuing the story; therefore, the *Los Angeles Times* should publish what new information it had uncovered. Thomas told the CIA that he was allowing his reporters to continue their investigation because "their personal journalistic reputation is in question." But he assured the agency, according to CIA notes, "that their findings will never be in print and additionally volunteered to furnish to us their results, although no names could be mentioned." Thomas later said he made no such offer, though he agreed to suppress the story.

Late in February Thomas heard from Colby that the *New York Times* was reconsidering its hold on the story, Seymour Hersh having concluded that Jennifer had been largely a fiasco. Thomas was getting edgy: the *New York Times*, like his a morning newspaper, would beat him into print by three hours if it broke the agreement. Thomas personally wrote a detailed piece about the CIA project and placed it in his office safe—to be launched like a missile if someone else fired theirs first.

Always meticulous, however, the *New York Times* put its bargain with Colby in writing. On March 3 the Washington bureau acknowledged the *Times*'s decision to withhold publication on condition that it be notified in advance "if you have knowledge that any other news medium is preparing to publish." The *Times* was edgy, too, but still keeping its word.

But word of Jennifer was spreading. Lloyd Shearer, West Coast editor of *Parade*, had the story; *Time* and *Newsweek* were onto it. Colby had more rounds to make. He informed Mrs. Graham's *Newsweek* of her commitment for the *Post* and phoned an old friend in the upper ranks at *Time*. Both newsweeklies agreed to go along with the CIA.

"This thing is really traveling," Lloyd Shearer phoned his CIA contacts on the afternoon of March 17. Talk of the *Glomar Explorer*, said Shearer, was "all over" the National Press Building in Washington and the journalism review *MORE* was asking newspapers if they had killed it. National Public Radio and C.B.S. got the Colby treatment: a dose of patriotism and assurance that everyone else had taken the vow of silence.

It had been six weeks since the *Los Angeles Times* reported the attempt to snare the Russian sub. Colby, a slight, unpretentious man, won most of the big news organizations to his side. Then abruptly on March 18 Colby's carefully knit cover started unraveling: syndicated columnist Jack Anderson had the story—and he had no bargain with Colby. A month earlier the CIA had deflected an inquiry about the project from Les Whitten, Anderson's associate, by telling him there was "nothing to it."

At 5:25 in the afternoon, with deadlines nearing for the big morning papers that he had deals with, Colby phoned Whitten who said, "I just cannot believe that this damn thing will hold."

". . . I would agree that the odds are against me, but I have to fight like hell because it is so important," Colby replied. "I have gone to everybody who has a finger on this, and everyone has said they will hold.

I feel like the boy in front of the dike, and I am running out of fingers and toes. . . ."

Colby urged Whitten to "sit with it a little bit. You are in good company. Everyone else is sitting on it. That is one of the most fascinating parts of it—the whole press . . . has been just splendid."

"We are all doing a half-assed job," Whitten declared.

Colby, like the hero in every spy tale, faced a seeming dilemma: If he alerted his co-conspirators that Anderson seemed about to break the story, they might rush to publish themselves rather than risk being scooped; if the director didn't tell them and Anderson reported on Jennifer, Colby's honor, a matter of pride to him, would be blackened. Through the dinner hour Colby busily phoned the editors.

At 9 o'clock that night Colby's dam burst. Anderson broadcast that the agency was trying to cover up an expensive failure rather than a successful intelligence operation.

It was puzzling: Had the *Glomar Explorer* actually gained valuable secrets from the Russian sub? Was the mission the costly failure some reports alleged? Had the supposedly skeptical press been cleverly played by Colby so that when the story inevitably did spread, the CIA generally appeared heroic rather than bumbling or evil, an image it was trying to overcome? Was the national interest harmed by the *Glomar* stories? "The only place where you could get that information is the CIA itself, and I'm not sure I'd believe them anyway," said Ben Bradlee.

Simons's devil theory was that Colby wanted a paper like the *Post* or the *New York Times* to give the *Glomar* a huge splash, showing the agency masterfully pulling off a highly technical spying mission in the hope that news of such a feat would give the beleaguered CIA a public relations lift. "I never heard of an intelligence chief telling an editor more about a matter than the editor knew," said Simons. An experienced former intelligence officer saw Colby's effort as standard operating procedure to convert a blunder to advantage: "By telling everyone, he assured the story would get out." The *Post* reported that the agency had succeeded in getting what it wanted from the sub, including part of the communications system. The paper's editorial praised Jennifer as exemplary of the CIA's true strength.

Still the questions gnawed, and so Bradlee, Mrs. Graham, and Howard Simons, after the story broke, drove out to CIA headquarters —entered past St. John's quotation on the lobby wall, "And ye shall know the truth and the truth shall make you free"—to see if there was more, or less, to Jennifer than they had printed. Colby was cordial and grateful. But they left with their uncertainty intact.

Some journalists suspected the motives of Colby's collaborators in the press had as much to do with their concern about their own image as with national fealty. "Since Watergate," Jack Anderson later commented, "the editors themselves are going along with the establishment. The establishment has been shaken with what happened, that the press can topple a president. The press itself is shaken by it . . . trying to prove that they're not against the establishment, the government, that we're not all gadflys." Roger Wilkins, a former government attorney who wrote the *Post*'s editorials on Watergate before joining the *New York Times,* reflected: the press cooperated "in large measure to prove in the wake of Watergate that they were not irresponsible, that they did have a real sense of the national interest, that they had wandered out of this corporate club. . . . But that essentially they were members in good standing of the club and they wanted to demonstrate that."

In the spring of 1979, eight years after the Supreme Court ruled against the government in the Pentagon Papers case, the government stopped the presses at the *Progressive,* a seventy-year-old politically liberal monthly in Madison, Wisconsin. At issue was an article scheduled for April about the workings of a hydrogen bomb. In running the piece, which was based on information available to the public, the magazine sought to persuade readers of the folly of the nuclear arms race.

The government lost the Pentagon Papers case primarily because its argument rested on no specific statute. This time it cited a specific law, one whose press curbs had never before been tested in court. The Atomic Energy Act of 1954 was designed to clamp the tightest kind of lid on nuclear weapons information; it empowered the government to restrain the press in advance from publishing anything about atomic energy that the government had classified secret. Federal District Judge Robert W. Warren, acting on the government's request, ordered the *Progressive* to refrain from publishing the controversial article. His order remained in force for seven months while the First Amendment twisted slowly in the wind.* Journalists and publishers who had been largely of one resisting mind on the Pentagon Papers issue divided sharply over this case. The *Post* came down on the government's side.

Two days after Judge Warren restrained the *Progressive*, the *Post*, in an editorial titled, "John Mitchell's Dream Case," declared:

> If . . . the *Progressive*, has what the Department of Justice says it has—secret information on how a hydrogen bomb works—it should forget about publishing it. . . . As a press-versus-government First Amendment contest, this, as far as we can tell, is John Mitchell's dream case—the one the Nixon administration was never lucky enough to get: a real First Amendment loser. . . . If it does have such material, the magazine, on its motion, should decide now against printing the piece, or at least its troubling sections. It will be doing everyone—including the friends of the First Amendment—a great service if it does so.

As the government tightened its hammerlock on the *Progressive*, the *Post* again commented: "Judge Warren's order, especially if it is sustained on appeal, will set a precedent on which other orders will be based. Once the door is open to advance judicial scrutiny of what the press may publish, it will never be closed. The loss will be immensely destructive." "There are times," said Ben Bradlee, "when common sense should prevail over some theoretical right. I would not publish this thing." There was a sense of great foreboding in this line of reasoning that had nothing to do with the fear of spreading nuclear power. The *Post* and others in the publishing and broadcasting business feared the current Supreme Court. Richard Nixon was gone, but he had left behind a high court dominated by his appointees, including Chief Justice Warren Burger, and a number of other conservatives.

---

*The injunction was lifted in September after the government decided to drop the case after the "secrets" said to be in the *Progressive* article appeared in other publications, including the *Chicago Tribune*.

"Nixon's Revenge," some called it. Their decisions in recent years placed new restrictions on the freedom that the press had enjoyed and regarded as irreducible, if not absolute. The court, for example, had opened an easier route to police searches of newspaper offices. The rein–the–press spirit was infectious. Local and state courts across the country pressed news people to divulge their confidential informants despite laws designed to shield reporters from being compelled to do so. The Supreme Court ruled that reporters must give such testimony in certain criminal cases. Much of this hard-line judicial attitude stemmed in no small part from a widely held judgement that the press had become too powerful since Watergate. This turn of events undoubtedly pleased Nixon who blamed the press for his political destruction.

The *Post*'s editorials angered *Progressive* editor Erwin Knoll, a goateed, chain-smoking, plumpish man who had once been a reporter and editor on the paper. "They talk about poor judicial climate," Knoll said heatedly. "Well, what do you suppose helps build an adverse judicial climate? Editorials in the *Washington Post* and others like it in other papers. Judges read the newspapers, and if they keep reading that they're going to rule against the First Amendment, well, the momentum is there. And so, these editorial writers are engaged in creating a self-fulfilling prophecy." Later he wrote to the paper: "I've been sort of busy these last few days worrying about the First Amendment, so I haven't had much time to worry about the *Washington Post* editorial of March 11, 'John Mitchell's Dream Case.' But I did have a fleeting thought I wanted to share with you. Somehow the *Washington Post* has become John Mitchell's dream newspaper. How did that come to pass?"

His note provoked another thought. How might the Pentagon Papers episode have turned out if Richard Nixon or John Mitchell had phoned the *Post* and the *Times* and said, 'The papers contain dynamite. Can we talk to you before you decide to print them?' Would the newspapers have accommodated the president and the attorney general, and, perhaps, not published? To be able to say yes or no in such a situation is a great power. It was what the First Amendment fight was all about.

It was long after Watergate. Bob Woodward occasionally had a nightmarish fantasy about the future. The country was in a state of terrible economic and social decline. A weakened United States faced grim challengers abroad. The times were politically ugly. There was a growing sense that the country had been led to disaster by the removal of Nixon; Watergate looked different than it does now. "I might be called before a Congressional investigating committee," Woodward fleetingly speculated. It was only a fantasy. Woodward was convinced that the Watergate story was an accurate description of Nixon's misdeeds. But the world turns.

Howard Simons also had moments when he speculated on the perverse twists of public sentiment. "Just as the heroes of the fifties were the bums of the sixties," he'd say, "the good guys of the seventies may become the bad guys of the eighties." The rules that Ben Bradlee said had changed to make the press the inquisitor of government might change again. Some latter-day version of the Cold War, some terrible threat from real or imagined demons, and the press might once more adopt a passive role. The nation would be the loser if that happened.

SIX

Black and White

This business is dominated by middle-class, middle-aged white males.
—WILLIAM HILLIARD, ASSISTANT MANAGING EDITOR, THE *Portland Oregonian*

WASHINGTON IN THE early 1940s, though bustling with war-time activity, remained a lovely and provincial city encrusted with Southern mores. Only a few decent restaurants remained open after eight o'clock at night. Congressmen from Dixie controlled the civic affairs of the District of Columbia through their unchallenged domination of the committees that ruled the voteless city. The chief officials were cautiously appointed by the president so as not to ruffle conservative feathers. Schools and streetcars were racially segregated and within a two- or three-minute walk of the Capitol stretched blocks of decaying brick row houses with backyard privies occupied by poor Negroes. A few years after he bought the *Washington Post* Eugene Meyer described Washington's slums "as dismal in squalor, as primitive in living conditions as any architectural eyesore on the American scene. . . ." Elsewhere in the District, Negroes who were doctors, lawyers, business-men, teachers, and government clerks lived in attractive middle-class neighborhoods, including sections of Georgetown from which most of them were displaced by white liberals who immigrated to serve the burgeoning New Deal. The railroad station restaurant was one of the rare public spots where a black and white could dine together.

For some Negroes in otherwise comfortable circumstances cultural apartheid inflicted an exquisite pain. Frank Snowden, Jr., a Harvard-educated classics professor at Howard University, established after the Civil War to educate freed slaves, complained to the editor of the *Post* that he and his class were barred from seeing *Antigone* at the National Theater. The newspaper did not publish Snowden's letter until he wrote a second time.

Subsequently, the *Post,* alone of the city's four dailies, endorsed the campaign of playwrights and actors to integrate the National, the city's principal live theater, which peculiarly allowed blacks on stage but not in the audience. "The manager came in to declare he would create a race riot by desegregating," recalled editorial writer Alan Barth. Publisher Eugene Meyer encouraged drama critic Richard L. Coe's support of the campaign.*

Washington's dailies and the large corps of correspondents, except for a few reporters from the Negro press, were lily-white preserves, reflecting the ingrained racism of the city's paramount institutions. Eugene and Agnes Meyer, however, the owners of the *Washington Post,* were exceptions who were genuinely concerned about remedying the injustices imposed on blacks. Although the Post was sometimes halting and contradictory, the paper was to be an important force in the assault on those wrongs. Mrs. Meyer established the Wendell Willkie Awards for Negro Journalism to encourage higher standards in the country's 170 or so black-owned newspapers, almost all of which were weeklies. When it came time to present the prizes the only place in segregated Washington that the banquet could be held was the ballroom of the National Press Club. It was a modest step for the press club. Journalist I.F. Stone was barred when he tried to take a Negro judge to lunch there in 1941. It was 1955, though, and only after a sharp factional fight, before the first black journalist was admitted to membership in the club. In 1948 the *Post* became the first paper in town to abandon the practice of routinely labeling Negroes by race in all stories. Police and some businessmen saw the change as further

*Meyer also stuck with Coe later when several movie houses, yielding to organized pressure, pulled their ads from the *Post* because Coe favorably reviewed *Monsieur Verdoux* after its star Charlie Chaplin had incurred the wrath of various patriotic organizations for his peccadilloes and criticism of the United States.

proof of their conviction that the paper was leftist; some members of the news staff grumbled over the new policy.

Onto this racially ambivalent scene in 1952 came the *Post*'s lone black reporter. Baltimore-born Simeon Booker, a minister's son, had won a Wendell Willkie Award for reporting in Cleveland's black-circulation weekly *Call and Post* the abysmal school conditions faced by the city's black children. Black papers tapped a pool of relatively cheap labor because Negro journalists were foreclosed from the white news media which paid more. Unable to break into any of the three Cleveland dailies and defeated in his attempt to unionize the *Call and Post,* Booker applied for a Nieman Fellowship for a year of study at Harvard. He was pointedly asked by a Nieman interviewer if he was a communist because union-organizing in Cleveland had attracted some CP members. Booker became the second black to get journalism's most prestigious sabbatical in the program's fourteen years. Booker received a stipend that doubled his seventy-eight-dollar-a-week *Call and Post* pay; the other Niemans got similar stipends, which were less than their regular salaries—a measure of how far down the pay scale black journalists stood.

After his Nieman Fellowship Booker was hired by the *Post,* the first of his race in the newsroom since a public schoolteacher, Edward H. Lawson, covered "colored" news two decades earlier. Many years after he left the paper, Booker still seemed scarred by the experience; he looked back at the two years "almost as a nightmare. I suffered all kinds of tensions and frustrations." As Dodgers manager Branch Rickey had advised Jackie Robinson a few years earlier when he became the first Negro in big league baseball publisher Philip Graham counseled Booker: "Don't ever hit anybody. If it gets too bad come up and sit in my office." It got bad. One men's room was open to him in the *Post* building. He avoided the inhospitable company cafeteria; many other eating places were closed to him. Booker's editors kept him in the office for a long spell, but when they finally sent him out to cover a robbery the police nearly arrested him as a suspect. He had trouble getting white cabbies to take him back to his office in time to write his stories before the deadline. Booker's copy was sometimes scrawled with racial epithets.

Blacks began picketing Hecht's department store to desegregate the lunchroom. Booker was not permitted to report this demonstration against a major *Post* advertiser. When an editor assigned him to check a tip that communists were among the protesters, Booker refused, arguing that if the picketing itself wasn't newsworthy, communist involvement wasn't either. Downtown merchants were feeling the sharp pinch of declining sales as poor blacks replaced the whites who were exiting to the growing suburbs where they found attractive shopping centers. Acutely attuned to the ring of their cash registers, the merchants feared the uncertain consequences of desegregation. Washington's ten leading downtown department stores—the mainstay of the newspapers' advertising income—did $1 million less business in December 1951 than in the previous December. Further decline seemed certain—an unpropitious prospect for the *Post* which was badly trailing the *Star*'s advertising volume.

Philip Graham, who had succeeded his father-in-law Eugene Meyer as publisher, threw the weight of his newspaper and his own creative energy and political savvy behind altering the cityscape. In 1952 the *Post* like many dailies in other big cities began campaigning for a revitalized downtown area, with improved public transit, urban renewal, and expressways. Graham's strategy included creating a new organization, the Federal City Council, to offset the Board of Trade, a hidebound but potent center of civic power. "The *Washington Star* was the board's paper and mouthpiece, its ruling Kauffmann and Noyes families locked firmly in conservative step with the board," recalled Alan L. Dessoff, a former *Post* staffer. "The board of Trade and the *Star* dominated the city," Ben Gilbert, then the *Post*'s city editor, said of that period. "Phil didn't want to have the *Star*'s veto power, but he wanted the city free from being tied to a small group."

High on the Council's agenda was the replacement with modern housing of a vast tract of decrepit tenements in Southwest Washington occupied by Negroes. No local entrepreneur was prepared to take on the huge project so Graham persuaded New York developer William Zeckendorf to direct the rebuilding, for which the Eisenhower White House provided the first federal urban renewal money. As development got underway the National Association for the Advancement of Colored People criticized the absence of any plan to relocate in decent housing the thousands of blacks whose dwellings were being pulverized by the wrecker's ball. Unfortunately, there was scant good housing for them in Washington's segregated real estate market and many of them ended up worse off. Simeon Booker wrote an article about the upheaval but it was spiked. He complained to editor Russell Wiggins. The next morning Booker's story appeared—in the back near the comics. "I could tell where my future was," said Booker, who not long after returned to the black press. The newspaper was keenly sensitive to real estate interests. Until 1960 housing ads carried racial designations. A proposal from two reporters—one black, one white—to investigate discrimination in apartment rentals was vetoed.

As the costs of building the new Southwest housing complex soared, despite federal subsidies, the high-rise apartments and stylish town-houses predictably slipped from the financial grasp of all but the more prosperous. "In Southwest," said Ben Gilbert, "the plan was to make it 15 percent black, 85 percent white. We kept the [reporting] lid on that aspect because the rental agent feared if blacks moved in first, no whites would follow." The *Post* was engaging in social engineering rather than journalism. Late when the racial effects in Southwest were starkly visible, with most of the development white-occupied, the *Post* editorialized "in all candor it must be conceded that the motivation has been more economical than social. . . ."

By 1957 Washington was 50 percent black and growing more so as the white exodus to the suburbs accelerated, spurred, in part, by school integration. That September President Eisenhower summoned Arkansas Governor Orval Faubus to his vacation headquarters in Rhode Island to ease the racial crisis in Little Rock where the National Guard was barring nine Negro children from Central High School. Police guarding Faubus at his Providence hotel ignored the young black man in a waiter's jacket who walked through their cordon toward the governor's room. At the door, the man shed the coat he had borrowed, knocked, and announced to the startled segregationist that he was

Wallace Terry of the Brown University newspaper. Next day newspapers across the country carried a photograph of Faubus and Terry shaking hands. Alfred Friendly, *Post* managing editor, saw the picture and phoned Terry to offer the nineteen-year-old junior a reporter's job.

Being black himself did not immunize Terry against the distrust of those blacks who saw him as an agent of a hostile white establishment. Infiltrating the Black Muslim movement in 1960 under an assumed identity, Terry wrote a series that the *Post* slugged, "Cult of Hate." Angered by the reporter's deception, Black Muslims shadowed Terry and threatened him with death. Terry complained to Malcolm X, who had liked the perceptive and fair series, and the threats stopped. Nevertheless, when Nation of Islam members saw Terry covering civil rights rallies, they would shout, "There's the Uncle Tom reporter, the lackey for the white devil."

Other blacks came to the *Post* staff. Columbia University's Graduate School of Journalism, one of the most eminent institutions for training reporters and editors, reflected the overwhelming white and male bias of America's predominant press. This reality in 1960 did not deter Dorothy Gilliam from applying for admission after a year and a half in Chicago on the black magazine *Jet.* She was searching for answers to the searing questions and terrible conflicts that raged for a generation of blacks coming of age in the mid-1950s. Journalism, she believed, would provide the means for her quest.

Graduates of the Columbia Journalism school interview applicants from their areas, screening out those they deem unqualified for one reason or another. Gilliam was interviewed by a Chicago newspaperman who sent this confidential impression to Columbia:

She is a well-groomed, personable young lady, with considerable spark and sparkle. In case you were wondering, she is quite dark—no borderline race question here. The matter of race did not come up in the interview, except through her reference to an interest in Africa. Therefore I assume she is not overly belligerent on the subject. We did discuss the class limitation on women, and she expressed some mild resentment that being a woman should be a handicap in journalism. There was no suggestion on her part that being a woman and a Negro might place her under a double handicap. . . . She seems straightforward, intelligent, and speaks moderately well (though the South Side accent does come through). . . .

The letter—"It reeked of 'this person is worthy to become a member of the club,' a club kept intact by the screening system," Tennessee-born Gilliam later said, resentment still in her voice—came into her hands by happenstance seventeen years later when she was chosen an "alumni of the year." But "the club" took her in; she was one of two blacks and a dozen women in the class of seventy-five students.

As a lanky youngster Dorothy Gilliam had snickered at the heathen savages in Tarzan movies on the screens of segregated theaters. "Mine was white America's comical and nonsensical view of Africa," she said. "It was one of the tragedies of my young life that this distortion was my only exposure to my complex, historic and exploited motherland." She spent the summer of graduation from Columbia in Kenya, then in its final period as a British colony, and greeted Jomo Kenyatta in her few words of Swahili when the rebel was freed from eight years of British detention. She made a discovery in Africa: "I went over thinking I was going home again, but many Kenyans had never seen an American black. There was no instant brotherhood or sisterhood; my home was New York, not Nairobi."

That autumn in 1961 the *Post* hired Gilliam and assigned her to the welfare beat. The newspaper paid unusual attention to the plight of Washington's poor because of the Meyer and Graham families' concern; Katharine Graham was then a rich matron wholesomely engaged in local good works. As a measure of welfare's high priority for the Post, three reporters covered the subject, only two covered Congress. Gilliam wrote about the shambles of juvenile treatment programs —which would persist exposé after exposé. Her stories often ran on the front page. "But they were negative stories about blacks," she recalled, "describing criminal ways and poverty. They never looked at the range of black activities as they looked at white activities. Just by exclusion, you ended up with this skewed picture, nothing else except welfare and crime."

"Assignments were not only being made on a racial basis; we had been pigeonholed in areas that were not competitive," said Luther Jackson, another Columbia graduate. (He, Gilliam, and Wallace Terry were then the three blacks on the *Post.*) "In welfare and civil rights the liberal *Washington Post* did not have to worry about the conservative *Washington Star.*" Simeon Booker, Wallace Terry, Luther Jackson, and Dorothy Gilliam came to the *Post* advantaged by Ivy League schooling—"white credentials," Gilliam called it.

But the *Post* still saw the world through white lenses. White editors had few contacts among the city's growing black population, which by 1960 far outnumbered whites. "We're going to be covering a city we don't know," said district editor John Anderson. The paper's intelligence gap had closed little since Simeon Booker, new in town, asked an editor who Washington's leading Negro was and the answer was Elder Michaux. "But he was just a radio preacher," recalled Booker, who set about getting to know scores of influential blacks who were invisible to his editors. A few blacks were relied on by the *Post* as Negro "spokesmen." At one point the *Washington Afro-American* disparagingly cartooned such a spokesman with a bandanna on his head sitting puppetlike on Ben Gilbert's knee.

Ben Gilbert was the youngest city editor ever at the *Post,* and he held the job for twenty-one years, longer than anyone else. Stamped from the mold of fire-breathers who legendarily boss local staffs, Gilbert was a fierce driver of reporters and was himself a driven man. Newsroom camaraderie ended at Gilbert. "He was not the kind of guy you'd clap on the back and say, 'Hi, Ben,'" one of his former reporters said. "You went to Princeton but you didn't graduate," Gilbert noted to a job-seeker as he impatiently leafed through the applicant's record.

"I got married," the job-seeker explained.

"We don't want quitters around here," Gilbert snapped, ending the interview.

After graduating from college in the middle of the Depression, Gilbert used his father's New York Central employee's pass to travel from New York to Chicago in luckless search of a newspaper job. Gilbert both disdained and envied those whose social cachet made so much possible. In 1948 a proper Bostonian named Benjamin Crownin-shield Bradlee, graduate of St. Mark's and Harvard, came to cover police and the courts for Gilbert. Long after, when Bradlee became executive editor and was encouraging Gilbert's departure from the newsroom, Gilbert suffered from stomach ulcers. Bradlee phoned Gilbert's wife, as the story is told, to inquire of his health. Her husband was going to have a blood transfusion. "Blue, I hope," quipped Bradlee to an unamused Maurine Gilbert.

Les Whitten worked for four and a half years for Gilbert, detesting him throughout for his tyrannical methods of dealing with his staff. Their shouting battles rocked the city room.

But there was another aspect to this complicated man. "Ben lived that paper," Whitten asserted. "He inspired it on behalf of poor blacks for years before blacks were fashionable. On his best days he brought to it the hungry fires of idealism that never burned out fully, even when he buckled to expediency on some stories." "Ben cared for the city and the paper—in that order," said a *Post* reporter. In one period of thirty months, twenty reporters left the paper for greener journalistic pastures, many of them unable or unwilling to endure the pounding on Gilbert's forge.

Police harassment of Negroes was an ugly fact of life in the nation's capital even after World War II. One afternoon a black worker who wrestled the heavy rolls of newsprint in the pressroom came upstairs to the newsroom, his head swathed in bandages. He said three policemen had beaten him that morning at police headquarters after accusing him of indecent exposure. A *Post* reporter, the editors learned later, witnessed the assault but reported nothing because such strongarm tactics were too common to be regarded as newsworthy. And life was easier, too, for police reporters who did not embarrass the department.

A police trial board called Gilbert to testify in the case. "Have you ever changed your name?" Gilbert was asked.

"Yes," answered the bespectacled editor, who had dropped his Jewish family name.

"Have you ever been a member of the Communist Party?"

"No," truthfully replied Gilbert, who had spent nine months in the

Young Communist League while an undergraduate.

Convinced after grilling Gilbert that he was not a communist, Phil Graham wrote an editorial defending him. The plainclothesmen were acquitted, the errant reporter fired. Gilbert later discovered that the police were given raw F.B.I. files including misinformation about him possibly to intimidate the editor and the *Post.*

Long after Gilbert's departure staffers still criticized his violations of the unwritten canon that a good reporter cannot be an actor in shaping the events he also chronicles. Gilbert was called "the fourth District commissioner" and it was widely assumed that officials consulted him on how a particular proposed decision would be greeted by the *Post.* He enjoyed the dual role he played, but he had not cast himself for the parts: "Phil Graham gave me an assignment. I was to watch the city. When something was happening that needed his attention—who is going to be a commissioner, the political jockeying—I was to see him."

John F. Kennedy was inaugurated president in 1961 in a city whose population was mostly black. At a White House Correspondents Association dinner, Attorney General Robert Kennedy shared with Philip Graham his concern that Washington was on the verge of a racial explosion. At Graham's direction Gilbert and welfare reporter Eve Edstrom prepared an unsigned eight-page report for President Kennedy on conditions in the District and suggested remedies. "The District of Columbia faces grave social, economic and racial problems," it warned. "Under the present governmental structure, it is likely that these problems will explode into a disgrace for the nation and a major embarrassment for the Kennedy administration." The White House, the report went on, had allowed "control of the city to fall into the hands of a few Southern reactionaries on the House District Committee. . . . If major social and racial disorders occur, the public responsibility will fall on the Executive branch."

The report proposed that the president install a special assistant to deal with the affairs of the District, which had no elected local government. Graham proposed, and Kennedy appointed to the strategically critical position Charles A. Horsky, an attorney in Covington &

Burling, a top law firm which represented the *Post.*

In 1967 the District government was reorganized to provide a presidentially appointed mayor and a modest measure of self-government on the way to home rule. President Johnson decided to appoint Walter Washington, a prominent housing expert and member of a patrician local black family. Informed by an insider of the impending action Gilbert, as he tells it, alerted editor Bradlee. Gilbert cautioned that he got the information in confidence and, therefore, no story could be published until Johnson's official announcement. As others recall, Bradlee then assigned a reporter to independently confirm Gilbert's tip. Joseph A. Califano, Jr., a Johnson aide, warned Bradlee that premature publication might cause the president to reverse his decision, a favorite LBJ anti-press gambit.

That gave Bradlee the unofficial confirmation he needed to run a story. He and District editor Stephen Isaacs were at Gilbert's house that night for a party. To keep their host unaware that the *Post* was printing the Walter Washington story, they headed off phone calls to Gilbert and hid the first edition of the paper that was delivered each night to senior editors. The next morning Gilbert raged at Isaacs, insisting on knowing the source for the story and denouncing Bradlee for breeching his confidence. But those who read newsroom "tea leaves" saw Bradlee's breaking of the story as a signal that the *Post* no longer would involve itself directly in the city's politics. Phil Graham was dead. Gilbert in time would become Mayor Washington's municipal planning director, attempting to mold the physical and social face of the city as he had tried to do when he was an editor.

North and South, the press had failed to convey the depth and nature of the black revolution that was rising in the land. Decent editors and publishers who were racial moderates handled the early portents of growing black discontent with such restraint—which they regarded as the responsible posture for themselves as journalists and community leaders—that their reporting provided no sense of the developing drama.

On Thanksgiving Day 1962 Robert Kennedy's warning about racial strife materialized in a wild slugfest after a *Washington Post*–sponsored football game attended by fifty thousand spectators in which a predominantly white Catholic high school defeated a black public school team. Thirty-two persons were injured, most of them by Negro toughs of whom few were students; some blacks were hurt defending whites. Police arrested fourteen persons. The *Post* carried a front-page story that played down the brawl's manifest racial character, telling far less than it knew about the eruption. *Post* sports columnist Bob Addie took a Pollyanna view of the clash: "It must be remembered that some of the college rallies often are more violent. For all of their tradition of dignity and learning Harvard students, for example, have been involved in dozens of battles with the police."

The dilemma for the *Post* was how far to go in reporting racial tensions without triggering worse strife. The paper's restraint was induced by its "institutional memory" of the old *Post*'s inflammatory coverage of a race riot in the summer of 1919 that left more than forty persons dead in the city. "We were frightened of unleashing something," Ben Gilbert recalled.*

As one after another Deep South state tried to block implementation of Supreme Court school desegregation rulings, the *Post* found its efforts to accurately report developments stymied by a reality of southern journalism. "The AP suffered from inbreeding in the South," Ben Gilbert said of that period. "In Virginia, the AP state editor was part of the Byrd political machine. (The arch-conservative Byrd clan owns newspapers in Virginia and dominated Democratic politics in the state for decades. Before he became a U.S. Senator, Harry Byrd, Jr., served five terms on the Associated Press board of directors.) Politicians, businessmen, and police ran southern towns. The papers were part of the establishment, and the AP got its news from its member papers. They weren't covering the race story. Everytime you went behind a wire story it was not accurate." In the 1940s when Gunnar Myrdal was

---

*Gilbert also remembered how a young and enterprising reporter named Ben Bradlee had written a detailed account of racial disturbances which followed desegregation of the District's public swimming pools in 1949. Phil Graham and Secretary of the Interior Julius Krug hastened from a dinner party in their tuxedos to argue for toning down Bradlee's story. The lesson of 1919 prevailed then, too.

researching his classic *American Dilemma,* southern newspapermen were among his most important sources of information about race relations; "they knew the story but could not write it," observed a 1969 report to the federal government.

Virginia waged "massive resistance" to school integration, encouraged by the Byrds and other Old Dominion powers, through complex legalisms designed to nullify the effects of the Supreme Court decision. Gilbert assigned to the story a tall, painstaking reporter with the oddly apt name of Robert E. Lee Baker—"on balance the best white reporter who covered the South," a veteran black journalist called him. As Baker struggled to make sense of the situation, Gilbert instructed: "Forget you're white. Write it as a green or blue man."

"We're going to have to cover this like a war," decided managing editor Alfred Friendly in ordering intensive coverage of the spreading civil rights conflict, which was becoming more violent as white supremacists sought to repel the "freedom movement." The *Post* often sent a pair of reporters—a more experienced white and a black—to cover a racial hot spot. In this bifocal way the newspaper presented a coherent and fair account of a rapidly unfolding, many-faceted, emotionally charged story.

White reporters from the North frequently were threatened by segregationist "angries"; black journalists understandably felt themselves in even greater jeopardy. Dorothy Gilliam was sent with William Chapman, a white staffer, to cover the clash between United States marshals and troops enforcing court-ordered integration of the University of Mississippi and white resisters. "Bill stayed at a motel in Oxford, I stayed at the black undertaker's." In the middle of the night, the mangled remains of a black man who had been killed by whites was carried into the mortuary. "I traveled with a thoroughly cautious black reporter from Memphis. He knew how to say 'yassuh,' but he kept a gun in the car. We were tailed by sheriff's deputies," Gilliam remembered.

On a reporting trip Wallace Terry drove across Georgia and Alabama with a supply of paper cups to urinate in so that he could avoid the humiliation of segregated restrooms and the danger of halting where he might attract trouble. "I was scared to death every day. All I could think of were the stories about lynchings and beatings I had heard as a child. Having all these dark fears about the South, I just wanted to drive through non-stop."

Birmingham in the early spring of 1963 was the malevolent redoubt of segregation. Scores of cross-burnings and anti-Negro bombings evidenced the fury of the steel-making city's response to civil rights activists. On May 3 police commissioner Bull Connor ordered police dogs and fire hoses turned on thousands of peaceful black demonstrators. Wally Terry stood right behind Connor. Dressed in a vested suit and carrying an empty attaché case, Terry did not take notes, hoping he would pass as a Justice Department observer. He even shouted encouragement to the police. His disguise worked as had his waiter's pose when it got him the 1957 interview with Orval Faubus. "I didn't want to get arrested," said Terry. "I couldn't write a story in jail. First of all, I was a reporter. It was so absurd, emotionally, it didn't grab me as much as it should have. I looked at the South as if it were Mars. I was a newsman. I didn't feel I should be a victim."

Terry had become a journalist who was black, rather than a black who was a journalist. The transformation could be agonizing. Many blacks in the white-dominated news business would be tormented by their identity crises.

By the next summer the racial storm thundered beyond the South, roiling northern cities. Conservative blacks grew alarmed at the turn Negro protests had taken in some places. In August Dorothy Gilliam reported the speech of Carl T. Rowan, director of the United States Information Agency and black, to the National Urban League: black street demonstrations "with possible rare exceptions have served their purpose for the time being. . . . The hour has come when bold, uncompromising efforts must be made to free the civil rights movement from the taint of street rioters, looters and punks. . . . I think there is a crying, almost desperate need for us to guard that movement jealously against inroads by those whose only desire is to create a chaos they see as America's undoing." A year later, on a sweltering August night, racial strife broke out in the Watts neighborhood of Los Angeles;

thirty-four persons were killed, hundreds injured, and $35 million in damage inflicted—the worst race riot in the United States since Detroit in 1943. It shocked "all who had been confident that race relations were improving in the North, and evoked a new mood in the ghettos," the National Advisory Commission on Civil Disorders declared.

"After Watts," said Gilliam of the mood she sensed then, "the poor black community was bringing in a whole new element. They didn't give a damn about whitey. Middle-class blacks had said assimilate. Black consciousness was so liberating, personally. I had always fought against being middle-class and really aligned myself with these people. It was the first breath of good air. Black reporters trying to report all this were caught by these changes. The poor blacks didn't trust black reporters representing white newspapers. White editors were not trusting the reports of their black staff. This had not been so earlier because they were not dealing with threatening topics. But now the issues were changing; the issue was changing the system. Voices that hadn't been heard before were being heard, and they were rough voices and uneducated; they knew the streets and they knew the score."

Robert C. Maynard has called Watts the event "to which virtually every working black journalist in America owes his or her employment . . . that made most editors across the country aware for the first time that there might be any imperative for even the token desegregation of their newsrooms." Eleanor Holmes Norton, chairman of the New York City Human Rights Commission, said: "It was undoubtedly the black rebellions which shut white reporters out to which we owe almost all of the modest growth in minority reporters, in particular. The daily media learned quickly that access to a growing population of hostile blacks depended upon the recruitment of more black reporters."

Most reporters move up to the major dailies from smaller papers, many of them in the South, that form a loose "farm system." The *Post*, for example, attracted a long line of reporters from the *Courier-Journal* and the *Louisville Times,* fine papers in Kentucky owned by the Bingham family. So many of them were on the *Post* that they were called "the Louisville Mafia." Blacks, however, were rarely hired by smaller papers so they could not gain the experience the big league newspapers required. Until the 1960s only two all-black colleges offered journalism programs. The chicken-and-egg proposition was at work: Papers generally didn't hire blacks, and blacks saw no future in journalism hence there was no pool of trained black reporters from which the papers could draw as they suddenly found themselves with a story that whites, no matter how skilled, were severely handicapped in covering. The press, unique critic of all other institutions, remained one of the nation's most segregated institutions.

When Washington began experiencing racial disturbances the *Post*, which had several black journalists, gave "battlefield commissions" as reporters to some news aides and library clerks who were black. A few months after Watts the *Post* hired Leon Dash as a copy boy—it served as indoor work which he sought for the winter in preference to his other job steam-cleaning the exteriors of downtown office buildings. Dash had gone to all-black Lincoln University, but rejected its code of nonviolent protest and its preferred racial designation of Negro instead of black. Dash was promoted to news intern as students launched a round of stormy protests at Howard University where he had transferred. "I would rush downtown to write about the dispute, then freeze at the typewriter in agony over choice of words. Was I being fair in saying the students were 'unruly' or was it better to say 'boisterous'?" If an editor seemed to be heavily marking the story Dash would boom across the room, "I'd like to see the copy before it moves" to make sure that his version of what had happened was going into the paper. "Black reporters were still an oddity; black reporters were still being second-guessed, still in a proving stage," Dash remembered. "Leon saw me as the Jewish storekeeper," said District editor Steven Isaacs, who wanted to drop Dash back to news aide for more seasoning. But Dash held on, soon writing a long feature on prostitutes and dope-pushers in the black tenderloin: "I didn't fear it. I grew up in Harlem. I didn't know there was anything else."

The *Post* "started bringing on ill-prepared blacks, many of them rhetoricians rather than reporters," said an editor from that time. "They didn't know whether they were blacks or reporters first." William Raspberry, a black who was first hired as a teletype operator and later became a widely respected columnist, counseled the neophytes: "You can be a black or you can be a journalist. Being a reporter pays a lot better than being a nigger." Some of them missed a newsworthy event simply because the cumulative impact of racism made them regard certain situations as commonplace. For example, when the school superintendent of the District, a black woman, accused opponents to her plans of being racists, the *Post*'s reporter, also black, ignored the episode though the official's charge was significant news. His editor exploded at the failure.

Black reporters might circulate in the ghettos with greater success than white newsmen; they were not necessarily safer. Leon Dash reported from New York's Spanish Harlem, turf he knew well, how tactical police trained to control riots had actually provoked rioting. Cruisers filled with tactical police suddenly arrived at the scene of vandalism as the crowd was peacefully dispersing. One of the drivers tried to run down Dash and his Puerto Rican interpreter. "As I jumped to the side of the car," wrote Dash in an account of the birth of a riot, "I started to explain that I was a reporter, but thought better of it. In that split second, I looked into the eyes of the driver and he looked squarely into mine. The hate mingled with glee was written all over his face and was all the explanation I needed. 'We've got you now, nigger,' was hardly out of his mouth before I was rapidly outdistancing my short-legged companion."

Probably the most widely held perception of the ghetto disorders conveyed by the press was that of pitched shoot-outs—the police and national guardsmen against gun-slinging blacks. In most instances there had been no sniping at officers, although the press often reported there was because that is what authorities said. To Ben Gilbert, the reports of how Negroes were being killed in Newark, in 1967, for example, smelled fishy. "A review of the Newark local press coverage generally would give the impression that it was simply a battle of 'good guys' in blues and fatigues against hordes of black snipers, bombers and looters," asserted the Federal Community Relations Service. The skeptical *Post* sent five interracial reporting teams to Newark to conduct a journalistic inquest into how each of twenty-three victims met death. Filling a full page and a half of the paper, they reported that the typical victim was an innocent bystander who died from police or national guard bullets sprayed wildly in response to shots from other officers thought to be snipers; the authorities, the *Post* concluded, were the "snipers." The *Post*'s investigative reporting stimulated more accurate press coverage of subsequent disorders elsewhere.

All of this was a prelude for covering the virulent torchings and looting that swept Washington and other cities after Martin Luther King was murdered on April 4, 1968. More than thirty blocks of the city's black neighborhoods were devastated on that warm Cherry Blossom Festival weekend. Into the city to back up police poured 13,600 soldiers. No deployment on this scale had occurred in an American city since the Civil War. Troops mounted machine guns on the approaches to the Capitol. Police made some 7,600 arrests, but looters were not fired on. A prominent Washington businessman complained that the *Post* was too soft on rioters: "The next time a policeman shoots someone, whether it is justifiable or not, you should not probe into the circumstances, but should propose him for a medal," the hawkish merchant urged.

Those were frightening and bewildering days, and black reporters were caught in an emotional whirlpool. Robert Maynard later wrote:

By the time a day in the street was over, between the hostile white police officer and the hostile and angry young black, a black journalist headed back to the newsroom in search of some sanity and reason, virtues our media prize greatly. But unfortunately, to many a black reporter, we were all to discover times within our own offices when the heat of the crisis had all but overtaken those of our white colleagues barricaded inside, wondering if indeed Armageddon had arrived. Even in the quiet moments, it seemed to us then that many of our colleagues had lost their perspective in the midst of the chaos. It was then that many of us looked about to ask where the blacks who knew and understood the city were working during those times of urban stress. They were all out on the street eating tear gas and ducking bricks and nightsticks almost simultaneously. The writers, the editors, the people with ultimate responsibility for portraying the event to the world, were all white.

Black reporters were sent out to sponge up the facts and mood of the rampage and squeeze it out to white rewritemen. Days went by with no black bylines on front page riot stories under the names of white rewritemen. (Bylines are important to reporters. Al Lewis, a police reporter for decades, once moaned when a story ran without his name, "Gladys won't believe what I was doing down here so late.") The blacks complained at this lack of professional recognition; editor Gilbert salved their wounded feelings by ordering the names of all reporters who contributed to a major story carried at the end, a practice that was retained. Four years later the black-white conflict erupted in the *Post* newsroom in a far more salient way.

Ben Bradlee opened the three-page letter that began in a peremptory fashion—not "Dear Ben," just "Mr. Bradlee"—which both angered and perplexed him as he read it: "We would like to have written answers to the following questions by Friday February 11, 1972, by 6:30 P.M." It was Monday, the seventh. Signed by nine of his local reporters, all of them black, the letter put twenty questions to Bradlee, such as, "Why are there no blacks in top editorial management positions?" "Why are there no blacks on the news desk?" "Why is the African bureau being closed temporarily?" Some of the questions concerned specific complaints of the treatment by editors of certain black reporters "I am against ultimatums on principle," Bradlee answered the next day. "They add one more barrier to the solution of problems that are already hard enough to solve," he concluded.

The following Monday Bradlee and managing editor Howard Simons came with written answers to a conference with the two women and seven men. Their questions did not address the real issue as he saw it, Bradlee told them. "You are here," he said, "because you feel seriously aggrieved, and discriminated against—because you feel that the *Washington Post* as an institution and some of its managers are consciously or unconsciously racist. . . . As professional communicators we have failed. We have lost our way in a forest of suspicion and misunderstanding. I hope this meeting . . . will leave nothing unsaid by anyone in this room . . . unless it all gets on the table, this meeting won't get as far as it must."

It all seemed at first hearing utterly incomprehensible, unbelievable more than ironic. Here was the *Washington Post,* a battler for equal rights when the other Washington dailies stood pat on segregation, with more black journalists than any other newspaper in the country outside the Negro press—almost 10 percent of the nation's black newsmen and women worked on the *Post*—and a large bloc of those staffers were accusing it of racism. The nine reporters, of varying levels of talent and accomplishment, listened but were not assuaged by Bradlee's ticking off of the paper's deliberate actions to bring more blacks into the newsroom. They could cite as evidence for their accusation the fact, for example, that there were no blacks on the sports staff while probably 50 percent or so of the rosters of major league basketball, baseball, and football teams were black players. The *Post*'s comparatively good record in hiring blacks was a decisive reason for the uprising because it provided the protesters both the critical mass they needed for impact on management and the expectation that a liberal management would do even more to redress their grievances once they raised hell.

Doing more for blacks confronted Bradlee with a dilemma: The *Post* news staff was not rapidly expanding as in the mid-1960s when a wave of blacks were hired to cover the riotous streets and few openings were expected to occur. Moreover, the ghettos weren't burning now. But the managers were not indifferent to creating opportunities for young black aspirants to journalism. Each summer the newsroom took on about sixteen interns. Blacks were given an edge in the selection process so that a black college student had an 11 percent chance of being accepted, a white has a 1 percent shot according to Bradlee. A young white copy boy complained:

"The blacks, the women, what's left for a nice Jewish boy like me?"

"You can always say you're homosexual," his boss advised.

Bradlee rejected unequivocally any suggestion of a quota—the protestors spoke of "timetables and goals"—to increase black hirings; to fulfill it would cost $2 million, he claimed. And what, the editor asked, would he do about a quota for women who were stirring in protest; women, too, were underemployed in the newsroom measured by their share of the population, and they were mostly in the lower ranks. One quota rammed against another. "This is a tough league here; quality, quality, that's the test," Bradlee would growl exasperatedly when quotas were mentioned.

Women were stirring, as Bradlee noted, asking for more jobs and a fair crack at major editing positions. Actually, they had been complaining about their underemployment to Bradlee before the blacks. But they sensed that he was more responsive to the black staffers because they were led by men. Also, the black protest embarrassed the racially liberal *Post* in a predominantly black city. Just as there were mind-sets that stood in the way of black reporters, there were also psychological barriers for women: Male editors tended to regard women as not tough enough to be good editors. A man who made a woman reporter his protégé was suspected of having a casting-couch motive. Married women, especially if they had small children, were simply assumed, without being asked, to be unavailable for certain assignments.

After the black reporters confronted Bradlee, a group of women, with some men joining in support, filed a sex discrimination complaint against the *Post* with the federal government. Just before they did, Bradlee pledged to the women and blacks that 50 percent of the future hires in the newsroom would be women or blacks, and he kept his word. The evidence subsequently gathered by the government supported the women.

It was ironic that an enterprise headed by a woman, Katharine Graham, should be the target of sex discrimination charges, as both the *Post* and *Newsweek* were. But even the women complainants felt that professionally it was correct for her to stay out of newsroom employment questions. The women activists, however, tried to enlist Meg Greenfield, then the deputy editor of the editorial page and later the editor, under their banner. She declined, explaining that she did not regard herself as a feminist.

Oddly enough, one of the women's complaints to Bradlee arose from his success in liberating the ghetto of the newspaper, the women's section. As Bradlee put it, this department "casually lumped women together as though they were concerned only with their hair, cooking and parties." In 1969 Bradlee installed "Style," a trendy, brightly written section covering entertainment, the arts, and social commentary. "Style" redefined society, from who was taking tea with whom to something far more catholic. An unforeseen consequence of this move was that the *Post* "literally abandoned any systematic coverage of the women's movement," observed Washington journalist Peggy A. Simpson. Before Style, reporter Elizabeth Shelton's articles on the rising national concern with women's issues were played on the women's pages. News about day care, abortion, and other issues of primary concern to women now were squeezed out of Style and rejected as "soft" news by the men running the other sections of the paper. Eventually the balance would be restored because the women in the newsroom pushed hard.

"On the numbers, the *Post* looked good," recalled Herbert Denton, one of the original nine blacks who confronted Bradlee, "but people weren't moving. They did not have first-class status. The feeling and reality was that black reporters were not getting the good assignments. Black reporters were doing leg work for white reporters. They were sitting here largely ignored and given petty assignments when they weren't being ignored." Part of the problem was the way the metropolitan staff was organized. Reporters in the suburbs had beats, "turf" for which they were responsible. Most of the District reporters were in a general assignment pool at the beck of whatever came along each day by way of news. "In the suburbs the editors were familiar with the terrain and were able to guide and steer reporters," Denton said retrospectively. "No editors on the city staff knew black Washington."

Metropolitan editor Harry Rosenfeld saw the issue differently. Bradlee decided the local staff was "too loose" and told Rosenfeld and District editor Barry Sussman to shake it up. "Some reporters were incompetent or lazy," said Rosenfeld. "The fact that they were black was only a circumstance. There were whites who were incompetent and lazy. The fault was in the early decisions bringing on blacks who were inexperienced."

Rosenfeld ran the metropolitan staff with the gentleness of a bull mastiff. He deserved his reputation as a "maneater." "You do very good, do more," Rosenfeld exhorted reporters through his cigar smoke. "What have you done for me lately?" he would challenge a reporter who had turned in a good piece the day before.

Born in Berlin, Rosenfeld was beaten in the street for being a Jew. The Gestapo carted off his father, a furrier, in the middle of the night. He, his mother and sister had huddled together as Nazi gangs smashed Jewish shops and synagogues. Rosenfeld was forty-two and grew a beard because several of his young editors and reporters were bearded; his, though, was mostly gray. He was "Uncle Harry" to reporters who sought his counsel on how to maneuver through the thickening bureaucracy of the news department, despite Bradlee's dynamic style of management. Rosenfeld found that he often had to protect his province from the incursions of the national staff with its experienced older hands and classy writers. "Everytime something major broke locally, [national editor] Larry Stern would establish an 'insight team' to cover it," said Rosenfeld. "It was hard on the local staff who saw themselves as hewers of wood and drawers of water."

The reporters who confronted Bradlee with charges of discrimination against blacks had no chairman, but there was an untitled leader. Late in 1971 Leon Dash returned to the *Post* from two years in the Peace Corps teaching high school in Kenya. He found younger black reporters still stewing over their feeling that they were being treated as second-class members of the staff. Dash perceived that things in the newsroom had not changed; the outlet for his idealism that he had found in Kenya was missing. He began drinking heavily, couldn't sleep, and suffered from a severe pancreatic disease; his marriage was crumbling. "I was an emotional time bomb." He was twenty-seven years old.

Tall, bearded, and sturdily handsome, Leon Dash was a powerful force with the dissident black reporters. The night before the reporters played twenty questions with Bradlee, they secretly retained as their pro bono lawyer Clifford Alexander, former chairman of the U.S. Equal Employment Opportunities Commission. As a boy Dash had admiringly watched Alexander play neighborhood basketball in Harlem. The group's tactics and strategy came from the confrontation politics of the 1960s. "We drew on the agglomeration of everything we had learned covering the civil rights movement," recalled Dash. "Change doesn't come about without pain, confrontation, and friction. Moral persuasion is not a great avenue of change."

Before each negotiating session they rehearsed their responses. Dash would play the tough Bradlee; Richard Prince, the talmudic Simons. They did not try to enlist older and more conservative newsroom blacks with families lest they be exposed to possible economic pressure and weaken the united front. They would meet long into the night hammering out their next move, shoring up a colleague whose commitment seemed to be wavering. Joseph D. Whittaker, a deeply religious twenty-four-year-old North Carolinian with Cherokee Indian ancestors, was the first to drop out. "I will pray for you," he told them. "God helps those who help themselves," Dash answered.

Angry at times and depressing throughout, the confrontation was a dispute between colleagues who mostly liked each other. At one meeting, Dash criticized a Bradlee statement: "This is superfluous and redundant."

"That's why we want to make you an editor," smiled Simons.

Another time Dash spoke of blacks being in bondage for two hundred years. "You've got four thousand years to go to catch up with us," said Simons, everyone in the room catching the reference to the managing editor's fellow Jews.

"I don't want to wait four thousand years," retorted the street-wise reporter.

Simons was forty-two years old. Cautious and intellectual, he was the ideal, the essential, deputy to the ebullient and trendy Bradlee. "Ben and I are an odd couple," said Simons. He had gone through college largely on a student loan; his grandfather, a shoemaker, had escaped to America from the Czar's persecution. Bradlee was old Boston; generations back some of his family had entered sailing ships in the South Seas trade. At Harvard Bradlee intended to reject a bid from A.D., one of the oldest and most exclusive clubs—it was the Lodges's club—but his father, who had belonged, persuaded him otherwise.

Simons, a former science reporter, was a birder and collector of Indian arrowheads. Bradlee spoke flawless French, conversed easily about modern art, and was an intimate of President Kennedy. Simons was a committed family man; Bradlee was twice divorced and later married for a third time. Heavy cigarette smokers through Watergate, Simons finally quit "cold turkey"; Bradlee had to go to "Smoke-Enders."

The deeper roots of the controversy seemed lost in the welter of individual complaints. Twenty-six other blacks in the newsroom, however, signed a letter to Bradlee that moved beyond personal grievances to "the heart of the issue" for them: "on this newspaper . . . and generally in this society, black Americans are painfully aware of the lack of their participation in the writing of the story of America in a time of change. We could not insist that all matters relative to blacks be written and reported by blacks, anymore than we could countenance the writing of all stories about women by women, all Catholics by Catholics, or all whites by whites. But the lack of black participation in the shaping of the news about the society in which they play so vital a role has led to unfortunate distortions of the basic posture of the community on such vital questions as crime in the streets and the busing of school children." Against the backdrop of the Nixon administration's demagoguery on busing and street crime, the letter stated, "the complexity of those issues has been masterfully distorted by politicians for political ends in ways that reflect almost nothing of the stake of the black community in those vital questions."

This letter was the work of reporter Robert Maynard, who checked it with Roger Wilkins—a recent arrival as the *Post*'s first black editorial writer. Wilkins, a lawyer, was a high-level federal racial conciliator in the mid-1960s; his uncle was Roy Wilkins, the grand old man of the National Association for the Advancement of Colored People. Passionate and temperamental, he relentlessly lobbied Bradlee and publisher Katharine Graham to open the paper fully to blacks.

But the negotiations were going nowhere. Meanwhile, Jimmy Hoffa, fresh out of prison, was in town one night and Dash, who had written about jail conditions, was assigned to interview the ex-Teamsters chief. Hoffa's lawyer would not let Dash into his client's Water-

gate Hotel room. Dash phoned Bradlee to intercede. Dash reached
Hoffa, but he said nothing worth a story. Disgusted, Dash stopped in
the Watergate bar. As he drank Manhattans, he brooded over the
newsroom dispute. He decided to violate the protestors' rule that no
member talk individually with management. He rang Bradlee again at
home and asked to meet with him.

As Dash walked in the door of Bradlee's big brick house, he announced, "Let's take off the gloves!"

"What do you drink?" Bradlee asked. Dash drank scotch and soda
and Bradlee sipped bourbon as their exchange grew louder and hotter.
Awakened by the bellowing, Bradlee's pajamaed children appeared at
the head of the stairs. Tony Bradlee reassured them their father was
not about to be murdered by the agitated black man downstairs.

"We are going to shake your tree," Dash growled at his weary host.

Early that morning Bradlee summoned to his place Simons, Rosenfeld, and Philip Geyelin, editorial-page editor and his close pal—until
Bradlee's divorce from Tony and their competition for prominence at
the paper wore away their friendship. The protest was serious, Bradlee
told them. Dash had complained that District editor Barry Sussman
yelled a lot at black reporters, proof, he claimed, of Sussman's racism.
Rosenfeld said this was ridiculous but he sensed that Sussman would
be offered up as a sacrifice to the protestors.

On March 10 Bradlee said that he would hire another black reporter
for the national staff, another black assistant District editor, and two
more black news trainees. Too little, replied the "Metro Eight," as they
were now called. They decided to take their case to the Equal Employment Opportunity Commission.

Robert Maynard was basking in a mellow sabbatical in Northern
California and uncertain whether he really wanted to come back to the
regimen of the *Post* national staff. The festering dispute caught up with
him. Simons called for counsel; the dissidents phoned for advice. A
lawsuit, if it came to that, Maynard believed, appeared unpromising as
a remedy: "How would the court deal with things like an editor's
unfairness in giving blacks instead of whites night assignments? You'd
be asking the judge to sit in the editor's chair. I saw some real problems

between the First Amendment guarantee of free press and the Fourteenth's guarantee of due process."

Those who began organizing the protest did not expect Herbert Denton to join them. At twenty-nine he was the oldest of the group. He was Harvard. And he had a special friend at the Post and everyone there knew it. Denton went on scholarship to private school in Massachusetts after Orval Faubus barred integration of Central High in his native Little Rock. At Harvard, also on scholarship, he worked on the *Crimson* with an English and history major named Donald Graham whose family owned the *Post.* For a while after Harvard, Denton edited the *American Student,* which unknown to him was at that time CIA-financed, before the *Post* took him on in its spurt of hiring black reporters. Drafted in 1966, he took basic training with Graham. Their paths intersected again in Vietnam where together the two GIs filed stories from base camps and the A Shau Valley battles to the hometown newspapers of First Air Cavalry Division soldiers. When his associates asked the government to investigate their charges, Denton withdrew: "It was one thing to create a ruckus in the newspaper; another to take it outside. I thought about Don Graham and identified him with the paper and I couldn't say, 'You're a racist.' "

Don Graham returned from Vietnam in 1968 a few months after Washington was ripped by rioting after Martin Luther King's death. Don had grown up in Washington and gone to private school. But it was a city he felt he really didn't know. He wanted to teach in the public schools, which white flight to the suburbs had left in shameful straits for an almost solidly black student body, but he lacked the required teaching credentials. The police department was rapidly expanding to make the streets safe as both Lyndon Johnson and Richard Nixon urged. Don, tall and brawny, joined the cops, assuring his suspicious superiors that he had no intentions of writing a book about it. Tension ran high between black and white policemen, many of whom were recruited in rural small towns of Virginia and West Virginia. Don drew close to young black officers. He spent the next 18 months patrolling a largely black precinct before he joined the Post as a reporter. He took a strong personal interest in the efforts to resurrect the schools. It would be hard to stick a racist tag on him.

"I didn't think anything was going to happen at the EEOC," said Denton, "but it served as an ax over the paper's head. It kept their interest. What was important was that the seven stood up and said this great liberal institution, the *Washington Post,* is not so liberal on the matters of race. It pushed the paper toward getting serious about some of the issues [they] raised."

The Metro Seven declared into the television microphones during a press conference: "The lack of black participation in the shaping of news reported by one of America's most prestigious newspapers is to us an insult to the black community of this city and an insult to black Americans around the country." They expected to be sacked for filing the complaint with the government.

"What are you going to do now?" asked a wire service reporter.

"We are going back to work," they replied.

"Won't there be retaliation?"

"We are not afraid of anything."

Until then nothing about the conflict had appeared in print. Both sides—the blacks to show good faith bargaining, management for the same reason and to avoid public embarrassment—did not report a story that the *Post* would have rushed to publish if any other major institution were similarly confronted. Ben H. Bagdikian, the *Post's* press critic, broke the silence. "Newspaper corporations, like all others, hate to have their linen washed in public," he wrote in a long, passionate opinion piece the day before the protestors went public. "Except that laundering significant linen in public is part of the business newspapers are in, a goal frequently forgotten when newspapers themselves get into troubles with unions, inner finances and hierarchical struggles. When blacks' complaints reach formal negotiations and certainly when they come to an apparent impasse, as they seem to be at this moment, this is something a newspaper cannot conceal from a community that depends on the paper and in a city where race is particularly important, just because it is happening to the newspaper itself."

Bagdikian, a prolific magazine and newspaper writer, had critiqued the *Post* in a 1967 *Columbia Journalism Review* article. Bagdikian found the paper "irritating because it comes within a lunge of greatness as a newspaper but it is not great," flawed in letting its liberal views color coverage, and deficient in its sense of what news was important. Bradlee hired Bagdikian in 1970 as national editor. In June 1971 Bagdikian rescued the *Post* from the ignominy of being totally beaten by the *New York Times*'s revelations of the Pentagon Papers by obtaining copies from Daniel Ellsberg.

A month after his commentary on the newsroom dispute, Bagdikian was a panelist at a conference on black priorities in Cambridge. Militants there accused the mass media of "vicious racism." Bagdikian defended the *Post*'s civil rights record. The purpose of newspapers, Bagdikian then explained, is primarily to make money, not suppress blacks. This being the case, he continued mildly, changes in the press would come about faster in cities with large black populations if blacks boycotted newspapers instead of calling the publishers racists.

Bagdikian was back at his desk the next day when a grim-faced Bradlee tossed at him an Associated Press account of his boycott remarks. "Did you say that?" the executive editor demanded. Bagdikian attempted to explain the context of his suggestion. "That's the end of it! One of my lieutenants telling them to boycott the paper," Bradlee stormed. "I'm not one of your lieutenants; I'm writing for the readers," snapped Bagdikian. Bradlee demanded Bagdikian's resignation, but in a few days he cooled down and tore it up. Given the sulfurous climate over the discrimination case Bradlee, a master politician, may have judged it wiser not to appear to be taking reprisal for Bagdikian's pro-dissident article.

But the article and the boycott incident had put the ineradicable pox of suspected disloyalty to the *Post* on the fifty-two-year-old writer. Bagdikian also was in the throes of a divorce and in love with a woman on the local staff. His wife pleaded for Katharine Graham's intercession, and the publisher counseled him on the ugliness of divorce, recalling Phil Graham's threat a decade earlier to end their marriage. By summer's end Bagdikian resigned. His friend, an experienced reporter, was soon exiled to the night police beat. She considered it punishment, and quit.

Long after the two of them were gone from the *Post* and married, Mrs. Graham still reproved their affair. Asked how it differed from the widely-known romance of editor Ben Bradlee and one of his reporters, whom he later married, she answered, "They were discreet."

The complaint before the Equal Employment Opportunity Commission got muddled by legal technicalities. But soon things at the paper did change: More blacks were hired; several went off to Harvard on prized Nieman Fellowships; new reporters were given far more time and help to prove themselves and were not limited to night police with a three-paragraph murder every other day. Blacks moved up a few rungs on the newsroom ladder; Maynard was lured back to the job of press critic and then editorial writer; Matthew Lewis was given command of the photography department; Dorothy Gilliam became an editor on Style; and Herbert Denton became District editor.

The number of blacks on the *Post* news staff had almost doubled since the Metro Seven uprising. (In the newspaper business nationally the number of black and other minority professionals increased markedly, though in 1979 they still represented only 4 percent of newspaper reporters and editors.) There were some staffers who felt themselves losers in this process. When Maynard resigned from the editorial page to teach the news craft to young blacks and Hispanic-Americans, a veteran *Post* reporter applied for the job. Editor Phillip Geyelin turned him down: "That's the black seat. This is not the time for middle-aged white males."

Leon Dash had dreamed for years of reporting from Africa. Now he felt certain that his prominence in Metro Seven and his drinking had shattered that dream. The year after the dispute, Dash wanted to cover the mounting guerilla war in Angola. But he saw no chance of getting the arduous assignment. Howard Simons insisted that Dash go to Africa. His subsequent reporting had accurately forecast events in the Portuguese colony, and after Angolan independence, Dash spent seven and a half months with UNITA rebels who were still fighting the new regime. Dash, who trekked 2,100 miles with the rebels, was laid low by a temporarily crippling attack of chigger-like parasites which had been introduced to Africa long ago by freed American blacks who came to transport slaves to the South. In 1978 Dash, newly married to *Post* reporter Alice Bonner—a black from rural Virginia whose desire to be a journalist became reality in the aftermath of the Metro Seven— became the *Post* correspondent in West Africa, and his dream was realized.

Nevertheless, some blacks who had been on the paper for many years wondered whether the increased numbers of their race in the newsroom counted for a real difference. At the daily news conference where decisions are made on the play of stories, said a black editor, "almost all of those faces are fifties white faces." Kenneth B. Clark, whose sociological research helped win the 1954 school desegregation ruling, commented in 1978: "Newspaper management positions are very important power areas in our society. They are areas of influence. The people who control power areas don't want to run the risk of losing that rein." The movement of some of their number into top slots seemed glacial, as elsewhere in the society. But it is happening. "Young reporters want to know how far they can go; it's important that there be black stars in the firmament," said Herb Denton.*

By the late 1970s the American economy had turned torpid and the view took hold among many whites that blacks were being unfairly advantaged in competing for jobs and admission to college; there was a weariness, it seemed, with racial equality issues. Black nationalism had subsided to low water as the political and economic system responded to the grievances of better-educated middle-class blacks. There were older black journalists who puzzled about how their younger colleagues, who had not experienced the struggle to break into and survive in the white-run press, would use their access to signal that large numbers of blacks were still living in hard times. "I don't want to be poor and I don't want to be powerless and that becomes far more important than racial identity," said one black writer who had been at the *Post* for many years in talking about a new generation of reporters of his race. The melting-pot of assimilation was working, too. "Younger blacks have a commitment to the mainstream; it's class rather than race,"

*One such star is Robert Maynard, who became editor of the *Oakland Tribune,* a major California daily, in mid-1979.

commented another older black, John Britton, who had handled community relations for the paper.

How would younger black journalists tell, as blacks at the *Post* phrased it, "the story of America?" In the midst of the Metro Seven dispute one answer came from Tony Brown, dean of the Howard University School of Communication: "A black reporter should use his access to the media to tell the black side. All the rules of journalism calling for objectivity, balance and fairness are white people's rules that have been used in the past by white media to distort black news. While the black reporter should feel free to criticize movement leaders and their programs, he should never forget that his primary loyalty is to other blacks and the movement." Two years earlier Sheila Younge was cited for contempt when she cheered a Black Panther defendant in a trial she was covering. "I was a black for twenty-three years before I became a reporter for *Newsweek* and being black is more important than being a reporter," she declared. Movement leaders, naturally, advocated that priority and tried to enforce it. Andrew Young rapped the black magazine *JET* for heresy in reporting that civil rights leader Ralph Abernathy, a minister, had a glass of wine on an airliner. No black should write ill of another black, Young told *JET*'s editors, who were threatened with picketing.

The litmus test came when black reporters encountered blacks in public office or institutional prominence who were doing wrong. When a black reporter on the *Chicago Tribune* disclosed that the Reverend Jesse Jackson and the Southern Christian Leadership Conference were at odds over fund-raising—a story that a number of black journalists in Chicago knew but did not publish—she was accused of trying to destroy the civil rights movement and menaced.

"What are you doing writing this stuff for whitey's paper?" jobholders challenged *Post* reporter Milton Coleman as he made his rounds of District government offices. The 'stuff' Coleman, who had attended Malcolm X College, was reporting was the alleged corruption and widespread bumbling in Mayor Walter Washington's administration. The mayor responded that "waste" and "inefficiency" were code words meaning blacks; and contended the press was racially motivated in its hot pursuit of the failings of officialdom. A few white reporters perceived the investigative stories as the paper's post-Watergate instinct for the jugular. There was truth in that, but the Post was incisively covering the city as never before.

Black reporters like Leon Dash saw it more simply: "I don't know any black reporter here who wouldn't take a thief over the coals just because he's black. Older black reporters coached that they shouldn't cut anyone any slack because he's a black. It's hard ball and you cover a black like anyone else." He sounded a lot like Ben Bradlee: "A reporter must not only avoid emotional involvement, but the appearance of it." "For fear of being called racists, people here had not looked hard at the city government, . . . The old image of the *Post* that Ben Gilbert had left us was over," said Herb Denton.

In the summer of 1978 the District was electing a mayor. Incumbent Walter Washington and another black, Sterling Tucker, who had long enjoyed close ties to *Post* executives, appeared the leading contenders in the Democratic mayoralty primary, tantamount to final election in the overwhelming Democratic city. Marion Barry was regarded as running third.

Barry had chopped cotton in the West Tennessee bottomland. He had been a dashiki-wearing civil rights movement shock trooper and jailed repeatedly for his militancy, while the older and more moderate Washington and Tucker sought progress from within white-controlled institutions. The three candidates met separately with publisher Katharine Graham and her editorial board to plead their cases for the *Post*'s endorsement. Barry at first glance seemed an unlikely prospect for the paper's blessing. He once had suggested that Washingtonians shoot any policeman who entered their homes without a warrant under the city's "no-knock" law, and urged that businesses in the District become majority-black–owned. "But Barry had cultivated the *Post* for a long time," District editor Denton recalled. "His strategists were convinced that he needed that endorsement to win. Marion had this street image that had to be blunted."

A few weeks before election day the *Post* endorsed Barry in a series of enthusiastic editorials praising his "talent for accommodation . . . [and] ability to deal with all elements of the community. . . ." Barry won by some two thousand votes; the *Post*'s editorials were crucial in his victory. "We made Barry respectable," said Katharine Graham. In fact, Barry had made himself "respectable" by adjusting his political strategy and tactics over the years to the realities of power in Washington. One of those realities was the power of the *Post* to persuade people that the city would be safe—and better—in Barry's hands. Barry's complaint a year later, when the *Post* probed the city's affairs, that he'd rather have liberal white reporters covering City Hall because they were easier on him than blacks delighted Bradlee.

More than thirty years have passed since the *Post* turned its editorial columns against the evil of segregation. It had failed for much of that time to break the racial barriers in its own newsroom. When it finally did, by enabling black journalists to share in reporting the story of America, the paper made the portrait of a mixed, ambiguous, and complex society far more authentic; it made the paper a more telling instrument of redress of pervasive wrongs. Not just blacks, but all Americans are the beneficiaries.

SEVEN

Stretching the Empire

I am in business to make money, and I buy more newspapers to make more money to buy more newspapers.

—ROY THOMSON, A NEWSPAPER CHAIN TITAN

MEN LIKE Eugene Meyer, William Randolph Hearst, and Robert R. McCormick owned newspapers for a purpose other than pure financial profit. More than money they wanted influence, although the former gave them the means to gain the latter. Their operating styles and politics were different, but each of them used his journal like a potter's wheel to shape public opinion and mold the judgments of political leaders. Their papers, as they intended, made them more powerful figures in society.

Warren E. Buffett of Omaha was different. Buffett owns the largest block of Washington Post Company stock outside the Graham family. He is a major influence on the company's affairs. For this multi-millionaire newspapers were first a business, like candy, trading stamps, or insurance (in which he also dealt). He was by no means indifferent to the quality of his publications. He respected well-edited newspapers and first-class writing in their own right, but he also expected higher profits to be the reward of higher quality. He could rattle off the circulation figures of newspapers that he had tried to buy years before like a baseball fan recalling batting averages from long-past seasons. He came by his interest naturally. Buffett's maternal grandfather had owned the weekly in Cuming County, Nebraska, and his mother ran the linotype and gathered news from passengers at the train depot. She met his father when they worked together on the University of Nebraska student paper.

Omaha suited him perfectly. Solid and unpretentious. He lived with his family in a large old house surrounded by shade trees near the Missouri River. Some Omahans perceived him as a political liberal, but he reportedly concluded that George McGovern in the White House would be bad for business and declined to contribute to his 1972 presidential campaign. He could accomplish most of his work on the phone. Washington, New York, Los Angeles, or Buffalo were only a few hours away by jet when his enterprises required his presence.

Buffett would have made a good reporter. For a while his investment partnership owned 5 percent of American Express. Buffett bought the stock after he went through the receipts of an Omaha steak house in order to sample the volume of credit card business American Express was doing. He once stood in a Kansas City railroad yard counting tank cars as they rolled from a plant that interested him. "I understand you're the Woodward and Bernstein of Wall Street," Ben Bradlee, the executive editor of the *Washington Post,* greeted him when they first met.

Omaha's widest known institution was Boys Town, celebrated in a forties Spencer Tracy and Mickey Rooney film. One of Buffett's companies owned a chain of Omaha weeklies that began investigating hints that Boys Town was raising tens of millions of dollars from public solicitations while spending only a small part of it on needy youths. The reporters were stymied in finding credible financial information that would reveal what Boys Town actually was doing with its wealth. Like many extremely wealthy persons, Buffett had established a charitable foundation so he was familiar with the laws that governed philanthropies. "Get Boys Town's annual report from the Internal Revenue Service in Washington; it's a public document," Buffett advised the frustrated staff.

"The light lit when Warren mentioned the IRS return," recalled reporter Mike Rood, who worked on the investigation. "The minute we got that in the mail," he added, "I knew we'd get a Pulitzer prize." They did win a Pulitzer, a rarity for weeklies, for their carefully documented account of abuses in Boys Town's operation.

Money was Buffett's game, and he was a nonpareil at it. "The soaring stock markets of the 1960s created many a star among professional portfolio managers," the *Wall Street Journal* observed, "but few shone as brightly as Warren Buffett." The investment partnership that Buffett put together in 1957 was the envy of the stock market. For twelve straight years Buffett's partnership never lost money. The portfolio grew in value at a combined annual rate of 30 percent so that ten thousand dollars invested in 1957 was worth about three hundred thousand dollars by late 1969. It was a phenomenal track record. He presciently liquidated the investment pool that year just before the market began a long downslide.

Buffett was thirty-nine years old. The partnership's stock was worth $100 million; $25 million of it was his. From managing money he turned to managing companies that he had acquired control of by stock purchases. Their assets totaled $1 billion by the mid-1970s. He controlled Berkshire Hathaway, a New England textile company that had diversified into banking and insurance and owned the seven weeklies in Omaha. Berkshire, in turn, owned Blue Chip Stamps Corporation, a conglomerate stew that included a trading stamp company, one of the country's largest fresh candy manufacturers, a savings and loan association covering South Carolina, and interests in newspapers such as the *Boston Globe* and the giant Knight-Ridder chain, as well as the *Washington Post.* Blue Chip in 1977 bought the *Buffalo Evening News* for $34 million, and Buffett went on the masthead as chairman.

Most of the 1,760 daily newspapers in the United States are monopolies; either they are the only daily in town or they have the evening or morning field to themselves. Competition between papers with different owners has shriveled to only thirty-five of the fifteen hundred or so cities where dailies are published, and that small number seems likely to dwindle.

A monopoly or dominant newspaper was the kind of investment Buffett pursued. "There's no business like it. . . . It compounds money," he was heard to say. One of his business associates implied that such papers were as precious as Rembrandts. In most cases they offer their owners, who increasingly are big communications conglomerates, protection against the punishing effects of severe inflation. Their capital needs tend to be modest; even when expensive printing and newsroom electronic systems are installed they soon pay for themselves by sharply cutting labor costs and yielding other economies. David Gottesman, a senior partner of the First Manhattan Corporation, remarked that "Warren likens owning a monopoly or market dominant newspaper to owning an unregulated toll bridge. You have relative freedom to increase rates when and as much as you want."* Local advertisers really had no place else to go but the newspaper; television and radio simply were nowhere nearly as effective for them. Nor do the competitive rules of classical economics apply to monopoly or dominant newspapers. When the *Washington Post's* advertising lineage fell during the 1974–75 recession, the paper raised its ad rates to keep income up, rather than cut them to lure business.

In the summer of 1970 Warren Buffett received a letter from Jay Rockefeller, a scion of one of America's richest families. Rockefeller, a Democrat, had been elected secretary of state of West Virginia and there was immediate public speculation that it was his first step toward the White House. After the election Buffett asked Rockefeller if there was any way that he could help him. Rockefeller asked if Buffett would aid the *Washington Monthly,* a new muckraking magazine that desperately needed a transfusion of cash to stay alive. The magazine was started by Charles Peters, a former West Virginia lawyer. Rockefeller was one of his first investors. Peters was hesitant about asking his wealthy friend for more money; Rockefeller was reluctant to invest more and risk the appearance, at least, of controlling the politically independent journal.

Buffett came to Washington in September with his two closest

---

*This analogy was ironic. One of Buffett's companies held almost 25 percent of the stock of the privately owned Detroit International Bridge Company, which operated a profitable, though regulated, six-lane toll bridge linking the Motor City and Canada. Buffett sold the stock when he couldn't acquire control of the company.

friends, Fred Stanback, who had been his best man, and Joseph Rosenfield, an Iowa businessman. Rosenfield lavishly praised Peters for his editorial the previous autumn which urged the United States to withdraw from Vietnam. At that Peters thought he could expect the money. Peters's politics, however, mattered less to Buffett than the *Monthly*'s prospects for turning a profit. He began grilling Peters about the magazine's operations. It was the toughest questioning any investor had put him through. Buffett put $82,000 into the *Monthly*, which eventually made a little money, but not enough to return to investors. He was a life raft for a maverick editorial voice that, as it happened, frequently criticized the *Washington Post.*

Over the years, Buffett asked Peters for only one favor: would Charlie call Katharine Graham to see if she had time to talk to Buffett? It was 1971. Buffett didn't know the chairman of the Washington Post Company. Peters got Buffett an appointment. The editor had struck out earlier when he asked Mrs. Graham to invest in his magazine. Later when the *Monthly* received the prestigious George Polk Award for a report on the army's spying on American civilians, Mrs. Graham was on the rostrum and smiled at Peters, "Maybe we should have given you the money."

Buffett told Mrs. Graham that his company owned stock in the *New Yorker* and he'd heard that it might be for sale. In his opinion, the *New Yorker*'s rarified class and the Post Company's high journalistic standards would make a marriage. Buffett mentioned that his family had lived in Washington when his father was a Republican congressman. As a teenager Buffett had delivered each morning some four hundred copies of the *Washington Post* and the rival *Times-Herald.* He facetiously claimed that he thus had "merged" the two newspapers before the *Post* bought its competitor in 1954. Mrs. Graham was intrigued by the *New Yorker* possibility, but they discovered that it was not for sale. Nevertheless the Post Company kept a covetous eye on the half-century-old weekly with its almost half-million circulation and high-priced ads. "We would leave it unmolested in its editorial direction," said one executive who had been intimately involved with *Post* acquisition plans. "It's profitable and we believe we could make it more profitable."

Soon after Buffett's fifteen-minute meeting with Mrs. Graham, the Washington Post Company went public, for the first time selling its non-voting shares on the American Stock Exchange. Beginning in 1947 when Eugene Meyer formed the *Post* corporation, the company issued non-voting shares to members of the Meyer and Graham families, and also gave or sold such shares to certain employees. Other blocks of stock were put in a profit-sharing plan as a form of pension for employees. The arrangement obligated the *Post* itself to operate a "market" in these shares, buying them back when a shareholder wanted to sell, or when the profit-sharing plan needed money for retirees. This unproductively tied up the company's capital. It also left the Meyer and Graham heirs potentially vulnerable to stiff inheritance taxes in the future. Going public erased these problems. By holding all the voting stock the family, namely Mrs. Graham, retained firm control of the company. They had their cake and could eat it, too.

Buffett kept close watch on the Post Company. The stock in his judgment was selling at bargain prices. Continuity of management appeared assured under the Grahams. He began buying shares through his Blue Chip Stamps Company, acquiring more than 10 percent of the Post Company stock. By the end of 1978 Buffett's $10.6 million investment was worth $43.4 million. As evidence of his confidence in the expected next head of the corporation, Buffett authorized Donald Graham to vote the Buffett shares for ten years. He had hit the jackpot again. He was elected a director and chairman of the strategically important finance committee.

Full of energy and business wizardry, Buffett was a formidable presence in the *Post*'s executive suite. He prepared a huge volume on future prospects in the communications industry. One of the company's principal officers found it all quite threatening. Buffett, in his eyes, was "a Wall Street buyer and seller, but with no sense of the operation or the need to nurture properties. His intimate relationship with Katharine compounded the problem." Buffett stayed at Mrs. Graham's home when he was in Washington. They were seen on occasions holding hands, and tongues wagged. To him she was the best publisher in the country because she cared about the quality of a newspaper, not just owning more. Heritage, he sensed, made her this way. But she wanted more papers, too.

For the Washington Post Company, 1974 was not a financially happy year. The national economy was stagnant and although the Washington market was hurt far less than most areas, the *Post*'s advertising lineage was sharply down. Moreover, the advertising department forecast the same for 1975.

Newsweek was in a deeper slump than the *Post.* Westinghouse and CBS, hearing of the magazine's distress, thought Mrs. Graham might be disposed to sell. Inside the Post company some voices prophesied a depression as deep as that of the thirties. Some bankers cautioned the company to behave conservatively until the economy bounced back. The company, however, was a long way from the bread lines: Its profits were respectable, though below the year before, and it had plenty of cash.

Other big media companies were scrambling to buy more newspapers. "In the sixties newspaper acquisition was a fad," remarked the *Post*'s deputy managing editor, Richard Harwood. "By the mid-seventies it had become hysteria." Newspaper chains were hungrily gobbling up smaller ones for the big profits that monopoly papers offered. Twenty years had passed since the *Post* took over the *Times-Herald.* Recession or not, the *Post* company was laying plans to purchase six or so papers as part of its expansion. Despite the prophets of gloom, Mrs. Graham went shopping for a paper in Trenton. The city was something of a journalistic museum piece: It had two separately owned, hotly competitive dailies—a situation that did not exist in most places.

Once a year or so septuagenarian S. I. Newhouse would drop in on the owners of the *Trenton Times* to inquire if the paper were for sale. Newhouse owned twenty-nine newspapers with a total circulation of 3.5 million, plus a stable of magazines and broadcasting properties. Newhouse was once described as "a graveyard superintendent [who] goes around picking up bones, preying on widows and split families" and "the leading volunteer family counselor to troubled journalistic households." His inevitable counsel: Sell, to him. The *Trenton Times* seemed ripe for him.

The Kerneys were a prominent family of Irish Catholics who had owned the *Trenton Times* since the turn of the century. James Kerney, the late family patriarch, was in the old mold of activist editors. "The real business of a newspaper," he declared in 1930, "is protecting the public from outrages from politicians and rich highbinders, who live as smug leaders of the community while they lift your watch." His heirs had been skirmishing in and out of court for years over control of the newspaper and the money it represented. In 1955 Kerney's devoutly religious widow deposed their son, James Kerney, Jr., as editor after he divorced his Catholic wife and married a Protestant. Kerney, a witty and urbane lover of good living, was restored as editor a decade after his mother's death.

Virtually all of the family's assets resided in the newspaper, whose profits were slim. It wasn't yielding enough cash to support the growing clan. In 1973 dividends totalling $421,282, virtually all of the *Times*'s income after taxes, were paid to the principal heirs. "However, there are twenty-two grandchildren in this fertile, fecund family," a non-Kerney overseer of the estate commented. "Seven of the twenty-two grandchildren have produced their own twenty-eight children, with two more on the way and probable pregnancies yet to be announced. What happens when this ($421,282) is divided by twenty-two, and more?" The unstated answer was to sell the paper. James Kerney, Jr., the strong man in the family, had more than a financial reason for thinking this was the remedy. When he learned that one grandchild, a nun, had left her share to the Bishop of New Haven, the editor snapped, "We have to sell. I'm damned if I will have a bishop as a stockholder." Kerney wanted to sell "to a company I wouldn't have to apologize for." The eminence of the *Washington Post* in the wake of Watergate placed it high on Kerney's list of prospects.

As Mrs. Graham and her key associates examined the Kerney proposition, they were well aware of the deepening distress in the evening newspaper field. Morning papers like their *Post* were growing. Big city "P.M.'s," however, were losing circulation. Several of them had recently died including one not far from Trenton, the *Newark News;* at home, the *Daily News* folded in 1972 and the *Washington Star* was bleeding millions. The newspaper doctors ascribed the "P.M." disease to a number of causes, some beyond the ability of publishers to alter. More women were working, and instead of shopping at midday they did their marketing in the early evening, a time when afternoon newspapers were read. In those hours and later, television enticed erstwhile readers. Morning papers carried the previous day's sports results and the closing stock market reports, as well as the news that occurred in early afternoon after the final editions of the evening papers. Work patterns were changing, too, with many more Americans starting their white collar jobs around 9 A.M., leaving time to read the morning paper. Trucks delivering the "P.M.'s" were often slowed by city traffic snarls, while the "A.M.'s" were dispatched when traffic was lightest.

The *Post* company knew all this and learned more. The *Times*'s rival was the morning *Trentonian,* a lively paper that won a Pulitzer Prize in 1974. The *Trentonian* enjoyed tweeking the stodgy afternoon paper. "When the *Times* ran a series of pompous editorials calling for the closing of known gambling joints," Dan Rottenberg wrote in *MORE,* "the *Trentonian* gleefully printed a picture of a *Times* reporter placing a bet with a State House elevator operator who was a notorious bookie; the picture was accompanied by an editorial calling on the *Times* to demand the closing of the State House." The *Times* was ahead of the *Trentonian* in circulation and advertising, but the gap was closing and if the morning paper caught and passed the *Times,* the game would probably be over for the Kerneys. There was competition, too, from the Philadelphia and New York dailies. It was risky, but *Post* executives concluded that with the right management the situation could be turned to the *Times*'s favor. Moreover, the *Post* could easily pay the Kerneys the $16 million they were asking with no dilution in the Washington company's earnings. But two *Post* editors were skeptical after they looked over the *Times*'s newsroom and production facilities. They encountered Post Company president Larry Israel as they boarded the Metroliner back to Washington. In unison the two editors exclaimed, "Sixteen million for this?"

"Refer to it as 'the valuable property,'" Israel smiled. To the company's chagrin, it later learned the Kerneys would have sold for $12 million.

The Washington Post Company announced in June that it was buying the *Times.* Several months passed, however, before the deal could be closed. Judge Kerney's will barred sale unless "some extraordinary emergency shall arise and then only if all of my trustees agree to the sale." The emergency, the *Post* lawyers finally satisfied the probate court, was the paper's declining value because of the continuing family warfare and shaky management.

By the *Post* editors' lights, the *Trenton Times* was a lackluster newspaper, a defect that they felt could readily be overcome by putting in one of their own as editor. Richard Harwood got the job. He was the third-ranking editor in the newsroom. In Trenton he could run his own show. Ben Bradlee was sensitive to the frustration that many of his editors experienced when they found no place higher to climb at the paper. Newspapering, of course, was not peculiar in this regard, but Bradlee saw a possible escape hatch.

Bradlee said that the company's buying of more newspapers would open top management jobs elsewhere for some of his editors. Celebrated dailies like the *New York Times,* the *Chicago Tribune,* and the *St. Louis Post-Dispatch* bought smaller papers as very profitable investments. "Cash register operations," the trade called them. Bradlee told Harwood that "we shouldn't just buy the Trenton paper and punch the cash register. We should try to export the *Post*'s excellence." Going to Trenton would be like propagating the Faith to the heathen. A Washington attorney who was deeply involved in efforts to relieve the pressures on smaller publishers to sell out doubted that anything but profits motivated big companies to buy newspapers. "The Roman legions didn't establish distant outposts to educate the colonials; they did it for tribute," he observed.

Harwood wore a Montagnard bracelet that he got while covering the Vietnam war. He kept in his office at the *Post* a photograph of his wife at an anti-war rally with a sign urging peace negotiations. He was a Marine at the age of seventeen in World War II. He had been a poor boy and had little sympathy for the sons and daughters of the comfortable who were so bitter in denouncing a country that he believed had been good to them. One Christmas Day, as the wrath over the war flamed higher, he presented to a dovish old friend a record of the country tune, "Okie from Muskogee." They laughed over the opening verse:

> We don't smoke marijuana in Muskogee,
> And we don't take our trips on L.S.D.
> And we don't burn our draft cards down on Main Street
> But we like living right and being free.

Harwood took to Trenton as his deputy one other *Post* editor, Joel Garreau. They were probably the most interesting newspaper pair since Hildy Johnson and Walter Burns of *The Front Page*. "I didn't want to clone myself," Harwood said of his choice. Hardly. With his scraggly, full red beard, pony tail, and country-and-western haberdashery, twenty-five-year-old Garreau seemed utterly miscast as an agent of a Fortune 500 conglomerate. Garreau had dropped out of Notre Dame in 1969 two hours short of a degree. He was a conscientious objector to the Vietnam war, who escaped conscription when Richard Nixon halted the draft calls eight numbers from his. In 1970 the *Post* hired Garreau to do layout.

Once a year Bradlee and his top editors retreat for a few days from the newsroom to ponder the state of their paper. Bradlee asked Garreau to talk to the group about graphics. There was much drinking at the gathering in a country place on the Susquehanna River and it was four in the morning before Garreau and his roommate dropped into their beds. Just as Garreau was about to fall asleep, his roommate growled, "Hey, hippie." For the next two hours Garreau and Dick Harwood argued ramblingly across the room and across a generation. If Harwood was going to enliven the *Trenton Times*, he wanted with him this graphics whiz, Garreau.

For weeks Harwood and Garreau spent most of their nights alone in a motel. They were reluctant to get socially close to the *Trenton Times*'s reporters and editors, some of whom Harwood might decide to fire. The *Times* was a paternalistic, easy-going place with long lunch hours and unpressured thirty-seven-and-a-half-hour weeks. "The staff didn't know if we were the U. S. Cavalry come to save the paper or the vengeful God of the Old Testament," Garreau said.

Some of both. Harwood rewarded those who excelled with praise and pay raises. As for the others Harwood said: "Good journalists are born, not made, so why give incompetents another year to improve? Reporters tend to be insecure; they fear punishment. Some are workaholics and you can still help them. Some are tired, their legs go, their eyes glaze over, they don't have fresh eyes." Over time half of the eighty-nine persons who were on the staff when Harwood arrived quit, retired, or were fired. He fired two of the three Kerneys on the staff. After Watergate there was no shortage of eager replacements for the *Times*'s ranks. "Everyone wanted to be a reporter and they all wanted to work at the *Post*," said Harwood. Young reporters saw *Trenton* as their first step to the *Post*—as it was for several. One young woman reporter who worked on the *Times* then called it Camelot.

Back in Washington at the Mother Church, they weren't so sure. *Times* circulation continued to slide, advertising was off and the Post Company was spending several million dollars to re-equip its new acquisition. In frustration with *Trenton*, Mrs. Graham asked, "Who ever decided to buy this thing?"

"You did, Kay," answered Larry Israel.

The ink was hardly dry on the agreement to buy the *Times* when a band of furious automobile dealers protested the paper's columnist writing that the high price of a new car made him keep his klunker. Sales were off because of the recession, they complained, and the *Times* was making things worse. "This paper is not for sale," Harwood told the dealers who wanted him to censor their critic. They replied by pulling their ads for a while. It was not the best of times. Sears, Roebuck had switched more than one million lines of advertising to the *Trentonian*, and the closing of two large stores cost the *Times* another big block of advertising.

While Harwood and Garreau brightened the paper with bolder typography, more aggressive reporting, and better writing that won awards for the *Times*, the *Trentonian* continued to gain on the paper. The battle was joined. For years the *Trentonian* carried the popular Los Angeles-Washington Post News Service. The service refused to renew the *Trentonian*'s contract when it expired. The *Times* picked it up.

The *Times* started a Saturday edition—a day the *Trentonian* previously had to itself. The *Trentonian* began publishing its first Sunday edition. The *Times* weighed producing a morning paper but hedged, said a former Post executive, because "we could have had some image problems if it looked like the *Washington Post*–owned *Times* was running the poor little *Trentonian* out of business."

By the spring of 1976 the *Times* looked better and read better. Its net income was up; the corporate managers wanted it to be higher. The paper continued to lose circulation, however, while the *Trentonian* gained readers. Tension increased between Washington and Trenton. The company had bought the *Times* without a carefully drawn business plan and market studies. "It was an impulse buy," a *Post* editor said. "The assumption was we would do it with the product, the newspaper itself," recalled Mark Meagher, a *Post* vice-president at the time. Meagher was an accountant and a systems analyst. He believed that a successful corporation didn't run by impulse; it ran by planning; it shaped events to gain its objectives. For anyone from Meager's disciplines, this was Holy Writ. Journalism ran differently. Often its greatest successes were the result of luck. Reporters were real life Princes of Serendip. Ben Bradlee once wished for a moment that he had a precise set of management objectives, like the Harvard Business School preached. It would spell out how many Pulitzers the paper expected to win, how many Overseas Writers awards, and so on. But he knew that newspapers didn't work that way. He could set out to produce thoughtful, responsible editing, insightful reporting, and brighter copy and make money for the paper by accomplishing it. But it wasn't a plan, it was too visceral, too much the creature of events.

Some critics said the *Times* was too much under the spell of the *Post*. Meagher contended Harwood was missing the market by trying to produce a national rather than a local newspaper. Katharine Graham had no desire to recast the *Times* in the *Post*'s image. "There is something in the Judeo-Christian ethic about humans developing their own potential; I believe that applies to newspapers, too," she philosophized and added, "That's why I want them to run autonomously." It was not a view hostile to excellence; indeed, it could restrain chain owners from homogenizing their newspapers, stamping all of them out with the same cookie cutter. A newspaper had to be tailored to its market.

"You can't produce a *Washington Post* in a small town," Harwood later remarked. "You have to pay attention to chicken suppers. I brought to a small town a large town mentality."

In the summer of 1976 Harwood returned to the *Post*. Mrs. Graham decided it would be "too traumatic" to succeed him with another editor from the *Post*. His successor was a man who had worked on the *Times* for years and spent most of his life in Trenton. The competition with the *Trentonian* continued unabated. Looking to the future, Harwood asserted, "We didn't go there to drive out the *Trentonian*, but we believe that it's in the cards that one paper will survive and we want it to be us." Time would tell whether this forecast would come true, as it had in most cities.

The *Trenton Times* in 1978 began returning modest cash dividends to the Post company, which encouraged the company to continue buying more newspapers. The DuPont Corporation owned papers in Wilmington, Delaware, then were on the block for reasons unrelated to their profitability. Mark Meagher saw the deal as "risk-free" for the *Post* because the Wilmington *Morning-News* and *Evening Journal* were a monopoly; advertising space could be priced at virtually any rate that would yield the owners' desired return on investment. Gannett— the Great White shark of the chains with the most newspapers, nearly eighty—was in a feeding frenzy for more papers and moved in on Wilmington.

Mrs. Graham, though she believed the papers were worth only $40 million, was authorized by her directors to bid up to $60 million. She bid $55 million. "We expected when Gannett got involved that they would be the high bidder, their usual practice," she explained later. "We thought that they'd bid fifty-seven or fifty-eight million dollars and it would be negotiable at that point." She and her executives anticipated that DuPont would give preference to their company's publishing distinction, in the wake of Watergate, in choosing among close bidders. But DuPont, to the *Post*'s surprise, speedily accepted Gannett's offer of $60 million. "We called it wrong," Mrs. Graham admitted. Asked why she bid less than the figure sanctioned by her directors, she said, "Five million dollars is a lot of money." Apparently, DuPont thought so, too.*

While the Post company was busy in Wilmington, Time, Inc. bought the *Washington Star* for $20 million and declared its intention to pump in another $60 million to improve the shaky paper. The *Post* was so far ahead of the *Star* in circulation and advertising that it would take a $2 billion conglomerate like Time, Inc., to make a race of it.

By 1976 the Los Angeles Times-Washington Post News Service that Phil Graham and Otis Chandler had established fifteen years earlier was a huge success. The number of clients exceeded the founding fathers' expectations by twentyfold. It was a vigorously competitive system for carrying news to clients that included the Argus Group newspapers in South Africa, more than one hundred newspapers in Germany and Switzerland, *Yomiuri Shimbun,* one of Japan's two largest dailies, and scores of papers in this country. From its base in the *Washington Post* building, the service transmitted forty-two thousand words each day. This mass included stories from Chandler's two other major dailies, *Newsday* on Long Island and the *Dallas Times-Herald,* and from *Agence France Presse* and Great Britain's *Guardian.* The Times-Post service rivaled the older New York Times News Service and at times pushed the redoubtable Associated Press and United Press International off the front pages of some clients.

The longstanding alliance between the two press empires, however, was verging on death at the hands of the *Post.*

When they formed the news service Chandler and Graham had put in charge of their new offspring British-born Rex Barley. He already headed the Los Angeles Times Syndicate which sold features and comics to other papers. Barley quickly signed some forty-five clients for the news service. What Barley apparently was doing, the Washington half of the partnership uncovered much later, was using the joint wire

*At the time it was negotiating for Wilmington, the *Post* was buying Everett, Washington's only daily, the *Everett Herald,* for $25 million. Mark Meagher predicted it would be worth twice that within a decade.

news service as a "loss leader" for the *Times*'s own syndicate; the news service was being offered at bargain prices to papers that agreed to buy the syndicate's material. The syndicate, it seemed, also was unduly charging certain of its own expenses to the news service.

In the autumn of 1976 the chickens came home to roost. On October 12 William Dickenson, head of the Washington Post Writers Group met for three hours at the Brown Palace Hotel in Denver with Robert D. Nelson, executive vice president of the *Los Angeles Times*. * They agreed to fire Robert Keith, Barley's successor at the news service. Nelson and Dickenson would become co-directors. The next day Dickenson reported to Katharine Graham that "as a result of a recent audit" the Los Angeles Times Syndicate charges against the news service would be fifty to sixty thousand dollars less in the coming year than in 1976, a measure of how heavily the syndicate had milked the news service.

The accommodation did not appease Bradlee. In a letter to Nelson, Bradlee wrote that syndicate boss Tom Dorsey "told us the syndicate had overcharged the News Service half a million dollars" in payroll alone since 1970. Bradlee continued that Dorsey had "misrepresented" the good first quarter financial showing of the service as the result of his efforts when in fact it was the payroll cuts resulting from the long *Post* strike in early 1976 that produced the gain. The clash reflected what Bradlee labeled the "gnawing" problem in the relationship between the two newspaper giants over their joint venture. He was annoyed at talk in Los Angeles of "repatriating" the news service from Washington to the Chandler bastion on Times Plaza. Moreover, he viewed the syndicate's relationship to the news service as a "conflict of interest."

In the midst of this management storm, the *Times* questioned the *Post*'s journalistic ethics on a different matter. The *Times*'s Washington bureau complained that the *Post* was purloining its exclusive stories. The bureau used the leased wire of the Times-Post news service, which was located in the *Post* building, to notify editors in Los Angeles

*The group is a vehicle invented by Bradlee so the *Post* can market the work of its best writers. It splits the fees with them. This is a way to hold on to talent.

of upcoming exclusive stories its reporters were pursuing. At that time the news service operated in a corner of the *Post*'s newsroom and *Post* editors had ready access to all of the information moving on the wire since they were collaborators in the service. The complaint was that the *Post,* tipped by the *Times* bureau's messages to Los Angeles and aided by the three-hour time lag between the capital and the West Coast, had beaten the *Times*'s Washington reporters on their own stories. An executive later admitted privately that the pilferage had occurred several times, once involving a Watergate development, another time a story about political harassment by the F.B.I.

A few days before Christmas 1976, in order to dampen the rising anger between the *Los Angeles Times* and his paper, Bradlee sent this note to all *Post* editors:

They say we have been known to appropriate their stories. They feel we regularly ignore stories from them, which merit our attention and use.

If the first happened, it will not happen again. We should always credit them. As a general rule, if their stories are worth citing, they are worth running, not rewriting. As for the second, *Post* editors should recognize, appreciate and use the tremendous asset available to us in the twenty-three reporters now filing regularly in the Los Angeles Times Washington Bureau.

"They'd do it again if it was the right story," a veteran of the *Post* newsroom predicted.

Bradlee's memo relieved the cribbing problem. The *Times,* however, had been caught financially in flagrante delicto; the moment was ripe for the *Post* to assert itself regarding the future of the Times-Post service. Bradlee wanted to put the operation in the hands of "a take-charge guy" who, by his specifications, would know the business, be tough enough to stand up to the Times Syndicate, and be diplomatic enough to get along with both sides. Through his office window the editor could see his choice for the job. Bradlee walked across the busy newsroom to where the national staff worked and stood over a tall, beefy reporter whose thining hair was closely crew cut. Steven D. Isaacs was typing a story on the 1976 election then winding toward an end. Isaacs came to the *Post* in 1961, two years after graduating from Harvard and working as a reporter in London. Within a year he was city editor of the *Post*. His father, Norman E. Isaacs, was a highly regarded editor who had been president of the American Society of Newspaper Editors. "This is important," said Bradlee interrupting Isaacs. Bradlee told him to take a hard look at the troubled news service and recommend what should be done.

Isaacs was a tough editor—"Are you a prick?" he was known to challenge prospective reporters—enormously self-confident and outspoken. His relationship with Bradlee was mercurial. A magazine article had quoted a *"Post* editor" as saying "Ben Bradlee is the most brilliant driving dynamic talented energetic professional and amoral man I know." "That's Isaacs," barked managing editor Howard Simons, believing he recognized the comma-less cadence of Isaacs's speech. Isaacs did not deny he was the source. Isaacs's father later reflected on the assessment of Bradlee that "Amorality may be the common denominator of all good editors."

Sometimes the encounters between the two men had the taste of farce. Once at Bradlee's place in West Virginia where he had gathered his senior editors to talk about the newspaper, the newsmen, full of drink and acting like schoolboys at recess, divided up for touch football. Isaacs, six-foot-three, close to 250 pounds and seventeen years Bradlee's junior, sent the boss sprawling in the dirt with a stiff brush block. Bradlee, a well-built six-footer, raced for a shed to find a farm tool appropriate for an assault on Isaacs. His amused teammates restrained him. Bradlee's retreat of some 150 acres ran along the heavily wooded banks of the lovely Cacapon River. When one of his neighbors asked permission to fish the waters that flowed by the place, Bradlee granted it with the good-humored caution that he and his lover, *Post* reporter Sally Quinn, whom he married in 1978, enjoyed swimming in the buff and the angler should please take care.

On another occasion, Bradlee might have been forgiven for committing mayhem on Isaacs for a costly lapse of editorial judgment. Soon after Isaacs became editor of *Potomac*, the *Post's* Sunday supplement, he bought for reprinting a seemingly innocuous article that had first run in an obscure magazine called *Mind-Fuck*. The piece explained how to fashion a superior bacon-lettuce-and-tomato sandwich. The author cautioned against using Wonder Bread, describing it as "a substitute for toilet or blotting paper." *Potomac* then was printed in Louisville and shipped to the *Post* three weeks before publication date. James Daly, general manager of the *Post,* spotted the indecorous phrase and complained to Bradlee. Wonder Bread is an incongruous product of International Telephone and Telegraph, a multinational conglomerate that also happens to transmit the *Post's* copy worldwide via IT&T Global. The *Post* was a possible candidate for a libel suit, Daly warned. Editors hastily shifted copy and ads. Some seven hundred thousand copies of *Potomac* were reprinted without the risky piece at a cost of $35,000. Isaacs apologetically explained to Bradlee that he had scheduled the "B.L.T." article without fully reading it. "How do you think I feel every night?" softly replied Bradlee who often had time to read only the highlights of the major stories that the *Post* would publish after he left the newsroom.

Isaacs spent two weeks sorting through the muddled affairs of the Times-Post News Service before concluding that the marriage could not last as it was. A council of war was convened in Katharine Graham's office. Bradlee, his shirt sleeves neatly rolled up to his elbows, Isaacs, Dickinson, and Phil Foisie, whose older brother was a *Los Angeles Times* foreign correspondent, reviewed the situation with Mrs. Graham. They considered the possibility that the *Times* and the *Post* might launch competitive news services if the partnership were dissolved. After an hour and a half, Mrs. Graham agreed to tell Otis Chandler the *Post* would pull out from the news service unless there was a new deal. One of the key conditions was that Isaacs would become director of the service. The bookkeeping would be cleared up so that the operation would be run truly fifty-fifty; the *Post* would have its man in the driver's seat to assure it.

Chandler accepted the *Post's* terms in a special delivery letter to Mrs. Graham's home on Sunday. A California editor who had known him for years observed that Chandler believes "prestige is power." The news service, as originally intended, added to the *Los Angeles Times'* prestige. Also, it was a paying proposition. Nothing would be gained, Chandler undoubtedly concluded, by ending an enterprise that was likely to be even more rewarding ahead.

On the day in January 1977 when Steve Isaacs became the director of the Los Angeles Times-Washington Post News Service, Mark Meagher, the president of the Washington Post Company, asked him to celebrate at lunch at the aristocratic University Club near the *Post.* Isaacs said he would not go there because he understood that the company treasurer had been blackballed because he was Jewish. When Isaacs later reported to Katharine Graham that he had pushed news service revenues 35 percent over budget projections, Isaacs, the grandson of a London butcher and part-time cantor, quipped that the money-making ability "is in my genes." She understood. Her father, Eugene Meyer, was the grandson of an Alsatian rabbi who counseled Napoleon I on Jewish rights. Meyer, however, had given up his religion when he married Agnes Ernst whose paternal ancestors were prominent Lutheran clergymen. Kay Graham did not hear that she was part Jewish until she enrolled at Vassar. "Kike," Phil Graham had shouted at her from the dark pit of his insanity.

It was not that Isaacs was a devout practicing Jew; he was not. He had grown up and was raising his own family with his Jewishness of no seeming consequence. In 1972 he was assigned to do a series on Jews in politics. The articles were expanded into a seminal book. In the fall of 1974 General George S. Brown, chairman of the Joint Chiefs of Staff, told a Duke University audience that "Jews own, you know, the banks in this country, the newspapers. . . ." President Ford rebuked Brown. Isaacs found himself being interviewed by other reporters as an expert on the issues raised by the General.

In *Jews and American Politics* Isaacs traced the charges of Jewish control of the news media back to the anti-semitic wave of four decades ago. He noted that in 1974 Jews owned 3.1 percent of the country's 1,748 dailies, comprising about 8 percent of the circulation. The old accusations, however, still resurfaced periodically. In August 1978, Bert Lance, heavily involved with Arab financiers since resigning from the Carter administration, suggested that the "great Jewish ownership of the press" might be the cause of the "hurrah" over Arab investments in the United States.

Isaacs was frequently assigned stories about Jews until he snapped at national editor Harry Rosenfeld, "I'm not your house Jew." Many

Jews lose their ethnicity in journalism. Isaacs found his identity through his work. His personal discovery did not conflict with his perception of why Jews enter the press. In his book Isaacs wrote: "Journalism offers a haven to the secular Jew who wants to assimilate and yet has a typically Jewish passion for involvement in public affairs. American journalism's oft-proclaimed goal of 'objectivity' places the serious practitioner above the fray stripping away attachments that can be construed as conflicts of interest, material or ideological. Thus the Jew in journalism finds that he cannot be 'Jewish' and at the same time be a good journalist in terms of the value system that the mass media in the United States have built over the years."

Newspaper jobs were hard to come by for anyone during the Depression and a Jewish name was no godsend for employment. Ben Gilbert, a former assistant managing editor at the *Post*, took his journalism professor's advice in the 1930s to change his name from Goldberg and landed on a St. Louis daily. Alfred Friendly grew up in Salt Lake City where his father, Edward Rosenbaum, was a clothing merchant. He took his mother's maiden name, Friendly, to help get on a newspaper in the thirties. "It was hard enough to get in someone's door if you were a reporter," Friendly recalled and added, "It was even harder if you had a Jewish name." In 1967 Friendly, who was neither a religious Jew nor a Zionist, covered the Israeli-Arab war for the *Post*. After the Israelis captured the Old City of Jerusalem, Friendly accompanied the first troops to the Wailing Wall. He was swept up in the emotional drama of a victorious Jewish army standing reverently at the site of the ancestral temple. "I touched the wall; wild horses couldn't have kept me away; I'm a Jew," he said with sudden emotion long after that exulting moment. His dispatches bore no trace of his Jewish roots.

While the controversy over the Los Angeles Times-Washington Post News Service was coming to a head, another press chain giant, Rupert Murdoch, unknowingly was moving toward clashes with Katharine Graham and Otis Chandler. Australian-born Murdoch was twenty-two when his father died in 1952 leaving him a small newspaper in Adelaide. By the time he was forty-five Murdoch owned a media empire of eighty-seven newspapers, eleven magazines, and seven broadcasting stations that spanned his native country, England, and the United States. Murdoch was a conservative, an Oxford graduate, and reportedly a good family man, none of which seemed to have any connection to the fact that many of his papers played up gory crime and sex with photos of lush women. Fleet Street had crowned him "the Aussie tit and bum king." Under a headline "Terror Victim Fleeing," his *San Antonio News* ran a story that began: "A divorced epileptic, who told police she was buried alive in a bathtub full of wet cement and later hanged upside down in the nude, left San Antonio for good this weekend. The tiny, half-blind woman, suffering from diabetes, recounted for the *News* a bizarre story filled with rape, torture and starvation."

In mid-November 1976, Murdoch bought for $30 million his third American daily, the *New York Post,* the city's only evening newspaper. Then in early 1977 the Australian acquired *New West,* a regional magazine published in Los Angeles, Chandler's home base. Chandler had tried to buy the magazine a few months before Murdoch got it. When Otis Chandler was asked about Murdoch's journalistic style on a Los Angeles radio talk show, he said: "Mr. Murdoch does not believe in the kind of journalism I believe in. He does not believe in publishing good newspapers. He will do anything to get circulation." Chandler, who had decidedly improved the *Los Angeles Times* and the *Dallas Times-Herald,* speculated that if the Aussie shopped for more American newspapers "maybe second- or third-rate papers in small cities will sell to him." In the early 1970s, Murdoch offered $20 million for the badly sagging *Washington Star.* Turned down, Murdoch inquired if the *Daily News* building was still available, but learned it had been razed after the tabloid folded in 1972.

Chandler had a puritanical reputation. "Otis wouldn't say 'shit,' " Mark Meagher, president of the Washington Post Company, once remarked. The *Los Angeles Times* had stopped accepting ads for X-rated films, a ban that cost the paper several hundred thousand dollars a year in revenue. "We have been dealing with an indefensible product, one with no redeeming values," Chandler declared on the radio, sharpening the supposed contrast between himself and Murdoch. The porno theaters "are a blight upon our beautiful city; I hope they close their doors," intoned the publisher.

A few weeks after Chandler's blast, Murdoch got in a riposte on the same show. Murdoch drolly questioned his critic's right to demean his professional standards when, indeed, a Chandler subsidiary had distributed *Penthouse* in Great Britain. How, Murdoch asked, could Chandler disdain Murdoch's papers which used the Los Angeles Times-Washington Post News Service. Chandler angrily decided not to renew the expiring contract between Murdoch's *New York Post* and the news service, and to offer it instead to the *New York Daily News.* When he came East, however, editors at *Newsday,* Chandler's tabloid on Long Island, argued him out of his plan. They regarded the *Daily News* as a more serious competitor than the *New York Post* and did not want the *News* to receive the same service *Newsday* carried. Mrs. Graham sent her ruffled partner in the news service a hand-written note counseling him against acting in pique. She might have concurred with Chandler, indulging her own possible wish for reprisal. Murdoch, after all, had outmaneuvered her in a rough match for ownership of *New York* magazine.

Unlike Katharine Graham, Otis Chandler, and Rupert Murdoch, Clay Felker inherited neither wealth nor the foundation of a publishing dominion. Felker came from a middle-class family in suburban St. Louis. Felker parlayed his $6,575 severance pay from the *World Journal Tribune,* a last-gasp mélange of three New York dailies, and his editorial incandescence into a magazine that from its founding in 1967 both anticipated and shaped the currents of New York City's high life. Judith Adler Hennessee in *MORE* magazine called *New York:* "The house organ of Rome before the fall, a magazine everyone is aware of. Even people who say they don't read it somehow manage to know what's in it." The weekly magazine focused on Felker's fascination with power—who presumably has it and its employment—and money, the same. Felker skillfully orchestrated writing and editing talent; frequently he made space for a sociological piece or serious reporting.

Eventually even the straight-arrow *New York Times* would incorporate *New York*'s trendy approach and layout in the special life-style sections it started publishing in the late 1970s to attract readers and advertising. Earlier the Felker treatment influenced the content and makeup of the *Washington Post* Style section and its Sunday magazine, *Potomac*. When Steve Isaacs became *Potomac*'s editor, Ben Bradlee, who called *New York* "boutique journalism," sent him to see Felker and Milton Glazer, the magazine's designer. "Use light and frivolous covers and you can get away with serious pieces inside," Felker advised Isaacs.

Sometime before Rupert Murdoch loomed on the American newspaper scene, Mrs. Graham reciprocated for his hospitality to her in Australia by inviting him to Glen Welby, her estate in Virginia. Another guest was her friend, Clay Felker. That pleasant weekend in the rolling hunt country, where scores of multimillionaires with such names as DuPont and Mellon own large fiefs, was the first meeting of Murdoch and Felker. The two men, each fiercely ambitious and exploring for new publishing ventures, got on well. They talked about magazine and newspaper enterprises that they might take on together, although they were wary of one another.

In 1974 New York Magazine Company bought the *Village Voice*, a profitable weekly tabloid with excellent writers. The next year the company okayed Felker's plan to publish a carbon copy of *New York* in California. Starting *New West* was projected to cost a little over $2 million; before Felker was through these expenses would more than double, and the company was sliding financially.* By summer 1976, the company reportedly had lost two hundred thousand dollars on Felker's unsuccessful attempt to publish a national edition of the Manhattan-based *Village Voice*. The financial problems were coupled with a growing animosity between Felker, who owned 10 percent of the company, and the other board members, particularly Carter Burden. Burden held 24 percent of the New York stock, the largest block. Burden was the great-grandson of shipping and railroad tycoon Cornelius Vanderbilt. He was active in liberal Democratic politics; in 1978

---

*Part of the money went to furnish *New West*'s offices in Beverly Hills with desks and other equipment that had been used for the simulated *Washington Post* newsroom in the film *All the President's Men*. After the movie was completed Felker bought the props.

he would spend $1.1 million of his own money to be elected to Congress, and fail.

Things got worse at *New York* and by autumn prospective buyers, among them Otis Chandler, were making passes at stockholders. In mid-November Rupert Murdoch arranged to buy the *New York Post.* Early in December he talked with Felker about buying the New York Magazine Company. The figure mentioned was five dollars a share; a few months earlier *New York* stock was at two dollars. He then, reportedly, would sell *New West* to Felker. But the two men could not agree, and Murdoch soon was talking seven dollars a share with an agent for Burden. Felker had an agreement with Burden that gave him first refusal if the socialite ever decided to sell his stock. Felker had until December 31 to top Murdoch's offer. He phoned Katharine Graham just before Christmas. From time to time Felker and Mrs. Graham had discussed the possibility of the Washington Post Company buying *New York* or hiring him. They also talked about her buying *Esquire* and making him editor. "I had listened to him for years about his directors, but I knew he wanted to be independent," she recalled. "He didn't want us or anybody to control him. He was having the same discussion with Murdoch." Then Felker discovered that Murdoch was going ahead without him; "Clay couldn't believe it," said Mrs. Graham.

Donald Graham had said earlier that he wanted to acquire *New York* more than any magazine the company had considered. If management and money issues could be worked out, he would have his wish. In the days since the Post Company's pursuit of *New York, New West,* and the *Village Voice* began, the discussion had narrowed to two central questions: Were the publications worth buying? Could Felker be managed within the Post corporate family? Larry H. Israel, president of the Post Company, had opposed the deal. He wasn't in New York. Scholarly and sober in nature, the fifty-seven-year-old Israel argued that the purchase would diminish Post Company earnings by forty-five cents a share. (Since 1976 produced record earnings for the Post Company it apparently could well afford the purchase.) More risky to the company, Israel contended, than the questionable financial impact of the deal was Felker himself. *Newsweek's* profits were sickly in 1974 and 1975. The magazine division was now doing well again and the absorption of *New York* and its forceful editor might reverse this trend, Israel feared. Mrs. Graham and other directors chose to plunge: The company had the money; Felker was a friend; and Ben Bradlee could help keep him in line. In the midst of this corporate scrambling Felker stunned Mrs. Graham by abruptly telling her that he desperately needed to escape it for a few days. He had just returned from a wrenching visit with his father who was dying in Webster Groves, Missouri. Felker left for Nassau.

"We decided to make a good, big solid offer," Mrs. Graham said, "but not get into a bidding match or a courtcase. We didn't want to start takeover proceedings." Nevertheless, her small circle of strategists included the man who Wall Street hailed as the "dean" of corporate takeover specialists, Felix G. Rohatyn.

Felix Rohatyn is one of the titans of global investment banking. He put together many of the deals that made International Telephone and Telegraph a global corporate superpower. He was born in Vienna to a family of prosperous bankers who fled when the Nazis seized power. He was a close friend of Mrs. Graham. Lazard Freres & Company, in which Rohatyn was a senior partner, was the main underwriter when the *Post* went public in 1971. Mrs. Graham's paternal grandfather had been a Lazard Freres partner. Rohatyn was forty-eight and chairman of the Municipal Assistance Corporation, the instrument he helped to fashion to stave off New York City's fiscal ruin when he stepped in to help Felker, who in many ways personified the city. Rohatyn has said of his deal making: "You put two companies together, you're dealing with money, you're dealing with egos, you're dealing with power, you're dealing with lawyers, you're dealing with accountants, and you're dealing with pressure."

It was the last day of 1976 and the deadline for Felker's counter offer to Carter Burden. The pressure was intense among those gathered in *Newsweek*'s executive suite above Madison Avenue, including Mrs. Graham, Rohatyn, Felker, *Newsweek* executives Peter A. Derow and Kenneth Auchincloss, and assorted lawyers. Derow and Auchincloss had been up all night talking with Felker about how he would fit in.

At seven-thirty that morning Derow phoned Mrs. Graham at her hotel. She was needed back at *Newsweek*. They were having trouble contacting Burden who was skiing in Sun Valley, Idaho. Later in the morning Rohatyn took the *Post*'s check for nearly $3.2 million, representing an offer of $7.50 a share for Burden's stock, to Burden's attorney, Peter Tufo. Tufo would not accept it. "Burden was so furious at Felker he would not consider anyone allied with him," Mrs. Graham remembered.

Gail Sheehy, a *New York Magazine* writer who was "very close," as she put it, to Felker, described in *Rolling Stone* the closing hours of this fervid competition for *New York:*

It is three o'clock on December 31st . . . Felix Rohatyn is fit to kill . . . On the other end of the telephone is Peter Tufo, who has been saying all day long that he couldn't reach Carter because his client is on the slopes.

"Peter," says Felix, "there is no snow on the slopes. Stop bullshitting me."

"You're going to have to give me more time," Tufo says.

"We'll give you till four," Felix says darkly.

The humiliation level in the room rises considerably during the next hour and three-quarters. Katharine Graham, queen mother of one of the most highly respected publishing organizations in the world, has been waiting for two days for the phone to ring. It doesn't. Carter Burden is treating her like a jilted dance-hall dolly.

At 4:45 Tufo calls back and tells Felix, "Look, I've talked to Carter, and it cannot go your way."

"You mean it can't go our way at any price?" Felix asks in astonishment.

"I can't tell you more than that," says Tufo. Felix says he will extend the deadline until 5:30.

* * *

And so here in the *Newsweek* offices in the last dying hours of 1976, the air of unreality is stifling. At 8 P.M. Katharine Graham takes the phone with its last feeble connection to Peter Tufo and she implores, "What is it you really want? Should I fly out to see Carter. I'll do anything."

"Kay, don't." Felix whispers, "It's demeaning to you. The whole thing is obscene. At least keep your dignity."

"Is there anything humanly possible?" Katharine Graham pleads.

Rupert Murdoch topped the *Post*'s tender with a bid of $8.25 a share, Burden accepted and Murdoch flew from his Hudson River

Valley estate on a chartered jet to close the deal in Sun Valley. The contest was over, save for a brief challenge of the outcome. On Monday, Felker went into court to prevent Murdoch's takeover of *New York*. On Thursday many of the magazine's staff walked off the job in a display of support for their embattled editor, who the next day ended his lawsuit by settling with his erstwhile friend. Murdoch agreed to pay Felker $8.25 for each of his 178,150 shares of *New York* stock, the same price the publisher paid others, as well as Felker's $120,000 a year salary for two years and other benefits in his contract.

It was the quintessential *New York* story: a cast of beautiful people, clashing corporate empires, slivered egos, wealth pantingly engaged in acquiring more wealth. There were ironic touches, too. Clay Felker earlier had brought Rupert Murdoch together with Dolly Schiff, from whom the Australian bought the *New York Post*. Murdoch used nearly $6 million of the *Post*'s cash to help buy *New York* away from Felker. In the summer of 1977 Felker became editor of *Esquire* when it was bought by British publisher Vere Harmsworth. *Esquire* was the magazine that Kay Graham had thought of buying and on which she would install Felker as editor.

Twenty-one days after the Post Company's whirlwind campaign to take over *New York Magazine* failed, Larry Israel suddenly resigned as president and chief operating officer. He had opposed the venture. The company issued the slimmest public explanation for his abrupt exit.* The resignation was a surprise only to those outside of the *Post*'s corporate throne room. Relations between Mrs. Graham and Israel had been eroding for some time. Israel felt edged aside by Warren Buffett who as a director and large stockholder was playing an increasingly significant role in corporate decisions. Mrs. Graham had turned to Buffett for counsel before she bid for *New York*. Israel's departure route

*Katharine Graham was livid when she read a column by Charles B. Seib, the *Post*'s commentator on the press, criticizing his own paper's "barebones coverage" of the resignation of a major figure in the communications industry. Readers of the *New York Times* were "told more about Israel's departure than were the *Post*'s readers," wrote Seib. Newspapers rarely report on their own operations except to announce price increases, honors received, or, in blankest outline, major personnel changes. Seib's agreement with the *Post* left him free to criticize any aspect of the news media; although the *Post*'s editor can veto a column it has not happened so far.

was paved with gold: His termination agreement would bring him seven hundred thousand dollars by January 1979 as well as other handsome benefits; he could hold on to the thirty-six thousand shares of *Post* stock that he had acquired, which would greatly increase in value. This lucrative package was a measure of Israel's accomplishments for the company and seemingly Mrs. Graham's great desire to have him gone. Nine years earlier it had been different.

On the evening of June 6, 1968, *Post* company chairman Frederick S. Beebe and company attorney William P. Rogers dined at the Waldorf-Astoria in New York with Larry Israel, a rising star in the broadcasting industry. (In seven months Rogers would become President Nixon's secretary of state.) Across the continent in Los Angeles Robert Kennedy was dead of an assassin's bullet. St. Patrick's Cathedral three blocks from the Waldorf was being readied to receive his body. The three men and their wives spoke gloomily of the tragedy.

Beebe and Rogers asked Israel to become head of the Post Company's broadcasting subsidiary, Post-Newsweek Stations, which operated radio and television stations in Washington and a television station in Jacksonville. The stations were slackly managed. Israel, Beebe and Rogers hoped, would change that. He had advanced rapidly to the presidency of Westinghouse's Group W, a mini-broadcasting network with a record for profitability and excellent programming. If he took the job, Israel told his hosts, he would try to acquire more television properties; they could be electronic gold mines if run smartly. It had been fifteen years since the Post Company had bought a television station. The Federal Communications Act allowed a single owner to have up to seven TV stations; the company had only two.

Philip Graham regarded broadcasting as a likely source of profits for the company. Eugene Meyer, on the other hand, "viewed broadcasting as a problem industry that sooner or later would run into complications from government control of the air waves," according to his biographer Merlo Pusey. Meyer supported the purchase of the company's first TV station, in Washington, but he initially strongly opposed Graham's plan to buy a station in Jacksonville because that "would be going too far afield," Pusey relates. Finally persuaded that it was a sound business deal and important to his son-in-law, a Floridian, Meyer agreed.*

Beebe readily agreed to Israel's expansionism and his request for autonomy in directing the subsidiary. In effect, the forty-nine-year-old Pittsburgher wanted his own satrapy within the *Post* empire. A few years later when the Post Company was considering becoming a publicly traded corporation, Israel suggested that the broadcasting subsidiary be spun off as a separate company which he then would acquire, perhaps with the Post Company retaining a partial interest. Lazard Freres & Company, underwriter of the stock offering, however, concluded that without the broadcasting stations, the company would not be attractive to investors.

When he arrived in Washington, Israel quickly discovered the truth of a veteran broadcaster's diagnosis that the Post Company's stations were "suffering from hardening of the arteries." WTOP-TV's studio floor was so pitted that the cameras could not be dollied properly; Israel's first act was to order construction of a new floor. A half million dollars worth of steel had been bought for a new transmission tower, but the station hadn't submitted the applications to build the structure. When the tower was completed, the station's telecasting reach was so vastly extended, bringing higher rates for commercial time, that it was comparable to adding overnight one million in newspaper circulation.

One of Israel's decisions rankled broadcasters across the country. A year or so before the federal ban on radio and television cigarette commercials took effect in January 1971, Israel ordered an end to such advertising on *Post* stations. His edict cost the stations several million dollars in ad revenues. Some of his industry brethren accused him of being "moralistic," as though it were a perversion.

Israel replied that the federal requirement that anti-smoking ads be

---

*In the early days of radio, and later television, the federal government encouraged newspaper owners to get into broadcasting because they were experienced in handling advertising and news. In recent years various government policies, some of them in conflict with one another, have been expressed to cope with an issue that the earlier stimulative policy had helped to produce—the cross-ownership by single companies of newspaper and broadcasting outlets in the same city. Until 1978, the *Post* was such a company. That year it sold WTOP radio in Washington to another company and swapped its TV station for one in Detroit. Many observers saw cross-ownership as a real or potential danger to the free flow of information in a community, especially in areas where the principal news media were controlled by one owner.

aired in response to cigarette commercials was destroying the credibility of all broadcast advertising. Israel, who had carefully read medical reports on the harmful effects of smoking, was trying to persuade his own children to shun cigarettes. The *Post* ran an editorial criticizing the broadcasting division's prohibition. "Smoking is so pervasive in society it doesn't accomplish anything to bar ads for cigarettes," argued Robert McCormick, the *Post's* vice president for advertising. As it turned out after the broadcasting ban, the cigarette makers simply multiplied their spending on magazine and newspaper space, to the profit of the *Post* and *Newsweek,* along with others.

Three months after Israel joined the Post Company, he got a tip that one of Miami's television stations, saddled with heavy debt and running last in that market, might be for sale. Israel and Beebe made a secret midnight inspection of the station, arranged by his informant, in order to cloak the Post Company's interest. On a handshake that held the deal firm against another company's subsequent offer of several million dollars more, the Post Company bought the Miami station and an allied radio station for approximately $18.5 million. The television station's call letters were changed to WPLG, in memory of Philip L. Graham.

A few years later the Post Company bought its fourth television station, this one in Hartford, from a subsidiary of the Travelers Insurance Company. At an initial meeting in the Travelers' suite in the Carlyle Hotel in New York, Israel's jaw dropped when Travelers' vice president Eli Shapiro told him and Fritz Beebe the price for the Hartford station was $60 million, far beyond both the Post's "going-in" figure to start the negotiations and its fall-back offer. With the Post Company and Travelers so wide apart on price, Beebe and a dejected Israel left the hotel. Outside Beebe sought to buoy up his colleague by telling him that it was in the Carlyle that Phil Graham had clinched the deal seven years before to buy *Newsweek.* It might still work out, Beebe smiled.

Shapiro phoned a few months later and suggested another session back at the Carlyle where he told Beebe and Israel that the price was now $40 million. The two Post executives went into the bathroom to consider their response. They decided the radio station that was included in the Hartford package could be resold for about $5 million. They emerged and agreed to Shapiro's price. Israel had projected that the company's investment in the Hartford station would pay off in six or seven years; the turning point came in three years.

By the end of 1976 the value of the Jacksonville and Hartford stations had doubled since their purchase by the Post Company and its other stations were booming. When the *Washington Post*'s profits sagged because of the long pressmen's strike in 1975 and 1976, the rising earnings of the company's broadcasting operations and *Newsweek* insured the corporation against a lean year. The company seemed invincible.

EIGHT

The Padilla Affair

In all American business and industry today, there is probably no instance of such bitterness, such conflict, such hatred, such opposition, and such war to the throat as between the newspaper workers and the newspaper owners.

—GEORGE SELDES, *Lords of the Press,* 1938

AT THE MAIN ENTRANCE TO THE *Washington Post* building sits a red-and-silver painted machine which looks as though it were created by a sculptor gone bonkers. Thomas Edison called an earlier version the "eighth wonder of the world" when it was first used at the *New York Tribune* on July 4, 1886. A plaque on the *Post*'s machine declares that it was the "very heart of the newspaper production process." The true genius of the linotype, an occasional printer named Mark Twain once said, was that it never went on strike.

Along with the high-speed press the linotype and its operator, often a deaf person who was not bothered by the incessant clanking as molten lead was cast into lines of type, were the instruments that made mass circulation newspapers possible before the turn of the century. Automation did away with the need for the linotype operator: In the early 1960s stock market quotations were being transmitted at 1,050 words a minute from the Associated Press in New York and fed directly to computerized devices in distant newspaper composing rooms that converted the information to a perforated tape, adjusting for the end of a line and hyphenation. In turn the yellow punched rivulet, nicknamed "idiot tape," was fed into the linotype to command the typesetting sans operator. In 1450 Johann Gutenberg set a line of type by hand in one minute. The linotype, operated by one human, produced almost five lines of type per minute. The computerized tape sped up typesetting to fourteen lines a minute. Far more dramatic changes were descending on printing—what Martin Luther had called "God's highest act of grace."

The typographical upheaval pervaded the American newspaper business in 1963. A Typographical Union strike against four New York City dailies, rooted largely in the printers' justified fears of what further automation would do to their jobs, lasted 114 days. The papers lost an estimated $108 million in advertising; the workers, $50 million in wages. On Thursday, February 21, 1963, with that strike in its seventy-sixth day, President John F. Kennedy in a televised press conference criticized Bertram A. Powers, president of the New York Typographical Union Local 6, and the strikers for denying New Yorkers their daily newspapers. Kennedy declared that "the best solution is for the union to demonstrate a sense of responsibility and not merely try to carry this to its final ultimate of cracking the publishers, because if they do it they will close down some papers and I think will hurt their employment possibilities themselves." The president suggested that a third party making an "independent determination" could help break the stalemate. Kennedy didn't have in mind his friend, Philip L. Graham, president of the *Washington Post.* On his own, Graham plunged forward as a self-appointed conciliator, a role Mayor Robert F. Wagner, Governor Nelson Rockefeller, and others were already attempting to play. On Saturday Graham asked Powers to come to his Carlyle Hotel suite in New York. They made an interesting pair. Graham a Harvard-educated lawyer; Powers a Boston-born poor boy who quit high school after two years to become a printer. They were both tall, dapper, ambitious, and articulate. The two men talked for six hours, with Powers indicating his position on each point at issue in the strike and Graham filling a legal pad with notes, A. H. Raskin reported in the *New York Times* the day after the strike ended.

Graham telephoned Kennedy, who was vacationing in Palm Beach, and, in Powers's presence, told the president he was wrong to criticize the union leader. Graham "praised Mr. Powers and reviled the New York publishers," Raskin wrote. Kennedy later called Mayor Wagner to inform him of Graham's proposal for a mediation board to be appointed by Wagner with Graham as chairman and United Automobile Workers president Walter Reuther and a conservative businessman as members. Strike mediator Theodore W. Kheel told the *Washington Post* owner that the introduction of new faces might upset the negotiations. Graham, confident he could produce a solution to the costly strike, met with Wagner and Kheel at the mayor's residence. They finally told Graham that the New York publishers would walk out of the negotiations at City Hall if he walked in. It was no secret to Kennedy and the principals in the New York newspaper dispute that Graham was suffering from severe manic depression; in six months he would commit suicide.

The next day the lead editorial in the *Washington Post* blasted the striking unions. The editorial entitled "A Threat to a Free Press," was diametrically opposite to Graham's position. He had not seen the editorial before editor Russell Wiggins, who had once been assistant to the publisher of the *New York Times,* ran it. Its appearance on the page that reflects the publishers' sentiments revealed how irreversibly separated Graham had become from his paper. The editorial said that the strike disclosed that "nearly every newspaper in the United States can be forced into temporary or permanent suspension on the option of the leadership of unions—even those representing a tiny fraction of the employees. . . . No free society would tolerate the exercise of such power by government itself; its exercise by persons neither chosen nor responsible to a larger suffrage is even more intolerable. . . ." Labor alone, the *Post* asserted, was guilty of denying society "its right to be informed by daily newspapers of its choice."

The editorial mirrored Wiggins's proper zeal for freedom of the press. But the editorial omitted the fact that local broadcasters had stepped up their news reports and papers from nearby cities were filling the city's newsstands. It also ignored the salient fact that at least five of New York's papers were blacked out on command of their own publishers, not the unions. The New York publishers had agreed to regard a strike against one newspaper as a strike against all; in that event each newspaper would stop publishing. (More than a decade later Katharine Graham, faced with a strike, would try to forge a similar pact with Washington's other newspaper.) This was the publishers' answer to unions that would not cross each other's picket lines, giving a single union a powerful weapon against a publisher. The editorial also failed to mention that the *Post* itself was involved in bargaining with its printers, a fact it revealed a few days later by running a long, critical letter from Powers.

Of the nine New York dailies alive in 1963, five died in a few years. Their end probably had as much to do with population movements, altered life-styles, and the onslaught of television as with the strike and steep production costs. But their disappearance sent tremors through newspapers with strong unions.

John Diebold, who coined the word "automation," was advising publishers on the technological revolution that was already upon their industry. "Today we have a technology that can brutally affect the whole guts of the publishing business," Diebold warned. "It is a very explosive situation for all connected with it." On the streets outside three Toronto dailies where computers were beginning to set type, pickets carried signs pleading, "Help Printers Fight Automation: Your Job May Be Next." The *Toronto Telegram,* by converting to the new printing technology, cut eighty men from its composing room force of two hundred, a 40 percent savings. In nonunion papers with the cash to install the new apparatus, the change came by management's dictate. By the end of 1963 the *Los Angeles Times* was setting all of its wordage by computer. Even Bert Powers, the militant head of the New York printers, pronounced automation inevitable; "the question is how and when." While other newspapers were rapidly automating, the *Washington Post* dawdled; indeed, the company was signing labor agreements that locked it into costly and, in view of the new hardware, unnecessary production practices.

"In New York the publishers took on the unions by shutting down," a *Post* executive at the time recalled, adding that "At the *Post* the decision was if we can't publish without the unions then we're going to make the best deal we can." In the early 1960s, the *Post* was in the ascendancy, having overtaken and raced ahead of the *Evening Star*, becoming number one of the city's three dailies in circulation and advertising. Money was rolling in. "They were afraid that any strike long in duration would hurt that rise," the former executive said. "Negotiate, but for Christ's sake, don't let anything happen" was the unwritten rule at the *Post.* Those reasons were overshadowed by a central reality: The *Post* then could not be produced without union labor even if the company so desired.

Katharine Graham succeeded her husband at the *Post* in the year of the long New York newspaper strike with its inescapable message for her. By 1969 Katharine Graham's novitiate in business administration was over. Gaining circulation and bulging with advertising, the *Washington Post* for several years in a row had been yielding pre-tax earnings of at least 15 percent on gross revenues. That performance was better than most industries; nevertheless, Mrs. Graham was uneasy as she planned her newspaper's future. The darkest clouds on the horizon were the sharply rising costs of producing the paper and worsening labor relations. New management was urgently needed if a storm were to be avoided, the owner of the *Post* concluded.

In January she picked fifty-year-old Paul Ignatius as publisher. Ignatius, a former Harvard Business School professor, had climbed the Pentagon ladder during the Kennedy and Johnson administrations to become secretary of the navy. He had no newspaper experience; it was assumed that anyone who could run the fleet could run a newspaper. What apparently was decisive in his selection was that he carried the recommendation of Robert S. McNamara, the former secretary of defense who was a close friend and advisor of Mrs. Graham.

Ignatius had rough sailing. The paper's earnings slid $3 million in 1970 from the year before, which was not his doing. In 1971 the Newspaper Guild outmaneuvered him by rejecting management's two "final" proposals, holding out for and winning minimum salaries that doubled those of just five years earlier.

At the same time the printers were warming up to negotiate for a new contract in 1972. They slowed work in the composing room, a tactic they had used before as a bargaining lever. Deadlines in the newsroom on the floor above lost all meaning if the printers could thumb their noses at the schedules required to convert copy to type. The editors, who regard a deadline as sacred, were furious. Normally the presses were started at 10:15 P.M. When the printers were waging their war of nerves with the company, it was sometimes midnight before the presses could roll. On the *Post*'s loading dock the dealers protested to circulation men that they could not get the bundles of papers to carrier boys for home delivery by 6:30 A.M. because of late press runs. Advertisers complained that their copy was being miserably printed. All the while the maddening slowdowns were driving up overtime costs.

Ignatius correctly concluded that the printers were holding all the high cards in the contest with the paper. If even one of them were fired for willfully disrupting production, every other printer was likely to walk out in protest. Painfully aware that the *Post* could not publish so much as a handbill without them, Ignatius capitulated to the typographical union on a handsome new contract. He soon resigned, taking with him a severance payment of $150,000, which stockholders were told was a three-year consulting contract. (Ben Bradlee, the paper's executive editor, was said to be a candidate to replace Ignatius. He knew the business and was both tough and shrewd. But the newsroom was Bradlee's home. "I would rather crawl bare-ass down the street than take that job," he remarked.) The military, where Ignatius did well, was a wonderland of high technology. There was never a question of whether men would be willing to operate the increasingly sophisticated equipment. In the newspaper business it was the only real question. Computerized systems were now available that replaced skilled printers wholesale. That was the apparition staring at the hundreds of printers in the *Post*'s composing room; they were determined to resist it.

"Repro" or "bogus" or "deadhorse," as it was also known, was the most flagrant of the featherbedding practices in the composing room at the *Post* and many other newspapers. Under their labor contract, the printers reset advertisements that came to the paper in the form of mats, which otherwise required no processing by the typographical workers. As the *Post* ballooned with ads through the sixties, the backlog of reproduction work swelled geometrically. In 1967 thirty to thirty-five pages of "repro" every week were sitting in the composing room fore-man's office waiting to be reset. Within a few years, when entire advertising sections that were printed outside the *Post* plant for inser-tion into the paper were added to the "repro" obligation, the rate of backlog was more than two hundred pages a week.

"Repro" was the printers' security blanket; it assured them work without end. And there was so much of it that any union card-carrying printer could count on walking in and going to work. In truth newspa-per publishers were being hoisted on their own petard. They had developed reproduction long ago as a competitive weapon to compel work in their own plants that otherwise would be done in other print shops and delivered to them ready for use. The *Post,* of course, was passing along the unseen expense of "bogus" in its ad rates without any apparent discouraging effect on advertisers. By the 1970s the *Post* was getting 70 percent of Washington's daily newspaper advertising; it climbed to fifth place in advertising among America's newspapers. Nevertheless, the slowdowns and make-work practices in the compos-ing room were eating into the *Post*'s profits. Katharine Graham's head-aches would really be over if the *Post* could plug in the latest automated equipment. It would enable classified ad-takers, reporters, and editors sitting at electronic consoles to do the printers' jobs with remarkably more efficiency. Their copy would move into computers that spewed it out as photocomposed columns easily pasted up by unskilled hands into page forms. The forms would then be photographed and the negatives turned into plates for the presses. That would dispose of "bogus" and work stoppages by disposing of the printers. Many printers disbelieved in automation; others told themselves the *Post* would never trade them for machines.

Mrs. Graham's frustration with Paul Ignatius, a newspaper outsider, had cost him his job. She replaced him in late 1971 with an industry insider, John Prescott. Prescott wanted to be a journalist, but at Wil-liams College he found himself working with printers and selling ads to keep the nearly defunct school paper alive. After Williams, Prescott went to work in the commercial department of the *Baltimore Sun.* He found working conditions there so bad that he began organizing the place for the Newspaper Guild. He was an almost shy, methodical man who wasn't given to bantering. Before coming to the *Post,* Prescott was a prized executive of the giant Knight-Ridder newspaper chain. At the annual Post Company stockholders meeting in May 1972, Mrs. Graham made clear who she was holding responsible to cure the *Post*'s ills: "John Prescott and his able management team are determined to cope with the escalating costs of material services and labor." Prescott was to be new point man for her counteroffensive against the unions.

The *Post* and the city's other two dailies, the *Star* and the *Washington Daily News,* joined forces to plan for upcoming union negotiations under Prescott's chairmanship. The trio hired a public relations firm to help fashion their pitch to labor and give the campaign a slogan, "It's a new ballgame." The heart of their argument was that while the cost of living had increased 47 percent in recent years, wages on the papers had at least doubled. Unknown to Prescott his two allies were talking to each other on a more urgent matter.

The *Post* was doing well, albeit less well than Mrs. Graham insisted was possible. The *News* and the *Star,* however, were sinking into financial quicksand. The tabloid *News* had lost money from its founding in 1921 to 1942, but Jack Howard insisted that his Scripps-Howard newspaper chain needed the prestige of a voice in the nation's capital, no matter the cost. The *News* was the paper of Ernie Pyle, the best known correspondent of World War II. In the years when the *News* did turn a profit, the best it ever did was half a million dollars in 1963. In 1967 the paper was back in the red to stay and in 1972 it lost $2 million. As for the 110-year-old *Star* it lost $4.5 million in 1971 and again in 1972. The *Star*'s owners had been negotiating secretly for months to buy the *News* in expectation of adding much of its 217,000 circulation to the *Star*'s 301,000. The *Star*'s owners, undoubtedly remembered how the *Post* had bought the *Times-Herald* eighteen years before, beginning the *Post*'s ascendancy.

In July the *Star* bought the *News,* which ceased publication. (The

News's death left New York the only city in the country with three independently owned newspapers.) John H. Kauffman, president of the Star Company, said, "If we didn't do something in Washington, we'd have ended up as a one-newspaper town." While the *Star* did gain about 100,000 subscribers from the acquisition, it picked up only about one-third of the *News*'s advertising. The *Star* still lost $5 million in 1973 and even more than that in 1974. Combined, the *Star* and *News* had less circulation and advertising than the *Post.*

Among the *Daily News*'s weaknesses was that it sold primarily in the District of Columbia while metropolitan Washington's huge population growth was concentrated in the suburbs of Maryland and Virginia. By the early 1970s the District's population was 76 percent black. Newspaper advertisers were pursuing the more affluent newspaper readers in predominantly white suburbia. Many of them also wanted a newspaper more sophisticated than the tabloid *News.* The riots that ripped through the central business district and black neighborhoods in April 1968 after the murder of Dr. Martin Luther King, speeded the end of the *News* by further diminishing downtown shopping.

In October 1969, another event occurred that was to be one of the final nails in the *News*'s coffin and was a precursor of subsequent labor troubles at the *Post* two blocks away. Union pressmen simultaneously struck the *News,* the *Star,* and the *Post.* The *News,* the smallest of the three dailies, spunkily printed fifteen thousand copies of an abbreviated edition with the help of supervisors from other newspapers in the Scripps-Howard chain. It was the first time a modern Washington daily had been produced by nonunion workers. After a throng of pickets blocked delivery trucks from leaving, the *News* stopped its presses. While Scripps-Howard was in court seeking an injunction to restrain the pickets, the *Post* and *Star* reached agreement with the pressmen to work at the two papers for five days while both sides tried to produce a new contract. Knowing the *News* was going to attempt to publish despite the strike, the *Star* and *Post* seemingly concluded there was nothing to gain by their staying shut. The *Post,* in particular, was in a far better position to pay the higher labor costs than the *Star* and the *News.* Less than three years later the *News* was gone. Some senior executives at the *News* felt the *Star* and the *Post* had helped wittingly, but not cooperatively, to bring about their paper's death by making separate deals with the striking pressmen.

The end of the *News,* the straits of the *Star,* and the slight downturn of the *Post*'s profits told the newspaper unions that, indeed, management was going to play a "new ball game." John Prescott hired men who shared his commitment to rein in the unions. One of them, James Cooper, as a young man had carried a stereotyper's union card, but he gave it up and later worked for the *Miami Herald* after the paper rid itself of organized labor. When word reached the *Post* composing room in the summer of 1972 that Cooper would be the new production manager, signs appeared branding him a "scab." The stereotypers threatened to fine any member ten dollars who so much as talked to him. The silent treatment was lifted eight months later after Cooper improved conditions in the stereotype shop.

Had Kansas-born Lawrence A. Wallace, another Prescott recruit, been less impatient as a young man, he might have found himself on the other side in the *Post*'s battles with the unions. In graduate school in the 1950s, Wallace thought about working later for a newspaper union. When he was told that union executives came up through labor's ranks, Wallace chose to work for the publishers' side. A year after Wallace joined the *San Jose Mercury* in 1958, it was shut down by a 128-day strike and lock-out of union pressmen. It took nine months for the *Mercury* to regain the circulation it lost because of the stoppage. That episode led Wallace to adopt the bargaining principle, "Never take a strike over wages." The long-term costs of such a strike are far greater, he concluded, than the cost of a settlement for higher pay. He was the labor relations director for the *Detroit Free Press* when it suspended publication in 1967 during a 268-day strike which almost killed the paper. Labor knew Wallace as a well-prepared, dogged negotiator who studied the politics of the other side. Political divisions between the locals and the parent international newspaper unions could complicate bargaining, or be turned to management's advantage. A local can't strike or propose contract charges without the international's sanction. On one occasion when the Detroit newspapers anticipated a stiff fight over a new printers' contract, Wallace induced international officers to meet secretly with him and other management emissaries in Florida to hear the publishers' case against the local's demands. The tactic worked to prevent a strike. The meeting, arranged by the Federal Mediation Service, was kept secret from the local for fear its members would rebel against the backstage support of the owners by the international. The coming of Wallace hard on the heels of Prescott and Cooper convinced the unions that the *Post* was preparing to deal with them in a wholly new and aggressive way. The evidence, alarming to the unions, was not long in coming.

The printers were the chief target of the *Post*'s hard line strategy to cut blue-collar labor costs. At the Post Company's *Newsweek* a new system for computerized photocomposition typesetting would soon so reduce labor costs that the price of the equipment was repaid in the first year—a lightning-quick 100-percent return on the company's investment. Clearly the *Post*'s composing room offered the certainty of the quickest and largest gains in manpower savings if the fiercely individualistic and proud printers could be persuaded, for a price, to accept wholesale automation. The printers were the godfathers of newspaper labor. In 1778, printers went on strike in New York: the Franklin Typographical Society of Journeymen Printers was formed there in 1779. Until the turn of the century the pressmen and other newspaper crafts had belonged to the printers union. Even some reporters and editors had once been members of the "typos."

The seven hundred or so printers at the *Post* were caught in a collision between man and machine. The inventiveness of some men was ending the need for the skills of others. In October 1973, a *Post* printer, Eugene Mueller, told reporter William Greider: "Automation, we talk about this every day. We're talking about people, humanity. How much further can they go? The upper echelons of the *Washington Post* have lost complete touch with the working people in this building. We're human beings, we got problems, we got families. We're not a bunch of wild-eyed radicals." Greider quoted Mueller in a long Sunday feature. Greider, one of the *Post*'s best writers and an essayist, a rarity in daily journalism, presented a sensitive and balanced analysis of both sides of the brewing controversy.

The next day Greider, whose face bears a Lincolnesque sadness, was talking with other reporters in the newsroom when Katharine Graham appeared beside them. She irritatedly braced Greider for "romanticizing those bastards." Taken aback, he replied that he had talked to Prescott and Wallace and apologized for not interviewing her. Even Wallace in talking to Greider had resisted attacking the printers because of the volatility of the negotiations. Whether Mrs. Graham would have been less restrained in talking for attribution is conjectural. As her criticism grew sharper, Greider's colleagues retreated as though someone had dropped a sputtering grenade among them. She left Greider embarrassed and dismayed. In the weeks that followed the printers continued their exasperating snarling tactics. Ben Bradlee told Greider, "Your friends, the Ben Franklins, are at it again." Actually, some of the printing problems were caused by bugs in the limited computerized systems the *Post* was experimenting with.

When printer Eugene Mueller asked rhetorically, 'How much further can they [management] go?' he did not have to wait long for the answer. Management waged its own war of nerves. A dozen or so printers were selected for training as supervisors, a job category not covered by the union contract. Other printers suspected their co-workers were being groomed to be a loyal corps to run the composing room in the event of a strike. They ridiculed the training as a "charm school." Workers noticed that a wooden catwalk had been erected to span a narrow alleyway between the roof of the newspaper building and the adjacent Pick-Lee House, which a hotel company leased from the *Post*. They concluded that the *Post* in the event of a walkout, would billet non-strikers in the hotel and use what union workers quickly called the "rat walk" to avoid picket lines. In mid-September John Prescott sent a letter to each printer warning that anyone who intentionally disrupted operations would be fired. The printers were enraged that the notices were mailed to their homes in an obvious attempt to raise anxieties within their families.

Prescott's staff planned for a "worst case" strike in which they would try to publish with only three hundred or four hundred of the

Post's regular 2,600 employees. They assumed that even with this decimation of the ranks, they could turn out, with nonunion workers, a forty-page daily. There might be minor vandalism to production facilities, they speculated; they worried about the building's power supply. Acid or explosives dropped through a steel grate could knock out the vital underground electric transformer in the alley behind the *Post* building. If the transformer were disabled, the Russian Embassy just across the alley would also be blacked out.

While negotiations to obtain a breakthrough for massive automation in the composing room dragged on, the *Post* was clandestinely readying Project X, the company's ultimate weapon against the craft unions' ultimate weapon, the walkout.

The key, of course, to getting out the paper during a strike was the availability of competent surrogates for the strikers. Newspaper publishers around the country for decades in the past made use of a Philadelphia firm called H. W. Flagg, Open Shop Division, which furnished strike-bound papers with flying squads of strike-breakers. The *Post,* liberal in its world view and for years anything but meanspirited toward its employees, in 1973 was desperate to install labor-saving systems. It found an ally in a union-busting organization that was a spiritual descendent of H. W. Flagg: the Newspaper Production and Research Center in Oklahoma City. Financed by approximately five hundred newspaper publishers, the Center was started in 1951 by Robert H. Spahn, the production manager of the *Daily Oklahoman* and the *Times.* Spahn had eliminated the eight unions at the two newspapers. The same thing happened at many other dailies whose people were trained by Spahn to replace striking news and production workers. The *Sunday Times* of London labeled the place a "school for scabs." Newspaper owners, through Spahn's center, had what amounted to a publishers' NATO. Spahn arranged for nonunion papers to send skilled hands to strikebound journals in a smooth-running mutual assistance pact.

In 1973 the *Post* sent sixty trusted white-collar employees to Spahn's school. Most of them worked in the advertising and commercial departments which are covered by the Newspaper Guild. The *Post*'s contract with the Guild exempts a small percentage of workers from compulsory membership in the union; from their ranks came the Project X recruits. Those who were willing to go to Oklahoma for three weeks were asked to keep their destination and mission secret even from their families lest the unions learn prematurely of the *Post*'s plans.

On the *Post*'s seventh floor, three tiers above the composing room and hidden from general view, was a machine the size of an office water cooler with a computer for a brain. It could do the work of 115 printers without getting overtime or a pension or sick leave. Project X also involved secretly training nonunion employees to use the device. Called an optical character scanner, it could read copy by computer and convert it to type. Such preparations, however, could not be kept secret for long. Prescott soon outlined Project X to the unions in an attempt to convince them that the company now had the means to print without them and, most essentially, intended to do just that if necessary. The unions were disturbed by the notion that an ad-taker or secretary with only three weeks' training might replace a pressman or printer whose apprenticeship lasted four years. Disturbed, but disbelieving.

At 7:45 A.M. on November 2, John Prescott made good his written warning that any *Post* printer who intentionally snagged production of the paper risked dismissal: A foreman fired Michael Padilla, who had been at work since before midnight on the "lobster" shift, for a willful slowdown. Immediately the other printers refused to continue working and they refused to leave the composing room. The company got a restraining order against them and U. S. Marshals hustled the printers from the building the next day. If they were to hold the company at bay, the printers needed the support of the other crafts.

Outside the *Post* the head of the printers, Bob Mason, climbed onto a parked car and appealed to a milling crowd of pressmen, "Don't betray us!" The pressmen agreed to support the typographical union. (Two years later the pressmen felt betrayed by the printers who eventually went back to work through the pressmen's strike lines.) On Saturday night union leaders met at a nearby hotel with John Prescott and labor relations director Lawrence Wallace to seek an end to the Padilla affair. There had been no *Post* that day; it seemed to the union chiefs Sunday would also pass without publication.

Early in the meeting, Charles Davis, the head of the stereotypers who were represented by the pressmen's union, asked Prescott, "Is anyone working in our jurisdiction?" Prescott replied no. That wasn't true. Prescott knew that some fifty Project X workers were busy in the building preparing to print a forty-page newspaper. The engravers, who make the metal plates that carry images of photographs and drawings, had entered the plant, ostensibly to work, but really to keep watch on any attempt to publish without the other unions. Every half hour or so an engraver telephoned the union executives at the hotel to report on the activities of the stand-ins. Prescott and Wallace left the meeting and walked to the *Post.* Before midnight, almost two hours after the regular time for starting the presses, Prescott phoned James Dugan, the thirty-four-year-old head of pressmen's Local 6. "We're going to go without you," Prescott told him. Dugan, cursing angrily, slammed down the receiver. He shot out of his chair. Prescott's blunt message was a declaration of war on the unions. Katharine Graham, who was in her office through the night, had approved Prescott's decision to publish without the craft unions.

Dugan was the most respected of the labor leaders at the *Post.* Clerks and ad-takers, Dugan realized, could be quickly trained to use the new automated apparatus to compose a newspaper. What he believed they were unprepared to do was to run the giant, high-speed presses without disastrous results. Dugan, his head bare to the cool night, led more than one hundred pressmen, who had been waiting outside the hotel for word of the meeting, back to the *Post.* Most of the pressmen believed they were going in to run the presses. Dugan's plan, shared with a few others in Local 6, was to occupy the pressroom, but not print the paper until the printers' demands were met. "We'll run those damn presses," Dugan told the husky six-foot-five Prescott who blocked the employees entrance with his body. Skeptical, Prescott hesitated; then he stood aside for the pressmen.

Inside the pressmen found fifteen graduates of Oklahoma City dressed in coveralls. To the pressmen's surprise, five presses had been "webbed up" with newsprint from 1600-pound spools threaded between the heavy cylinders on which curved printing plates were fitted into place. A press of the black start button would engage the presses. "Get those scabs out of here," the pressmen shouted. They left. Dugan told Prescott the price for running the presses was the return of all the unions to the building along with the fired Michael Padilla. Prescott's blue eyes narrowed angrily through his horn-rims. He reminded Dugan of his pledge without strings a few minutes earlier to have his pressmen work. "I lied to you," snapped Dugan. It wasn't much of a sin, he decided, because Prescott had lied when he told the unions that no work was being done on their turf.

Dugan had the *Post* in checkmate. Long after that tumultuous night Prescott said of his adversary: "Jimmy Dugan should have been selected to be a foreman. He was better than his boss and, therefore, the men followed him." Fifty marshals were waiting elsewhere in the building to clear a path if pickets blocked deliverymen from picking up the newspapers the *Post* had expected to print. Prescott said that the court order in the marshals' hands might be used to evict the pressmen since they were engaged, he believed, in an illegal work stoppage. Dugan warned that he would not be responsible for what his men might do in anger over nonunion employees working on "our presses." Facing the pressmen, Prescott became convinced that they would not leave peacefully. There was every chance of an ugly battle among the close-packed presses; they might be damaged in a mêlée between flak-jacketed police and workers.

Prescott left to meet with Mrs. Graham and others to take stock of their predicament. "They've got us by the ying-yang," one of the executives groaned in frustration. As soon as Prescott left the pressroom, the pressmen tore out the newsprint that nonunion hands had inserted preparatory to printing the *Post.* For the next two hours, Prescott met with Dugan and the heads of the other unions. Finally he explained to Mrs. Graham his decision to yield to the union. She endorsed it. The company reinstated Padilla, hardly saving face by placing a reprimand in his record. The pressmen then printed ninety thousand Sunday papers, about one-eighth of the normal circulation.

Before they did, they "censored" the *Post*'s story of the dispute by
chiseling from the page plates a sentence noting that type for the paper
was set by nonunion workers.

Prescott felt humiliated; the galling end of the affair seemed more
harsh to accept than his predecessor, Paul Ignatius's, capitulation to the
printers in 1971. At that time the *Post* had no way to publish without
the unions. Now they had Project X. They had carefully planned it as
though it were the invasion of Normandy. It gave the *Post* a counterweight to the unions' power; and they had actually employed it, almost
completely, only to be torpedoed by a stubborn Irishman. No one
would forget that night.

When the company backed down out of fear of violence, the
pressmen were convinced that the threat of force could be decisive in
getting their way. The unions, though, drew the wrong conclusion from
the wild events of that autumn night. Project X, after all, came within
a hair of producing a newspaper; next time, knowing it could be done,
the company might go all the way rather than be humbled again. For
all their blustering about "scabs," the pressmen knowingly printed a
paper composed mostly by strikebreakers. The explanation for this
grave breech of union dogma lay in the rivalry between the printers and
the pressmen and Jimmy Dugan's personal ambitions. Years ago the
pressmen had split away from the International Typographical Union,
believing independence would strengthen their own bargaining power.
The printers' wages still exceeded the pressmen's scale, but with their
considerable muscle, the pressmen might change that. Dugan had won
the typos' fight over Padilla; he had proved himself the most effective
union leader in the plant and was talking about the possibility of a
strong union bloc under his direction to face the *Post*. By printing the
paper that morning, Dugan demonstrated the printers' dependence on
him. Dugan was cock of the union roost at the *Post*.

Slowdowns persisted; management continued to stonewall union
complaints. "Bagging the webs" was one of the simplest and surest
ways to deliberately delay the presses. When the presses are running
the thin newsprint speeds tautly between the cylinders. A small dart
of paper or a paper clip fired with a rubber band at the stream of

newsprint could break the paper and shut down the press. During a normal printing of the *Post* there might be 26 or 27 web breaks, each one requiring about eight minutes or so for the pressmen to mend. On one night soon after the Padilla incident, according to a story in the *Post,* there were 72 breaks; on the night of January 31 and early the next morning, 147 web breaks were reported. The pressmen took as long as a half hour to restore the webs. Sometimes the press runs were so laggard that management cut off printing because it was too late to meet street sale and home delivery deadlines.

In the midst of the unrelieved strife, the unions and the company met hurriedly in an unsuccessful attempt to cool the situation. "This place is going to explode one day," Dugan told Mrs. Graham. She calmly replied that she thought he was overreacting. On another occasion Dugan and Charles Davis, the head of the stereotypers local, went to Mrs. Graham's office to ask, "What's the war for?" They were, she said, misreading the situation; there was no war. Nor was there peace. In April 1974, there was a most peculiar seventeen-day strike at the *Post* by the Newspaper Guild. It was the first Guild strike against the paper ever.

The Guild, the youngest of the unions in the newspaper industry, was established in Washington in December 1933, during the depths of the Great Depression. Journalists had tried for forty years to establish a union. With reporters and editors being laid off or suffering deep wage cuts as newspaper revenues declined, the time for such a union was at hand. The newsroom usually was the first place publishers cut expenses because the news staffs were unorganized. In June 1933 Congress passed the National Industrial Recovery Act which authorized codes to limit working hours and provide other benefits, industry by industry. Professionals were not covered by these codes; the newspaper publishers argued that editing and reporting were professional jobs, hence the new law did not protect them.* Heywood Broun, the *New*

---

*The American Newspaper Publishers Association asserted that editorial unionism was a threat to freedom of the press. The Supreme Court, in upholding the right of newsroom workers to unionize under the National Labor Relations Act ruled, "The publisher of a newspaper has no special immunity from the application of general laws."

York World-Telegram columnist who spearheaded the formation of the Guild, challenged this self-serving contention, observing:

The men who make up the papers of this country would never look upon themselves as what they really are—hacks and white collar slaves. Any attempt to unionize leg, re-write, desk or make-up men would be laughed to death by these editorial hacks themselves. Union? Why, that's all right for dopes like printers, not for smart guys like newspapermen!

Yes, and those "dopes," the printers, because of their union, are getting on an average some 30 percent better than the smart fourth estaters. And not only that, but the printers, because of their union and because they don't permit themselves to be called high-faluting names, will now benefit by the new NRA regulations and have a large number of their unemployed re-employed, while the "smart" editorial department boys will continue to work forty-eight hours a week because they love to hear themselves referred to as "professionals" and because they consider unionization as lowering their dignity.

Broun accurately perceived the source of much of the friction that has plagued the Guild for more than four decades. Unlike the newspaper craft unions which are comprised of workers with a single skill—such as the photoengravers, pressmen, stereotypers, printers, mailers, and paper handlers—the Guild is a mixed bag covering advertising, business, and circulation workers, as well as journalists. At the outset, many joiners of the Guild argued that it confine its membership to the newsroom. They believed the Guild should be a professional, as well as a collective bargaining organization. By 1937, however, ". . . the sad experience of bitterly fought strikes had by now taught them [the Guild] that alone they had little economic strength; that newswriters by themselves could not easily shut a paper down in order to enforce their demands for hours and pay." Preceded by a lengthy intraunion battle, the Guild voted that year to widen its membership to include all non-craft newspaper employees. "The move strengthened its negotiating position and made the union more attractive to some prospective members," a labor magazine recalled. "Conversely, however, it reduced its appeal to those editorial employees who were, and are, afflicted with a sense of their own professional superiority. Many of them preferred an elite craft membership, no matter how weak, to an industrial union, no matter how strong." These elements, recognized early in the life of the Guild, were still alive forty years later.

On April 8, 1974, at 4 P.M. when the tempo in the *Post* newsroom quickens as deadlines near, the Guild went on strike against the paper. They walked out almost gaily. Before the walkout the *Post*'s labor relations chief Larry Wallace and the Guild's negotiators led by Brian Flores, a thirty-nine-year-old former *Post* commercial artist, holed up for several days in a motel bargaining unsuccessfully over a new contract. The sessions had moments of street theater as Flores baited Wallace for being a union-baiter. Before Wallace's and Flores's day, the bargaining usually proceeded in a serious, but friendly, manner. When a sticking point developed over a clause, the union negotiator and the *Post*'s man might go to the men's room and settle the issue while standing at the urinals, an editor recalled. The editors wanted their staffs to be well and fairly paid. In 1971 Ben Bradlee congratulated a Guild officer on winning a handsome increase in minimum salaries; in four years the minimums had increased to $400 from $200 a week, a 100 percent gain. Management, however, always wanted some provision that would allow the editors to fire an employee they deemed "dead wood" but who was protected by the labor contract. Philip Graham agreed to higher wages, but in return he demanded what came to be known by the union and management as the "immoral clause." It provided a way to dismiss an employee even if an arbitrator had ruled in his favor. The company could get rid of the worker by paying him severance plus an additional sum. "It assured that a victorious employee would not prevail," Morton Mintz, an old Guildsman, remembered. "It took thirteen years to get it out of the contract."

Brian Flores, who ran the Baltimore-Washington Newspaper Guild which included the *Post,* played his cards tightly in 1974, sharing little of his strategy with the other Guild bargainers. There was, of course, a concern about wages: Wallace made clear that the days of the fat pay increases were over. Flores, ambitious to move up in the union hierarchy, was more intent on converting the loyalty of his members from the *Post* to the union. This he sought to accomplish by bringing the employees' health plan under Guild administration and substituting a retirement system with some union control, for the company-run profit-sharing plan.

The company established profit-sharing with *Post* stock in lieu of a pension plan in 1953. The news staff called it "The Melon," and it grew sweeter and sweeter as the company prospered. Eugene and Agnes Meyer three years later, separate from profit-sharing, gave almost $500,000 worth of their *Post* stock to more than seven hundred employees in gratitude for their service. (One share then was valued at about $60; before *Post* stock became publicly available in 1971, a share was worth $1,154. By mid-1979 the value of one of those 1950s shares had increased a hundredfold to $5,520.) Reporter Eddie Folliard was an institution on the *Post.* Fired in an economy move in 1932, Folliard was hired back after Meyer bought the paper. He had a slice of "The Melon" and shares from the Meyers. Folliard wrote to Meyer in 1958 after the *Post* stock doubled in value: "I suppose it sounds strange for a newspaper reporter to be talking about finance in this way. The Lord knows that I didn't start on a journalistic career with any idea of getting wealthy. What has happened, I suppose, is that we have something new in journalism, something that might be called Meyer's Law. It is this: that newspaper people can do good work and be happy, without at the same time being shabby and improvident." The company had its own reasons for wanting to end profit-sharing. The plan, once a way to inspire loyalty and greater productivity, wasn't spurring either, Mark Meagher said. Besides in the long haul a regular retirement plan would be cheaper for the *Post.* Flores and the company agreed to end profit-sharing over the protests of some of the other unions.

"What kind of a bullshit strike is this?" asked an incredulous Jimmy Ingraham, a rangy, cigar-smoking pressman. There was no picket line. Never before had the Guild struck a newspaper anywhere without setting up a strike line. This unorthodox strategy—the walkout was soon dubbed "the Polish strike"—was prompted by the printers' fear of implementation of Project X if they honored a Guild picket line. The printers, moreover, were still mired in negotiations over automation with no solution in sight. By some reliable accounts, the International Typographical Union told the Guild that the typos would work regardless of the strike. Others say the automation-vulnerable unions asked the Guild not to establish a picket line that would compel them as devout trade unionists to stay out. Jimmy Dugan, however, unthreatened by automation in the pressroom, pledged to the guildsmen, "Put up the line and there won't be a single pressman cross it." Dugan had the power to expel from his union any member who did so.*

The Guild, without a picket line, said its weapon was to "deny excellence" to the *Post.* "I don't know how long they can stand to have the big bylines off the front page," declared Brian Flores. There was one big but long absent byline on the front page the next morning. Benjamin C. Bradlee reported the sale of the *Washington Star* to Texas multimillionaire Joe E. Allbritton. Within a few days the Guild optimistically predicted the *Post* "will soon be a joke." The joke was on the union. Bradlee, reverting to the police reporter he was a generation earlier, chased down a murder case in the suburbs. Katharine Graham, who once was a Guild-card-carrying reporter in San Francisco, wrote articles and took classified ads. The senior editors and a handful of union-exempt staffers worked twelve to fourteen hours a day, seven days a week. It was exhausting. It also was exhilirating for a while for editors in their forties and fifties to prove their legs were still good. Some of the printers felt uneasy about handling copy during the strike; a few times they dropped into stories, "This paper is edited by rats." But they still handled the "tainted" copy and the pressmen continued to print the paper.

The Guild at the *Post* was riven by dissension. Reporters Carl Bernstein, Bernard Nossiter, Murrey Marder, and Laurence Stern tried to break the impasse on their own. They met at two o'clock on a Sunday morning with Bradlee and managing editor Howard Simons to seek a way out of the cave of the winds in which the strikers felt trapped. Distrusting Flores, they wanted to hear from their bosses the *Post*'s

*In the wake of events at the *Post* and other papers, the Newspaper Guild and the International Typographical Union began planning a marriage of the two unions as a means to possibly regain some measure of their quondam bargaining strength. Through the 1890s the I.T.U. regarded newsroom workers as a threat because many of them could also set type and the union wanted to eliminate "reporter scabbing." With the advent of computerized systems for editing, producing type, and composing whole pages of a newspaper, reporters and editors are doing much of the printers' previous work.

terms. This bypassing of the union bargaining committee measured the schism between Flores and the newsroom rank and file. Four days later, after agreeing to a pay increase that was about what the company had first offered, the strikers came back to work.

As the workers approached the main entrance to the *Post* after voting in a nearby church, Bradlee, Simons, and other editors waved a welcome from the fifth floor windows. "Why did we prove to the world they could get along without us?" mused reporter Karlyn Barker as she entered the building. The strike seemed futile. During the strike the *Post* lost more than $176,000 in advertising, but it actually made a quarter of a million dollars because payroll savings exceeded lost revenues. The strike destroyed any semblance of a union coalition at the *Post.* Moreover, many in the newsroom anticipated correctly that their future paychecks would be fattened as blue-collar labor costs declined with automation. This wasn't a disposition hospitable to worker solidarity.

The *Post*'s new city room occupied most of the fifth floor. Gone was the seedy grayness of the old newsroom; in place of bare floors and battered chairs and desks, like props for *The Front Page,* were wall-to-wall carpeting, color-coordinated furnishings, and recessed fluorescent lighting. It was, said one wry reporter, "the only newsroom in the country that looked like the John Hancock Insurance Company." A few irreverent souls tried to restore a bit of the déclassé that had been exorcised by interior designers. Under a glass-covered firehose on the newsroom wall, art critic Paul Richards taped a sign saying, "Porno mechanico. Sculpture in glass. By Jan Grossenscrotum." He labeled a wall picture of a black farmer and his wife, "Merican Gothic." They stayed that way until an outsider on a tour of the *Post* asked about the titles. Hank Burchard, a big, square-faced reporter, and Carl Bernstein played ping-pong between their desks until an editor ordered the net removed.

Beneath the ribaldry and antics was the vague unhappiness, more than any economic complaint, that had triggered the strike but that was left unrelieved by a settlement which dealt with money, not human relationships. Bradlee picked it up on his "radar," but he was puzzled about what to make of it. The *Post* had become a big institution and Bradlee had made it so. It worried him. He hated the stuffy leadenness and self-protectiveness of large and successful organizations.

He asked George E. Reedy, a journalism professor at Marquette University, a Jesuit school, to try to explain the strike and the moody newsroom climate and, perhaps, write a book about it. Mrs. Graham didn't think much of the idea. White-haired Reedy, a former press secretary to President Johnson, was a humanist and a candid man. He spent several weeks talking to fifty or so people on the news staff and some company executives. Everyone was assured of anonymity. "People bared their souls to me," Reedy recalled. "I thought I should go back to Marquette and get ordained."

"Almost universally, people felt it was a struggle between the forces of light and the forces of darkness," Reedy continued. "It was Armageddon. They were contesting for Ben Bradlee against John Prescott, a decent man." Bradlee wanted to open a Chicago bureau, and Prescott, the general manager, said no. The staff saw that as an example of the clash between journalistic excellence and the pressures of the counting house. Reedy probed the causes of the strike and concluded: "I can only say this—that the economic factors were totally irrelevant to the strike. The real causes were intensely personal and linked to the 'family' aura that still hovers over the newspaper . . . by that I mean the relationship of Ben and other executives to the employees and not just the position of Kay Graham." Reedy described the situation at the *Post* as a bit reminiscent of Russia before the Revolution when trusting peasants believed their suffering would be eased, "If only the Czar knew." In the newsroom unhappy staffers were saying, in effect, "If only the Czarina knew." Reedy told Bradlee another attitude he had discovered: "The allegation is that you 'play favorites' and glory in pitting people against each other to a point where the office resembles a snake pit. In many instances, this may well be nothing but the alibi of the second-rate. But nevertheless, it is a widespread perception."

Reedy decided not to write a book, he explained later, because "a true account involved the use of psychological revelations that cut deep

into too many personal friends." Reedy put his findings in a long letter
to Bradlee. Bradlee never answered the letter. The problem would
linger.

With the Guild strike settled, the focus returned to the *Post* printers whose negotiations with the company were a matter of vocational
life and death. Their union brothers in New York, Pittsburgh, Baltimore, and St. Louis also were struggling to soften the blow of automation. After a printers' slowdown had lasted for nineteen days at the
New York *Daily News,* America's leading circulation daily, nonunion
secretaries began processing copy through automated machinery, completely bypassing the printers. At 3 A.M. on May 6 police cleared the
tabloid's composing room of printers who had suddenly been super-
numerated by young typists. In a couple of hours the *Daily News* was
coming off the presses, composed for the first time in its history by
nonunion workers. The International Typographical Union shied away
from supporting the New York printers. Convinced that the printers
no longer could defeat automation, the international hated to see its
treasury futilely drained to pay strike benefits.

As John Prescott saw it, 1974 was a propitious time for the printers
to strike a bargain that would net them a piece of the gains that
management expected from imposing the controversial equipment.
Printers in New York and elsewhere had settled for guarantees of
lifetime jobs, if they wanted them, and phased introduction of the
computers. The handwriting was clear on the composing room wall:
"The issue, it seemed, was no longer whether the printer would consent
to his own passing," Patrick Owens, a former labor reporter wrote in
MORE. "He had accepted the inevitable, however grudgingly. The
question was the price he would be paid to agree to go. He was
bargaining away a right with slight claim in American law or philosophy
—the right to a job—and the whole question was what he should
receive from the huge savings his passing would make possible."

In September, fourteen months after negotiations started, the
printers union bowed to the inevitable and signed a contract ending
"bogus" typesetting. The forty thousand pages of backlogged reproduc-

tion work was valued by the company at $2.6 million. Within two weeks of the signing the company divvied up this kitty among the printers, some of them getting as much as nine thousand dollars. The contract met the burning issue of job security. Each of the 773 printers could keep his or her job, but financial carrots to leave were dangled in front of them; anyone who retired would get a pension plus a five-thousand-dollar bonus. Within six months 174 printers had taken the money and run. The following March, the company showed how eager it was to be rid of surplus printers by more than tripling the bonus to eighteen thousand dollars. A few months later, it sweetened the pot further with health insurance. "It was like wild card poker," said the *Post*'s labor negotiator, Larry Wallace.

By late 1977 there were approximately five hundred printers left in the composing room. By this wholesale buy-out, the *Post* achieved major savings immediately and opened the way to bigger, long-term savings from unimpeded automation. Each one hundred workers dropped reduced the composing room payroll by roughly $1.3 million. More men and women were leaving, often to escape the enervating boredom of trying to look busy in the composing room where the company believed it could do nicely with no more than 250 printers. What might be worse, of course, was having no job at all.*

By late summer John Prescott felt rather good as he surveyed things. He had accomplished a large piece of the tough task Katharine Graham hired him to do thirty-three months earlier. His colleagues bought fourteen hundred dollars worth of luggage to give him at an office party planned for the day after the printers ratified the breakthrough agreement. With no warning to Prescott, Mrs. Graham called Prescott to her office on the day of the party. She and Larry H. Israel, president of the Post Company, told Prescott that he was being made president of the newspaper division mainly to watch over the company's newly acquired financially troubled *Trenton Times.* It was a less consequential job, in Prescott's view. Disheartened and shaken, Prescott came back

*This outcome foreshadowed the 1978 victory of the *Post* and its partners at the *International Herald Tribune* over the printers union in Paris where the *Trib* wanted to employ the labor-slashing composition machinery. The union surrendered to the *Trib*'s offer of cash to severed workers and its threat to move to Zurich.

to a cheerless drink with a few associates in his office. He said nothing to them about his new job until the company issued an announcement. Prescott subsequently resigned.

"To this day many *Post* executives don't know what Prescott did wrong," reporter Robert Kaiser wrote long after the episode. A high *Post* official said, "Mrs. Graham regarded John as non-decisive or procrastinating, but his style is to win over subordinates rather than command them. One of the advertising executives was playing around and even though lineage was going up, Mrs. Graham wanted him replaced. She wanted Jack Patterson, the circulation director, to groom his successor. Prescott was moving too slowly for her." "Katharine Graham has a heroic idea, probably based on her Washington friends, about what a manager should be," said another close observer. Someone close to Prescott described the irony of an enterprise like the *Post* that had built its fame and fortune on its communication skills but was now suffering a kind of organizational tongue-tiedness. "The problem is severe because you have highly talented writers and artists at one end putting words and drawings on paper and the pressmen and paper handlers at the other end—all of them putting out a product that's more perishable than lettuce. Prescott was constantly trying to break through the walls between the operations." Still another person who intimately knew the situation said Prescott was "a scapegoat for the labor problems." He was reducing those problems but not fast enough, apparently, to suit Mrs. Graham.

In the newsroom, too, Prescott's contretemps was a puzzlement. With an unintended hint of chauvinism, a senior *Post* staffer laid it to the publisher's impulsiveness. "There is the good Queen Kate and the bad Queen Kate," he said. "It all depends on how she's feeling that day." After she forced out Larry Israel as president of the company early in 1977, Mrs. Graham refused to discuss the affair: "If people say I murder and use arsenic I still won't comment." A reporter with many years on the *Post* said, "Mrs. Graham set out to prove she was a better newspaper publisher than Phil. Having done that, she then set out to prove she was a better businessman then her father." In the year ahead, 1975, Katharine Graham would be challenged as Phil Graham and Eugene Meyer never were.

NINE

The Pressmen's Strike

Great strikes are determined by public opinion, and public opinion is always against strikers who are violent. Therefore, in great strikes, all the efforts of the employers are devoted to making it appear that the strikers are violent.

—UPTON SINCLAIR, *The Brass Check*, 1919

DONALD GRAHAM had been asleep for two hours when the telephone jangled him awake. It was 4:50 A.M. As he hurriedly dressed and waited for a taxi to take him back to the *Washington Post,* the meaning of the telephone message struck hard: The newspaper's pressroom had been turned into a shambles by rebellious pressmen. There was fire. A foreman had been beaten. As the cab carried him through the empty, early morning streets that first day of October in 1975, the thirty-year-old heir to the *Washington Post* communications empire had a gnawing sense of doubt about his managerial judgment.

For weeks Graham, assistant general manager of the paper, had been meeting frequently with other key *Post* executives to plan how they would publish the newspaper if the long negotiations with the pressmen's union ended with a strike. When the possibility of sabotage of the presses was occasionally broached, the soft-spoken Graham dismissed the suggestion as "utterly implausible." The pressmen, he knew, were tough; they had won a climactic power struggle with *Post* managers by an audacious threat of force just two years earlier. But he also knew that Thanksgiving and Christmas, the season of advertising-swollen newspapers, were approaching and with it the men in the pressroom could count on several paychecks of seven to eight hundred dollars a week because of overtime to get out the fat papers. Graham thought back to his optimism at one-thirty that morning when he confidently left the *Post* for his rambling old three-story house in Washington's Cleveland Park.

The *Post*'s contract with the pressmen had expired at midnight. James A. Dugan, the red-haired president of the pressmen's local, had then phoned the paper's labor relations director, Lawrence A. Wallace, from the nearby Post House bar to say that he was willing to continue bargaining later in the morning. "Anytime we feel like it we can hit the streets," Dugan added. A little earlier Dugan had handed Wallace a note saying, first, that his men were ending the contract, and second, "We are willing to work under the terms and conditions of the present contract only as long as meaningful negotiations continue." "We focused stupidly on the second half of the note," Graham thought as the cab reached the *Post.* He soon would be placed in command of the *Post*'s all-out struggle to publish.

His mother, the publisher of the *Washington Post,* was also hurrying back to her paper. She left her chauffeur asleep and drove herself the two miles from her home in Georgetown. Fire trucks and police cruisers, their red lights flashing, blocked Fifteenth Street in front of the *Post.* Katharine Graham had been through labor troubles before; the last several years they were chronic in the building. She sensed the anger that smouldered within many of the *Post*'s blue-collar workers toward her and the men she had hired to break the power of the unions over the production of her newspaper.

Nevertheless, an assault on the presses, the thundering engines of the newspaper industry, never entered the publisher's calculations for toughing out a strike. She could publish without the large corps of reporters, and had done so in 1974, and because of automation, also without union printers to set type and compose pages. But without the bank of nine marvelously engineered machines in the football-field-long pressroom, the *Post* was a helpless giant. No presses; no *Post.* As she edged through the scores of policemen, firefighters, and workers milling around the entrance, Kay Graham, fifty-eight years old, braced herself for the ordeal. The weeks and months ahead would be long and tense. When it was finally over in mid-winter and she had won she would be hailed as "the Iron Lady." Once inside the building, Mrs. Graham, worried that her car parked on the street might be damaged as the presses were, asked a young executive, Roger Parkinson, to move it to a safer spot. "Can you drive a Mercedes?" she asked, handing him the keys to the 450 SEL.

About a half hour before the two Grahams arrived, John Waits, the *Post*'s night production chief, phoned the pressroom foreman to ask why his own monitors showed that every press had stopped running although sixty-six thousand papers remained to be printed. No one answered. Waits surmised that foreman John Hover was already out in the pressroom seeking the same information.

Although Hover, a muscular, 190-pound Virginian, was a member of the pressmen's union, he was the immediate target of much of the men's antagonism to management. Hover, in the words of local president Jimmy Dugan, was "always like a bear with a sore ass. The production men would get on him and he passed it on to the pressmen." Dugan, a pressman at the *Post* for nine years, thought it was heresy for Hover to allow production supervisors to even sit in his office swivel chair, a symbolic defiance of the union contention that "the foreman always ran the pressroom." What Dugan really meant was that the union ran the place, controlling who would be hired, what they would do, and when they would work.

Unlike the composing room upstairs where automation had eliminated the need for skilled printers, experienced workers were still required to operate the high-speed presses. The company contended, however, that the union was forcing it to employ nearly double the number of pressmen that were actually needed to run the presses and to pay unnecessary overtime. Local 6 of the International Printing and Graphic Communications Union had amassed that power over two decades of bargaining with owners who were compliant, initially, because there was a shortage of pressmen at the expanding *Post;* then because the company was so profitable, there seemed no reason to change things. The shortage had long since passed. Profits had slipped.

Mrs. Graham said that the pressroom situation was intolerable and she meant to change it.

Negotiations between the Post Company and Local 6 had been underway since July. Anxiety heightened as the deadline neared with no sign that either the newspaper would bend its demands for sweeping changes in work rules or the pressmen would seriously consider such changes. Among the most militant pressmen were those who had come from other cities in recent years where their unions had been "busted" for refusing publishers' demands for cutbacks in manning and overtime. They had been replaced with nonunion workers. Those same demands confronted Local 6. If they yielded, these men counseled, it would mean the ultimate doom of the union. At a union meeting nine days before the September 30 deadline, a few members suggested that if a strike occurred fires should be set in the pressroom and key parts of the presses removed. After the meeting one journeyman was heard in the pressroom saying, "Well, if we do go out, maybe we should fix the press so it won't run no more. We're not going to win with strike signs, we're going to win it with baseball bats."

Now, with the deadline passed, John Waits' phone rang. "There's a riot down here," pressman foreman Hover blurted. "They beat the shit out of me." Waits called general manager Mark Meagher, who had decided to sleep on his office sofa in expectation of an early morning resumption of negotiations with the pressmen. He was pulling on his trousers as Waits entered with the forty-three-year-old foreman. Hover, bleeding from a deep gash over his right eye, was almost incoherent and crying in rage and frustration. Drops of blood fell on Meagher's orange shag rug. Hover had been hit repeatedly by one pressman while two others pinned his arms after he had discovered them and other pressmen vandalizing the presses.

Dugan had told the other unions as well as the *Post* negotiators that his men would not strike at midnight and would continue bargaining. A few hours later Dugan convened a chapel meeting (so called because the first printers and pressmen were priests who produced bibles in monasteries) in the pressroom. Dugan told the chapel that "every day they worked without a contract the company got stronger." He contended that a stiff-necked management would drag out the negotiations if the pressmen remained uncompromising but kept printing newspapers. Dugan and the six others of the local's negotiating committee unanimously recommended a walkout. The men loudly agreed. Dugan left to get placards for his pickets. Some fifteen or so members of Local 6 started an assault on the presses.

Eighteen months later, Donald Graham still kept on a closet shelf in his office a stack of 8 by 10 glossies to show to inquirers in detail the damage inflicted that morning: The slashed electrical wiring; jammed cylinders; sliced rubber blankets that cushion the heavy page plates on the cylinders; smashed gauges and controls that govern the flow of ink and missing tooled-metal nose cones that guide the speeding newsprint. One press was set ablaze, melting the lead plates on its cylinders. Automatic extinguishers had snuffed out the flames before they could spread to the three-quarter-ton rolls of newsprint in the reel room below.

At first glance that morning the pressroom looked like Attila the Hun had swept through. News accounts on television and in the newspapers persuaded the community, by and large, that the damage was devastating. While the *Post* was hurt for a time, the strike in the long run was actually a bonanza for the company. The sabotage of the presses—"our presses" the men had called them—also sabotaged the union. The pressroom was quickly repaired. Local 6 never recovered.

But why did Dugan give others to believe the pressmen would stay on the job? Dugan surely recalled the night in 1973 when the *Post*, using nonunion employees, made ready during a brief labor dispute to run the presses without his men. He suspected that the company was ready to do so again. Indeed, it was. Through the evening some 150 nonunion people in the advertising and commercial departments waited in the building to produce the newspaper if a strike occurred. They had been trained in Project X, which the *Post* unveiled in the 1973 labor trouble, to replace striking craftsmen. With the strike threat seemingly lifted around midnight, they were sent home. There now was no way to get out the paper that day without the pressmen. For the moment Dugan had outfoxed the company. Thus began what would be one of the longest and most bitter strikes in the history of the nation's capital. Its implications for the company and impact on many lives were deep.

Late in 1974 as Mark Meagher studied the documents in the blue loose-leaf binder he paused over the memos from the *Post*'s advertising department. The binder contained the newspaper's operating budget for the coming year. Advertising was expected to take a sharp drop because of a sagging economy. In Meagher's view this was further justification for the company's campaign to cut back the pressroom payroll. If there was going to be less advertising, there would be fewer pages of the newspaper, and thus fewer pressmen would be needed.

Without any advance discussion with the union—"we didn't feel it would do a helluva lot of good to sit down and talk with them," Meagher explained later—the company in late December posted a "markup"—an employee's instruction notice—on the pressroom wall that thirty-three regular jobs were being eliminated for 1975. The *Post* intended to convert the thirty-three regular pressmen into substitutes who would be required to work shifts at straight wages in place of other pressmen eligible for overtime pay. Jimmy Dugan met with Meagher for several days to argue against the reduction. A federal judge subsequently ruled that the *Post*'s unilateral action violated its contract with the local, and he ordered the old markup restored and the issue settled by arbitration. The judge also ordered the *Post* to pay the workers $72,000 in back wages. The victory cost the union $132,000 in legal and other expenses, according to Dugan. The episode reinforced Dugan's conviction that the *Post* was unscrupulous and out to break the pressmen's union. On a Saturday after the court decision Mrs. Graham appeared unexpectedly in the pressroom, apparently to evidence her willingness to talk. The pressmen turned their backs to her in silent protest. They began work slowdowns until the court told them to stop. For Dugan, further proof of the *Post*'s intentions toward Local 6 came when Meagher, referring to the contract, told him,

"Y'know what I'd like to do? I'd like to tear that book up and start all over again."

"I bet you would, sweetheart," the union chief retorted.

When Dugan complained about alleged violations of the contract, Meagher said, "Just be glad you've got a job." The remark provoked memories of hard times, and its significance was not lost on Dugan, the son of a union bricklayer.

The two protagonists appeared to be worlds apart. Dugan, an unpaid union official, in 1975 earned $17,300 working as a pressman, the most he ever made in one year. Meagher's contract then assured him at least $70,000 a year, plus attractive stock options and large cash bonuses if the company did well. In two years Meagher would become president of the Washington Post Company. At thirty-nine he had been the youngest director of the company, until the election of Donald Graham. Sometimes Meagher, now forty-four, would sit in a chair with his short legs crossed Indian style, punctuating his sentences with an occasional "Gee!" or "Christ." "Super," answered Meagher when an assistant asked how a business trip to Paris had gone. Dugan was more pungent in his expressions. *Post* managers conceded that he was the most effective of all the union leaders at the newspaper. Dugan was thirty-five. He had spent eighteen years in the pressrooms of three Washington newspapers. Meagher, whose father was a neighborhood druggist, grew up in the Catholic parish next to Dugan's in a middle-class neighborhood just over the Maryland line from Washington. "I'm a chaser," said Meagher of his rapid ascent in business. But as a young man he aspired to the spiritual rather than the corporate world, studying for the priesthood for a while.

After Meagher became general manager in 1974, he asked Dugan and Charles Davis, head of the stereotypers, who were represented by the pressmen's local, to have a friendly drink with him to discuss their differences. Davis and Dugan wanted to go to the Post House, a nearby bar where *Post* production workers congregated, but they ended up as Meagher's guests in the private University Club. They drank and it was all civil enough, but it left things unchanged. Meagher showed Dugan and Davis figures on the company's financial situation and the seeming high production costs. "You're making a lot of money; share the wealth," Dugan countered.

From the company's standpoint, the 1975 budget was a mix of

mostly rainbows and a few storm clouds. The payroll for craft workers
was projected to reach $26.4 million, an increase of $7.7 million from
1971. But there would be no overtime for the printers due to the
breakthrough contract signed the previous September, clearing the way
for full scale automation and sharply curtailing the composing room
crew. Indeed, the budget showed the newspaper's production payroll
as a share of its revenues actually had been declining, from 25.9 percent
in 1972 to 24.3 percent in 1974 with a further drop to 23.3 percent
likely in 1975. The newsroom budget, too, was taking a smaller percentage of revenues. Administration and the advertising department, which
generated the overwhelming share of the paper's income, got bigger
pieces of the operating budget. The 193 journeymen and apprentices
in the pressroom were expected to rack up more than $2 million just
in overtime and bonuses for special assignments. These pressroom
items led management's hit list. Another view of the pressmen's productivity came from Ben H. Bagdikian, former national editor of the
Post and an analyst of newspaper economics: "In the three years
preceding the [1975] strike, they increased their work hours five percent, far less than the eleven-percent increase in the paper's lineage,
a measure of pressroom work done."

Many of the pressmen took every advantage of the provisions of
their contract in order to get as much overtime and bonus pay as
possible. They would "shoot the angles," in their phrase, to work more
shifts at premium wages and fewer at straight time. This could sometimes mean working double shifts and for some it required putting in
three shifts back-to-back on weekends, starting early Saturday morning
and ending up the next morning with the final run of the bulky Sunday
Post. "Going to the whips," the pressmen called these triple-headers.
The pressroom was a noisy, possibly dangerous, factory. When the
presses were rolling, the air the men breathed was thickened with
newsprint dust and ink mist. There is some evidence in epidemiological
studies for suspecting a link between the spoiled air of pressrooms and
chemicals used in them and a higher rate of respiratory cancer among
a sample of pressmen. When the paper was being run off the roar of
the presses was intense. It was not uncommon for older pressmen to

be at least partially deaf as a result. One of them, Ray Foresman, who had been at the *Post* for seventeen years, said, "the noise and vibration make you irritable. There are a lot of quarrels. You still hear the sound of the presses at home."

From late night till dawn when the pressmen were the main inhabitants of the building, the quality and attractiveness of the food in the company cafeteria deteriorated. A top *Post* official agreed with the union that the pressroom was dirty and poorly maintained; the pressroom toilets, among other things, were in disrepair. Once when repeated requests to repair their soft drink machine went unheeded, Jimmy Dugan and his co-workers unplugged it, wrestled it onto an elevator and sent it upstairs with a note attached: "Mrs. Graham, please repair this machine." A security guard pleaded with them to remove the dispenser, lest he be fired, and they did; but the machine was soon fixed.

A handful of pressmen in 1974 shot the angles so artfully that their paychecks ran around $30,000, but they worked for it; it was "blood money," said a pressman's wife. That year the average wage in the pressroom was $22,500; at straight time a pressman would make approximately $14,500. Reporters and editors were making far more working straight time at what is variously called a profession, a craft, or a trade. No profit-oriented executive, many of whom were large stockholders in the company with an owner's stake in expanding profits, could be expected to long wink at angle-shooting. On one occasion Mark Meagher told a visitor, "I'm a high pricer," explaining that gains from manpower cuts along with higher advertising rates were the key to the *Post*'s big profits.

The *Post*'s manager-owners were quick to cast the first stone at the pressmen for gorging themselves on overtime; but the *Post* was not sinless. Years earlier when the Post Company planned its new nine-story building, the advertising and news departments were surveyed to determine what future press capacity would be needed. As a result the decision was to equip the seven old presses with new motors so each press could produce ten thousand more newspapers hourly and to buy two new faster presses. But both the revved-up and new presses could still print a paper no larger than 112 pages. When the *Post* ran to more than 112 pages—as it always did on Sundays, Thursdays and Saturdays—pressmen had to work day-runs to print advance sections of the paper, a system that is conducive to overtime. In contrast, the *Star* in the 1960s ordered presses with 144-page capacity for its own new building. The *Star*, for all its far-sightedness, was not rewarded with the volume of advertising that would require frequent weekday papers of 144 pages.

When the television and newspaper reporters asked Jimmy Dugan why his men vandalized the *Post* pressroom, he blamed the company's anti-union practices. He was belligerent and defensive. "Anything that has happened the management must take full responsibility for. . . . They have harassed and reprimanded the men. . . . They were stalling since December on a new contract." Pointing toward the buff-colored building behind him, Dugan said, "Anything that was done in there was born of frustration." His men "just went crazy and panicked"; the beating of foreman Hover and sabotage were "temporary insanity." Dugan had no chance to win at public relations.

Before all this, said John Dower, the *Post*'s public affairs director, "we recognized we would probably have a strike and it would be the toughest labor dispute we ever experienced because we were going to cut pressmen's income at a time when inflation was climbing." The company, assuming that public opinion would side with the strikers, hired the renowned J. Walter Thompson firm to help orchestrate its public relations.

Any possibility that the pressmen may have had for wide community sympathy went up in the flames that briefly threatened the pressroom. The shambles was indefensible; moreover, it was made to order for the television cameras. *Post* executives eagerly displayed the wreckage to outside reporters as well as the paper's own staff. They estimated the damage at anywhere from $1 million to $2 million, although the costs soon proved to be far less. A room was set aside with special lighting for television interviews and Mark Meagher made frequent statements regarding the tempestuous situation in front of the cameras. "We had this big propaganda machine," the *Post*'s labor negotiator, Lawrence

Wallace, recalled. (An opinion survey taken during the strike indicated that many people believed that there had been far more destruction than actually occurred, including employees' cars being blown up.)

For most of the news staff Fort Sumter had been fired on, the Maine sunk, Pearl Harbor bombed. They rallied around Old Glory.

A few hours after the strike began reporters Kevin Klose and Richard Cohen stood across the street watching the milling line of strikers and the police cordon in front of the *Post* building. Klose turned to Cohen, "I don't know about you, but I'm going through that line." As they wedged through the pickets they were called "scabs" and spat on. The two Newspaper Guild members felt a universe apart from the unionists carrying strike placards. Richard L. Coe, a drama critic at the *Post* since 1938, paced back and forth near the building carrying an article he had written at home for the Sunday paper. "I'm stunned by the violence, but I've never crossed a picket line in my life. . . . But I don't know if it's a legitimate picket line," Coe remarked. It was. A few minutes later with a *Post* editor Coe crossed the line to work. Reporter Don Oberdorfer, who had covered the Tet Offensive in Vietnam, went down to the pressroom. His dismay quickly turned to anger at the shambles.

At two o'clock that afternoon the *Post* unit of the Newspaper Guild gathered in the red brick African Methodist Episcopal Church around the corner from the paper. Oberdorfer, the southern softness of his voice hardened by his outrage, responded to a plea for the unit to support the pressmen's union: "They ask us to consider the future of the Guild. What about the future of the paper? Last night a bunch of guys who call themselves a union tried to destroy the *Washington Post.* I'm not about to stand on a picket line with a bunch of guys who went out there with crowbars and torches and tried to wreck our newspaper."

Oberdorfer spoke after Brian Flores had urged some 650 Guild members jammed into the church "to support our brothers in labor." Flores was the full-time executive of the Guild local that covered news organizations in Baltimore and Washington. He had been warned by some members from the newsroom that he didn't stand a chance of winning; anger at the pressmen was too intense to be overcome by a call to union solidarity.

As though the memory of the pressroom violence needed reinforcement, one striker followed Jules Witcover, a national political reporter, to his parked car one night and beat him. When his colleagues saw Witcover with a fractured jaw, chipped teeth, and an ugly black eye, their animosity toward Local 6 intensified. At three subsequent meetings over the next ten weeks the *Post* unit of the Guild voted to keep working, though some members stayed out. Fewer than fifty of the nearly four hundred workers in the newsroom did not work during the strike; most of the Guild members who joined the strike were in the business offices. The issue, said one Guild striker, is a "class thing, there is an elite within the Guild composed of the reporters and editors. They even call themselves the 'Fourth Estate.' "

The whiteness of Local 6 in a city that was more than 70 percent black, with a black mayor, a virtually all-black city council, and the same for the school board, injected racism into the dispute. A few years earlier John Prescott, then the paper's general manager, had the decrepit pressroom toilets repaired, but, suspecting the pressmen might segregate the restrooms, he refused to provide keys. "They've got no black pressmen," a black in the *Post's* PR office told an out-of-town reporter who covered the strike. He was wrong, but not very. The pressmen had not been champions of integration but they were doing better, just as the newsroom was beginning to open its ranks to more blacks. There were a few black journeymen; one of them, Lloyd Simons, had recently lost his hand when it was caught in the press. A dozen or so young blacks in Local 6 were training to be full-fledged pressmen.

Some blacks in the Guild sided with the pressmen. Walking the picket line, a black *Post* photographer told writer Nat Hentoff: "How come all those liberals never said a word about this being a racist union until being against racism at the *Post* became a way they could justify staying in to collect their paychecks? Most of them don't give a shit about racism unless they're covering a story somewhere else where they can make judgments on everybody but themselves." Local black labor leaders took up the pressmen's cause at rallies, convinced that economics and trade unionism were what counted, not whether the pressmen might at heart be rednecks. The Central Labor Council protested when the *Post* hired black high school students to substitute for the mostly black mailers who honored the picket line. The teen-agers were let go, and the *Post* brought in women from a local junior college.

Don Oberdorfer's fury at those who damaged "our newspaper" reflected the intense pride and consuming emotional investment of many reporters and editors in the *Washington Post.* These feelings widened the split between the Guild and the strikers. "For the mechanical unions the division of who is employer and who is employee is very clear," said editorial writer Robert Asher who once headed the Guild unit at the *Post.* "There exists a tension there which is good and true. For the Guild members have been invited to lunch with Katharine Graham, see each other and management socially, share decisions somewhat about the paper and policy, and may even consider the paper 'our' paper." Another *Post* writer saw the divisions in the building as mirroring larger distinctions: "The *Post* is a microcosm of this society, stacked floor on floor, from the janitors to the printers to the new professional class (us) to the corporate empire builders. Only nobody in the building quite realizes this. Each floor looks out at the world around us through its own lens, unaware of the multiple ironies contained within."

Jimmy Dugan had an uncluttered perception of the place. In 1971 after he was elected head of the local, Katharine Graham told Dugan she wanted him to meet executive editor Ben Bradlee. "I didn't even know who Ben Bradlee was," Dugan recalled sarcastically of the introduction in the stereotype shop. "Bradlee works at the *Washington Post.* I work in a factory."

Nevertheless, the Guild unit was splitting into rancorous factions over the strike. The newsroom bulletin board was quilted with announcements of meetings of one group or another and mimeographed declarations of sentiments. The free coffee and danishes the company provided in the newsroom did little to ease the tension. The usual 7:45 P.M. deadline was advanced to 1 and 2 P.M. to compensate for stretched-out production schedules. Editors, many of them weary from voluntarily working at production jobs after their editing stints, treated reporters with unusual politeness lest a rebuke drive the staffer into the arms of the strikers. Some *Post* editors surmised their reporters and subeditors were motivated to work by their paychecks rather than loyalty or abhorrence of the pressmen's violence or racism. Statements circulated by the strikers reminded working Guild members of the pressmen's contribution to their financial well-being: By winning pensions, company-paid health insurance, and cost-of-living adjustments in its contracts, Local 6 had made it easier for the Newspaper Guild at the *Post* to later get these important fringe benefits.

In the Newspaper Guild's international headquarters directly across from the *Post's* front door, president Charles Perlik concluded that a powerful force had kept most of the news people at their desks: "It was the apogee of Watergate. The accolades had rubbed off on everybody in the newsroom. They felt the preservation of the paper was vital. In the test of loyalties, Kay Graham won."

On the day after the pressmen struck the *Post,* four nationally prominent men in the newspaper business lunched amid the antique furnishings of the exclusive 1925 F Street Club a few blocks from the White House in order to discuss Katharine Graham's sudden distress. They were: Arthur O. Sulzberger, publisher of the *New York Times;* his Washington bureau chief, silver-haired Clifton Daniel; Joe L. Allbritton, owner of the *Washington Star;* and his editor, James G. Bellows. The previous morning Mrs. Graham had phoned Allbritton to ask him to print the *Post* on his presses until hers were repaired. This could be done every day except Sunday because the *Star* is an evening paper and its presses are idle from early afternoon through the night, the hours when the *Post* is produced. Allbritton, a Texan whose wealth Fortune estimated between $100 and $150 million, had been a publisher for only a year. He was attempting to pull the *Star* out of an extended and perilous financial slide running back several years and persisting under his ownership. Part of the profits from the Star Company's radio and television stations were being channeled into the paper to keep it afloat and Allbritton was pouring more money in. At the rate the *Star* was hemorrhaging money, however, these transfusions could not outpace losses for long. If Allbritton did print Mrs. Graham's paper his own certainly would be struck because the *Star* pressmen were in the same local as those at the *Post*. Some striking pressmen from the *Post*, in fact, got temporary jobs on the *Star*'s presses. If the *Star* didn't publish, it would pass up a crack at the advertising and circulation that the *Post* was losing. Allbritton said no to Mrs. Graham's request. He also said no to suspending publication in support of the *Post*, a request she had also made two weeks before the strike without success. She responded, said one involved in the episode, in rather "pungent language."

Sulzberger told Elliott Marshall of the *New Republic*, "I didn't go to persuade Allbritton of anything. This was just a luncheon that had been agreed upon a long time before anybody knew anything was going to happen to Mrs. Graham's pressroom." Mrs. Graham, Sulzberger said, hadn't asked him to intercede with the *Star*'s owner on her behalf; his purpose simply was to tell Allbritton, who was new to publishing, what had happened in New York when the newspapers had been "whiplashed back and forth between the unions" until they finally agreed that a strike against one would be considered a strike against all. Under this arrangement the non-struck papers would shut down rather than publish. Sulzberger said he appreciated that if the *Star* tried to print the *Post* it also would be struck. "That would be the whole name of the game, to blacken out the whole city and double the leverage on the union," explained Sulzberger. This strategy formulation by the publisher of the nation's premier newspaper illuminated, as the 1963 newspaper strike in New York previously had, a grand sham: That is, the solemn avowals of newspaper publishers that they have a moral responsibility to their communities to publish, while at the same time wielding nonpublication as an economic club against strikers.

Allbritton, a short, slightly built banker and lawyer, had been warned by Jim Bellows "against any cooperation with the big guys— because the little guys wind up second best." Bellows cautioned his boss against being seduced by the "country club atmosphere among publishers." The fifty-three-year-old editor with longish sideburns was no admirer of "Punch" Sulzberger and when the *Times* publisher mentioned the advantages of the publishers' alliance, Bellows interjected, "that wasn't the way it was in New York." Bellows was editor of the *New York Herald Tribune* before the brightly written, journalistically solid daily died in 1966, squeezed by stronger rivals, including Sulzberger's *Times.* He reminded his three companions that the *New York Post* had survived the protracted 1963 newspaper strike only by seceding from the publishers' plege to ally against the unions. Allbritton repeated to Sulzberger that he would not print the *Post* and would not shut down in alliance with his dominant rival.

A few days after the F Street Club lunch, which he had arranged, James Reston wrote about the *Post* strike in his *New York Times* column. Reston, whom Mrs. Graham once tried to lure away from the *Times* to edit her newspaper, began the column: "The pressmen of the *Washington Post* have finally succeeded in doing to their own newspaper what former President Nixon and his Attorney General John Mitchell tried and failed to do during the Watergate conflict: They have stopped the presses at the *Post.*" (Scotty Reston, himself a co-owner of a small newspaper, the *Vineyard Gazette* on Martha's Vineyard, echoed the theme he stated during the 1963 New York newspaper strike: "The President of the United States cannot censor the New York papers. But Bert Powers, boss of New York printers, can shut them down. What is free about a press that can be muzzled by one union leader?") Reston pointed out that publishers from many newspapers were offering help to the *Post,* "But the main burden has fallen on Joe Allbritton, the new owner of the *Washington Star,* who is now losing a million dollars a month. He has a problem. Should he come out against the sabotage by the *Post*'s pressmen, and offer to print the *Post,* making a common front against this anarchy, or concentrate on his own immediate interests?" Reston suggested that a joint printing agreement with the *Post,* unrelated to the strike, was the way for the *Star* to cut its operating deficits and assure the survival of two independent dailies. Allbritton's unwillingness to help the *Post* made such a deal unlikely, said Reston; "The *Star* needed the *Post* and the *Post* felt that the *Star* played the role of fearful bystander in the crisis. . . ." Reston applauded the *Post* for meeting "the two main obligations of any newspaper: to stay alive financially and to print the news," which was exactly what Allbritton was trying to do.

The *Star* buys Reston's column through The New York Times News Service. When it came into his office Bellows called on Jimmy Breslin, one of his writers on the late *Herald Tribune* who occasionally wrote for the *Star,* to counterattack. Bellows ran the two columns side by side. Breslin blasted Reston's argument as "A Washington gentleman's version of freedom of the press: Come along with us, you Allbritton, or we'll bury you." "These guys with drawing room manners," Breslin wrote, "either go to too many Mafia movies or they've had it in them to be tough guys all along." "Sulzberger," said Breslin, "did not say the *Times* was suspending its Washington circulation . . . in sympathy with the *Washington Post.*" As it turned out, the next day the *Times* shipped 35,000 copies of its Sunday paper to the Washington area, six thousand more than it normally sent in, and they were grabbed up by readers for whom the 24-page *Post* that day was exceptionally thin fare compared with the 318-page paper published the previous Sunday.

The *Star* might be a sinkhole for cash, but Allbritton knew that he had a veritable goldmine in the broadcasting properties owned by his parent company, Star Communications. He sold off several of the company's radio and television stations and held others. When he was through dealing, he had more than doubled the $65 million he had put into the *Star.* In one instance Allbritton outlined on a restaurant menu a proposed swap of television stations with Karl Eller, the chairman of Combined Communications Corporation. After signing the menu Allbritton handed it to Eller, who glanced at it and passed it to his attorney to review. "Karl," said Allbritton, "I'm making this offer to you. If you have to consult your lawyer, the deal's off." The incident illuminated the shrewdness, toughness, and brittleness Allbritton brought to the running of the *Star.* But he kept the paper alive.

The strike of the *Post* was a boon for the *Star.* Unable to publish its normal-sized paper, the *Post* watched advertising fall into Allbritton's lap. Advertising in the *Star* jumped more than 50 percent from a year earlier and circulation perked up. October was the *Star*'s first profitable month in five years. Allbritton tried to keep the ads flowing to his newspaper, warning gatherings of businessmen: "Everyone in this room has an economic interest in the *Star.* Without it the *Post* has unbridled power." (Eugene Meyer had argued the same case against the other papers before the *Post* became the city's dominant paper.) The message was implicit, but not obscure: Without the *Star's* competition—modest as it was with the *Post* normally getting 70 percent of Washington's newspaper advertising dollars and the *Star* the balance—the *Post* might be unrestrained in raising ad rates. The reality was not so stark. While the *Post's* ad rates were higher than the *Star's,* the far greater circulation of the morning paper made it more economical for advertisers. Whatever their political philosophy or feeling about monopolies, advertisers really prefer to use one newspaper.

In the *Star's* seedy newsroom across town from the *Post,* the staff's despairing mood about their paper turned revivalist at the report of an upswing in ads. A red and white sign lettered "One Way" with an arrow symbolically pointing up was hung outside editor Jim Bellows's office. In the first five weeks of the pressmen's strike, the evening paper picked up about $2 million more in advertising while the *Post* lost approximately $4 million. But by late November the *Post* was back in the black, printing about 80 percent as much advertising as a year earlier and on its way to glowing profits. How did it happen?

Thirty-six hours after the pressmen's strike began, Katharine Graham stood at the window of her eighth floor office, watching intently the first big gamble to rescue her newspaper. The autumn afternoon light caught the idling blades of the French-built Gazelle helicopter. Suddenly, they gained speed and the craft whirred up past the room of the *Post* building, rattling the air conditioning ducts. As it lifted off, Mrs. Graham beamed and clasped her hands over her head in a prizefighter's cheer of triumph: The *Post* would miss only one day of publishing. The leased chopper and others that followed carried photocomposed pages of the *Post,* to be sure an emaciated twenty-four-page *Post,* to six nonunion newspaper plants as far away as 115 miles. Workers there turned the filmed pages into plates and then printed the *Post* on offset presses. Trucks later that night and next morning hauled the newspapers to shopping center parking lots around Washington where distributors picked up the bundles for parceling out among the *Post*'s 6,500 carriers.

The printers who were not on strike had been locked out of the composing room from the day the pressmen's strike began. A notice said the *Post* had no work for them. But nonunion employees were setting type and composing pages protected by Wackenhut guards in blue blazers.* Management distrusted the printers because of their seizure of the composing room in a 1973 labor protest and work slowdowns.

Project X, the *Post*'s carefully orchestrated scheme for publishing in the event of a strike, had one gross flaw: It always assumed that even in the worst situation the presses would be workable. Now Project X's graduates were at work in the composing room but the presses, which they were also trained to run, were denied them. Late on the first day of the strike William Cooper, a *Post* executive, had an idea. Two years earlier Cooper had scouted newspaper companies that might print the *Post*'s growing number of advertising inserts that were swelling the paper and revenues. Perhaps they would print the *Post*, Cooper suggested. When Mark Meagher asked Mrs. Graham for her approval, she was concerned that the plan once started should not collapse. "Can we keep it going?" she asked. After she okayed it, Cooper began phoning publishers telling them, "Charge us what it costs you, plus a fair profit."

Someone remembered that aircraft are banned from a large block of airspace surrounding the White House five blocks from the *Post;* a helicopter might inadvertently intrude on that sanctum en route to or from the *Post.* With Emperor Hirohito in town for a state visit, the Secret Service was nervous about the buzzing choppers. The State Department also was asked to assure the Russians the helicopters were not about to attack their embassy behind the *Post.* For the first few nights, *Post* workers held flares to illuminate the roof; then sawhorses with blinking amber lights to outline the landing area at night were positioned at each corner of the roof. Washington had been hit by torrential rains in late September, but in the weeks the helicopters ferried back and forth the weather was on the *Post*'s side.

---

*Wackenhut employees, according to Senate hearings, have worked undercover to report on union organizing elsewhere.

Roger Parkinson wouldn't quite call it fun, but he did say it was all exciting: running the airlift, directing the hired fleet of trucks, holding tight schedules—a little like Vietnam where he had been a Green Beret planning officer. Parkinson was a thirty-four-year-old Harvard Business School graduate with horn-rimmed glasses and a curl of sandy brown hair that drooped on his forehead. Some shots had been fired through the masked windows of the *Post*'s composing room. When the choppers were at the *Post,* Parkinson would go up to the roof and scan the neighboring rooftops with his binoculars for any sign of danger to the craft. Mark Meagher had brought Parkinson to the *Post* six months earlier from *Newsweek* where he had proved something of a management whiz. His star was on the rise in the Post corporation. Precisely two years to the day from the start of the pressmen's strike Parkinson would be named vice president for administration of the Post. One day early in the strike when things had gone particularly well, Katharine Graham appeared in his office and hugged him and Angus Twombly, another young executive. "It's been sort of like the Battle of Britain," Mrs. Graham said later. And she was 'sort of like' the Queen Mother, cheering the troops.

The *Post* tried to keep secret where the paper was being printed. The *Star* apparently learned the locations and the *Post* got wind of this. Lynn Rosselini later reported in the *Star* that Mrs. Graham phoned Allbritton to accuse his paper of planning to publish the information.

"You bastards are going to get someone killed," she said.

"I'll have to get the facts and call you back," Allbritton answered.

"You mean you don't know what your goddamn news department is doing?" said Graham.

"No, I'll have to ask," Allbritton said.

"Then you don't deserve to publish a newspaper," she said and hung up.

She made other calls to Allbritton. Strike supporters began distributing *Star* subscription forms and urged people to drop the *Post.* Mrs. Graham phoned the *Star*'s publisher to complain that it was "the most unprofessional thing I'd ever heard." He told her the forms had been stolen from his paper. The practice somehow stopped.

Allbritton later decided to get tough with his rival. He ordered the *Star*'s profile writer, Lynn Rosselini, to prepare a gloves-off series on Katharine Graham. The pieces were written, but Allbritton grew so skittish about publishing them that he required his two top editors to pledge in writing that they would not run without his permission. They did not appear in the *Star* until after Time, Inc.'s purchase of the newspaper in February 1978. The new bosses unleashed the series after a heavy advance promotion, including a blurb on the front page with a quote, Katharine Graham is "an imperious bitch." It was *Time*'s way of letting everyone know that they were in town and ready to play tough against the *Post*. They did it again when they bought the syndicate that distributed the widely read comic strip "Doonesbury," lifting it from the *Post* to the *Star*. Ben Bradlee, driven wild by this, called the *Star* "the biggest challenge since Nixon."

The *Winchester Star* in Virginia's Shenandoah Valley was one of the papers that printed the *Post* during the strike. Senator Harry F. Byrd, Jr., owned the paper. The use of the Byrd presses to print the *Post* figured in a rather bizarre brouhaha a year later between *Post* executive editor Ben Bradlee, columnist Jack Anderson, and *Washington Star* editor Jim Bellows. Bradlee killed an Anderson column that alleged Byrd had seduced "one voluptuous Virginia constituent" because the story seemed neither reliable nor relevant, nor was there any apparent violation of law or interference with the Senator's public job. The dispute came in the wake of the *Post*'s disclosure that Congressman Wayne Hays kept Elizabeth Ray on his official payroll for his sexual pleasure rather than public service. There was a spate of similar stories about other congressmen.

"Ear," the *Washington Star*'s gossip column, suggested that Bradlee's spiking of Anderson's report was in thanks to Harry Byrd for helping the *Post*. "Ear" was editor Jim Bellows' invention. He once had told Bradlee that "the little paper has to attract attention, get the big paper into the little pond." The column reveled in taking jabs at the *Post*, which was always the O.P. (the "other paper"). "They were describing me in Ear as Marie Antoinette," Katharine Graham complained. "Ear exacerbated the tensions between the papers."

Bellows quickly apologized to Bradlee for the unsubstantiated morsel about the Anderson column. But Bradlee was infuriated by what he surely regarded as a slander of the *Post* and himself. A *Post* reporter was assigned to "find out everything he could" about the woman. He did, including her name, which Bradlee used in a long, lurid article across the top of the page opposite the editorials explaining why he had scrapped the column. Bradlee disclosed his reporter's findings, based on attributed statements from police and neighbors, that the woman had complained "that female neighbors were having homosexual affairs al fresco . . . that her husband had been beheaded and thrown into the river by the Mafia. . . ." "She used to tie her dog to a rope when it was in heat and stand in the doorway with her daughter and watch the dog breed with every dog in the neighborhood," a neighbor told the reporter. The woman, it turned out, had called the *Post* repeatedly two years earlier with a string of antic charges, the kind of calls city desks have attracted forever and routinely ignore. Bradlee left no doubt that he regarded the woman as a nut. As for the senatorial seduction, Bradlee concluded: "The question is whether newspapers should print such charges when the woman refused to identify herself, when no complaint was ever filed, and when no law was broken. I think they should not." Bradlee's fervid rejoinder, prompted by the *Star*'s suggestion of a quid pro quo in his suppression of Anderson's column and the notoriety the matter was getting in Virginia politics, violated his own stated judgment. He did, after all, print the woman's charges in a manner that guaranteed them wider attention. At the same time, Bradlee managed to titillate his readers with the piteous actions of a possibly unstable woman whose sole defense from undeserved public ridicule in this instance would have been responsible journalists.

On Monday night, October 6, five days after the strike began, the *Post* got the first of its presses operating and printed 100,000 twenty-four-page papers. Earlier in the day, Mrs. Graham told her employees who continued to work: "I have no illusions that you are here on some uncritical, automatic basis. I know that the same depth of conviction that caused you to make this difficult decision will cause you to go out in support of what we all know could be a very prolonged strike if you believe the position of management vis-à-vis the presemen is unfair." She told them "jobs would be lost . . . ultimately this would no longer be the great newspaper you have made it" unless the company could "manage our own paper." Some interpreted management control to mean, "This is our paper; you only work here."

Earlier in the life of the *Post* a genuine warmth existed between the craft workers in blue denim and khaki and the big bosses in banker's gray. Dominating the lobby of the *Post* today is a huge photo montage with a beaming Eugene Meyer wearing a pressman's folded-newspaper hat cocked over his high forehead. The pressmen's union made Meyer an honorary member so he could start the presses on the day he purchased the *Times-Herald*. Meyer's broad grin was the glowing symbol of an extended era of good feeling between the craft unions and the owners. Later, when the glow vanished as the company and labor began a bitter series of conflicts, newer production workers would sneer at those who harbored any affection for the owners as "Post Toasties." Within many of those who were working their regular jobs during the day and then producing the paper through the night, there evolved toward the strikers an animosity so deep that they wanted them barred forever from returning. The motives for these extra long hours varied. Anti-union sentiments rather than merely loyalty to the *Post* fired some. One hundred and fifty or so workers stayed in the building around the clock, sleeping on cots and office sofas, and eating catered meals served by waiters in tuxedos. Beer and wine were served, an electrician played his banjo while Donald Graham, who worked as a paper handler when he wasn't managing the *Post*'s operations, sang, and movies were shown. Outside the pickets continued to walk.

Aligning with Cesar Chavez's United Farm Workers, the strikers plastered litter cans and walls in downtown Washington with signs declaring, "No Grapes. No Lettuce. No *Post.*" Their sympathizers staged "informational picketing," to avoid possible charges of engaging in a secondary boycott, at stores that advertised in the *Post*. They appealed to merchants to shift their ads to the *Star* and a few large stores did for a time.

The pressmen got unsolicited help from unexpected quarters. Young members of the Socialist Workers Party and the Spartacists League, small leftist groups, were drawn by their view of the strike as a classical battle between a corporate giant and abused workers. Some pressmen immediately wanted to beat them up. A printer asked Dugan,

"What are you doing with these Reds?"

"They're on our side; that's all that counts," replied Dugan. At demonstrations Dugan ordered the radicals, "Get at the end of the line and yell what we yell."

"Without them," said attorney David Rein, "the pressmen couldn't have organized." Before long pressmen were attending lectures on sexism and racism taught by the youths; and the pressmen's wives, who in the beginning had been kept away from strike activities by their husbands, started speaking at rallies. James Ingraham, a lanky pressman, recalled that until the strike "we never had thought about questions of justice. We took it for granted." On the wall of the pressmen's shabby headquarters a poster proclaimed the plight of several *desaparecidos,* Chilean printers identified by name who had disappeared after the 1973 overthrow of Allende. Many of the pressmen had come to see themselves in a new light.

Several weeks into the strike Roger Parkinson went to dinner at Mrs. Graham's home. Others there included Donald Graham's wife, Mary, a lawyer, and retired *Post* columnist Joseph Alsop, an old Graham family friend. Over dessert Mrs. Graham, seated beside Parkinson, mentioned the possibility of some compromise with Local 6. Parkinson turned to the *Post* publisher at his elbow. He felt, he recalled later, "like I was on a huge high." He made the case other executives also had been pressing with her: "First, if you compromise, most of your top management will have to leave. They took the biggest risk and they will not be able to stay and deal with the unions. Second, it's working, the community is on your side. It's now or never. Third, you will make it impossible ten or twenty years from now. It will be impossible for Donnie. Don't back off because you've never had harmony anyway and you won't have it if you yield." As Parkinson tapped his palm to emphasize each point, Alsop concurred, "Hear, hear!" Katharine Graham listened intently.

On November 7, with the strike well into its second month and agreement between the pressmen and the company no closer, forty-one Guild members who had kept working in the newsroom, wrote to Mrs. Graham to express their anguish. Alluding to "the oppressiveness of the armed camp atmosphere," they said some Guildsmen could not support the pressmen because of the violence, others because a majority had voted to cross the picket line. "Some," they wrote, "fear reprisals if they don't work, despite your pledge that there will be no reprisals. Their bosses have led them to think otherwise. . . . Some tend to feel that a newspaper's right to publish is something sacred. . . ."

Ten days later Mrs. Graham, in a statement carefully crafted by Mark Meagher, Lawrence Wallace, and Donald Graham, replied that

. . . it would in my judgment be the ultimate act of irresponsibility on our part to permit the pressmen to return under the old conditions. I could not myself in good faith preside over a building or an enterprise in which people who had worked faithfully and to the point of exhaustion for the company were in continuing physical danger from fellow employees, in which those who committed the acts of violence resumed their control of a whole section of our building while those who had worked to repair the damage to the company and to get the paper out of harm's way, in which hiring and manning practices permitted not just the same kind of featherbedding, but also the same importation of men likely to commit the same kinds of violence should they be crossed . . .

Parkinson was right, "it" was working. More presses were being put back in operation. On the weekend before Thanksgiving, assistant production manager David Peebles flew with pasteups of a 104-page ad-laden food supplement to the nonunion *Miami Herald* where the section was printed and then trucked north in time for Thursday distribution. That morning the *Post* contained 184 pages. The *Post* actually made money in October, November, and December because of sharply reduced payrolls and the recovery of *Post* ad revenues. Insurance covered most of the losses resulting from the strike and the damage to the pressroom. The *Post* was more than enduring; it was prevailing.

The week before Thanksgiving, reporter Elizabeth Becker and John Hanrahan, an assistant Maryland editor, signed a flyer printed on yellow paper summoning news workers to abandon their typewriters: "The paper is getting fatter every week. That is your doing. Your presence lends false respectability to management's anti-union efforts. You are not monks, cloistered away in a monastery. Your actions do have meaning and impact. . . ."

Becker, who had covered the war in Cambodia for the *Post*, continued to work after the strike began. On a visit to Seattle she talked about the dispute with her brother, a fireman and a strong union man. "Which side are you on?" he asked her. She came back to Washington, joined the Rank and File Strike Support Committee, a small core of Guild members who obeyed the picket line, and began writing pro-strike statements. They spent their own money and cash slipped to them by Guildsmen who felt guilty about working, to print the leaflets.

John Hanrahan had been on the *Post* for seven years. He was a good editor, headed up, with many friends in the newsroom. Hanrahan and reporter Carl Bernstein had once complained together to managing editor Eugene Patterson about distorted coverage of a conservative patriotic rally. Liz Becker was going to a party where Bernstein, who was on leave to write a book with Bob Woodward about Watergate, was expected. Hanrahan wrote a note for her to carry to his friend saying, "Hope you'll be supportive of the strike," and signed it, "A fellow newsroom rebel." "I want to talk to John," Bernstein told Becker. Some strikers expected Bernstein's help because his book writing and other Watergate-related income left him independent of a *Post* paycheck. They also believed that the passionate trade-unionism of his parents would influence him. David Rein, an attorney who defended some of the pressmen against criminal charges stemming from the strike, went to Columbia Law School with the older Bernstein during the Depression. They had remained close friends and shared a distaste for the *Post* for what they believed was an undeserved liberal reputation. Carl Bernstein, who had seen himself as a militant unionist, and Hanrahan never talked. The violence and racism left both Bernsteins ambivalent about the pressmen's cause.

Most of the big labor unions have their headquarters or major offices in Washington. Across Lafayette Square from the White House is the white marble home of the A.F.L.-C.I.O., with 16.6 million members, whose president George Meany had been sedulously courted by presidents for over two decades. But Washington is not a labor town; the area's work force, mostly white collar, is roughly 12 percent unionized; the average for other big cities is twice that. Here there is no harsh memory of long and bloody strikes of the kind that gripped railroad or steel or mining towns. The pressmen's strike was an oddity.

In late November when the strike at the *Post* was almost two months old and no glimmer of a settlement was in sight, Jimmy Dugan and Sol Fishko, president of the international pressmen's union, went to see George Meany. They asked him to attempt to persuade Katharine Graham to agree to a fact-finding and arbitration procedure as a way to end the standoff. Meany interrupted them several times to ask if they were sure that the other international unions were still backing the strike. They said yes, but they had reason to believe that the International Typographical Union was manuevering backstage for a way out of a strike costly to its members for no clear gain. Meany later met with Mrs. Graham, but he was unable to convince her to be conciliatory toward the pressmen.

At 10 A.M. on December 10 the *Post* newsroom was crowded but grimly hushed. At one end of the capacious room, Katharine Graham, unsmiling, stood at a lectern to make her most important pronouncement on the strike. Her voice cracked occasionally as she spoke. "I want to say what a sad day this is for me and for all of us. It's tough as hell. It's not something we wanted to do. It's not something we like doing. . . . This company is not now and never has been anti-union. It will be said that we set out deliberately to break this union and I say that is a lie." She reminded the news staff of the events that had originally hardened most of the Guild members against the pressmen. Her words were possibly chosen to preserve the schism. "Responsible union members do not set fires or beat fellow workers or make midnight phone calls threatening to kill the wives and infants of their fellow workers," Mrs. Graham declared. "And they do not embrace people who do these things. They discipline them. Responsible union leaders give a damn about the well-being of their colleagues in other unions." The publisher outlined the *Post*'s last offer to Local 6: No one would be fired, although those guilty of violence would not be taken back; reductions in the pressroom force would be only by attrition; the pressmen would get a $400,000 bonus to divide among themselves in return for ceding to management control that would end needless manning and overtime, and the base pay without overtime would be raised to $22,500, the average pay of pressmen before the strike, from $14,500.

Twice in November, prodded by the national craft unions and mediators, Mark Meagher had met secretly with Dugan to tell him what the company's "bottom line" was for reaching an agreement. It was money in exchange for work rules. The meetings got nowhere. The pressmen subsequently rejected the *Post*'s "final offer," 249 to 5.

George Meany said that this offer was more unfavorable to the union than what the company proposed in August. He asserted that the *Post* had no illusions about what would happen to the offer. After the strike the *Post* published a long, detailed account of the strike by Robert G. Kaiser, which it nominated for a Pulitzer Prize. Kaiser related that when Meany at one point asked Mrs. Graham what she would have done if Local 6 had accepted the final offer, she replied, "Slit my throat."

The night before Mrs. Graham spoke to the news staff, the *Post* wired Dugan that it felt an impasse had been reached. Under federal law, the *Post* could not unilaterally break off negotiations with the pressmen. Only after a stalemate was reached could the company impose new working conditions in the pressroom. Dugan wired back that he was ready to negotiate any time, but there was no movement from the pressmen's side of the bargaining table. The company's proposals spelled income cuts for many men who frequently worked overtime; there was no amnesty for men allegedly involved in the violence; the union's new weakness, evident in the *Post*'s ability to publish without them, would be formalized; technical innovations in the pressroom, already in use elsewhere, would further cut the need for pressmen. Dugan and most of the pressmen wouldn't accept this. The company wouldn't budge either, it was too close to victory.

Many of the men on the picket line were Catholic. As Mark Meagher entered the building, some of them asked how he, a Catholic like themselves and a former seminarian, could treat working men in such fashion. One day an old man named John Shields, who ladled out food to the poor in a nearby parish, stopped Meagher outside the *Post* with the same question. Meagher brought Shields up to his office and they talked for hours about the moral issues in the strike. They, too, reached an impasse when Shields called him a "subjective relativist."

"What we are doing," Mrs. Graham stated in her newsroom statement, "is unquestionably legal. What has been infinitely harder for me to decide is whether we are acting in a way that is humanly right. I have thought about this long and hard, and I have concluded that we are. We have offered all we have to give. We are therefore today going to begin hiring temporary pressmen." Her decision was not wholly surprising; the company had notified the pressmen's union a week earlier of its intention. The reality of it, nevertheless, jarred many in the newsroom. Local 6 and the other unions could picket till hell froze over; without major, and unexpected concessions from the pressmen the company would not be moved. As she walked away from the lectern, Katharine Graham's hands were trembling.

That afternoon the helicopters were back, this time with a contingent of nonunion pressmen recruited through an anti-newspaper-union program to back up the Project X people and the new hires. Two other striking unions, the mailers and photoengravers, got Mrs. Graham's message: they spent most of the day in a friendly session with *Post* bargainers for the first time since the walkout began. Craft union solidarity with the pressmen was collapsing as other strikers prepared to go back to work.

The replacement of the union pressmen was a crucial point in the drama that was being played out at the *Post*. Having published a newspaper for two and a half weeks without the Guild in 1974; having subdued the union printers and sharply reduced their number, the company was now eliminating the remaining union that threatened the company's authority. Once more the Guild met to vote on whether to honor the picket line. After two hours of emotional debate the local voted, as it had three times before, to ignore the picket line. Austin Scott, a black reporter on the national staff who had continued to work, now warned the guildsmen that all *Post* workers "are in serious danger both in terms of job security and working conditions." But another black, columnist William Raspberry, asked if anyone was prepared to make a "long-term sacrifice on behalf of a thoroughly racist pressmen's union?"

Once applied to the pressmen, the racist label held fast among many in the newsroom, despite the contradictory presence of blacks among the strikers and their allies. The Newspaper Production and Research Center in Oklahoma City was the *Post*'s chief confederate in its campaign against the unions. Curious about the operation, Elizabeth Becker, a striking reporter, went there and interviewed the director, Robert H. Spahn. She identified herself as on assignment from a foreign journal. Spahn astounded her when he said labor and blacks— he called them "jungle bunnies," her first encounter with the aspersion —were bad for newspapers because they cannot read. The *Post* didn't exclude racists as its allies against the unions.

After Katharine Graham's announcement some two thousand unionists and their sympathizers marched past the *Post* building and burned her in effigy. That fiery rite did not disturb her as much as the sign held high by Charles Davis, one of Jimmy Dugan's chief lieutenants. It said: "Phil Shot the Wrong Graham"—an ugly reminder of Philip Graham's suicide.

Writing in the *Post*'s Style section a week after Mrs. Graham's somber declaration, columnist Nicholas von Hoffman chastised the pressmen for their "preposterous featherbedding." Von Hoffman, called by *Time* "a sort of William Buckley of the New Left," continued: "The union is to be smashed . . . by retaliating with that ancient management device, the lockout. Graham has accepted the pressmen's union's invitation to waltz back to the industrial warfare of the nineteenth century. The lockout was a standard management tactic in the face of the union violence characteristic of those miserable and bloody times." Katharine Graham's decision, von Hoffman lectured brashly, was "as socially and politically reckless as the pressmen destroying the presses. . . . More than the *New York Times* even, the *Washington Post* has been the editorial symbol of the liberal solution to labor-management conflict. . . . By breaking with its own past, the *Post* breaks with the liberal solution without offering any other but dire conflict." Von Hoffman wrote his column at home and sent it in to the paper so he never had to confront the choice of whether personally to cross the picket line. Editor Ben Bradlee read the column and retorted: "We're not talking about cruel management or an exploited working class. We're talking about a bunch of criminals who slash tires and smash presses and hit women over the head with two-by-fours. I have no lint left in my navel for that."

The full page ad in the *Washington Star* on New Year's Eve, "a time for new beginnings," as they put it, was signed by 107 liberal, political, civic, and religious eminences, including Hubert Humphrey, George McGovern, Andrew Young, and Shirley Chisolm. The Committee for a Fair Settlement urged the *Post* and the unions to engage "in intensive round-the-clock bargaining" to end the "ever-escalating hostility." If that failed, the committee recommended impartial fact-finding and then arbitration—procedures that had been applied in other protracted and volatile labor disputes. Joseph L. Rauh, Jr., a leader of American liberalism, was one of the signers. Rauh, a tall, ruddy-faced Harvard-trained lawyer, was a leader in the civil rights and the progressive labor cause for more than three decades. What distressed Rauh about the struggle at the *Post* was that it was "adding tensions to the already overloaded friction between liberals and blue-collar workers." Among the liberals Rauh counted those who guided the *Post.* He saw it as a rerun, in microcosm, of the political schism that had developed between organized labor and McGovern liberals in the 1972 presidential campaign.

On New Year's Day, Rauh dropped by two Washington parties. At both his judgment was confirmed that the strike was damaging the already weakened liberal-labor coalition. At Jerry Wurf's, the president of the American Federation of State, County and Municipal Employees who had met with Mrs. Graham on behalf of the strikers, Rauh heard the *Post* denounced. A few hours later he listened as the labor movement was attacked at the home of Robert Nathan, a founder of the politically liberal Americans for Democratic Action. Rauh voiced his fears that a wedge was being driven between traditional and essential allies. Hobart Rowen, the *Post*'s financial columnist whose son was married to George McGovern's daughter, was there and later reported Rauh's remarks to Katharine Graham. Mrs. Graham invited Rauh to her home to discuss the strike. They were long-time friends, easy with each other. When Philip Graham seemed to be emerging from a long spell of manic depression in August 1963, Kay Graham phoned Rauh to ask him to visit her husband the following week; Graham killed himself before that could happen. Now on the first Sunday of 1976 Rauh and Mrs. Graham talked for three hours about the Committee for a Fair Settlement's proposals for impartial fact-finding and arbitration. She was unbending: She would not have Local 6 back in her building; the striking pressmen would never be allowed back and she singled out several by name.

Almost a year later, in mid-December 1976, Rauh introduced Edward Sadlowski, the young anti-establishment candidate for president of the United Steelworkers of America, at a fund-raising rally in a Washington church. Jimmy Dugan was there and Sadlowski spoke warmly of the pressmen's cause. Dugan cautioned Sadlowski about depending on liberals whom he believed had deserted the unions striking the *Post.* Later in the church Dugan and six or seven other pressmen encircled Rauh. Dugan demanded that Rauh sign a petition to quash the further prosecution of fifteen pressmen for offenses during the strike. Rauh refused as Dugan undoubtedly knew he would. Rauh's son, Carl, happened to be the principal assistant U. S. District Attorney for Washington, one of the prosecutors of the indicted pressmen. Carl Rauh saw the incidents at the *Post* not as a labor dispute, but as "destructive acts needing to be prosecuted." "Your son is a whore for the *Post,*" Dugan muttered at Joe Rauh. "He calls Donnie Graham every day to get his orders." Rauh said that was absurd and he bet Dugan that Carl had never phoned Graham about the case. It turned out, as Rauh discovered from his son the next day, that Carl had indeed phoned Donald Graham after Attorney General Edward Levi expressed concern for Mrs. Graham's safety and asked to be kept informed on the case. Graham told Carl Rauh not to worry, his mother had a personal guard.

The Newspaper Guild unit at the *Post* lay in disarray since its 1974 walkout; divisions over the pressmen's strike further fractured it. The unit was the biggest wing of the Washington-Baltimore Newspaper Guild Local, but a coalition from a dozen or so other publishing organizations, including the *Washington Star*, dominated the local's governing board. Many on the board, it was believed, resented the *Post* for its higher wages and its fame. This feeling was compounded by the growing animosity of many on the *Post*'s news staff toward the Guild. After the *Post* unit repeatedly voted against supporting the pressmen, the governing board ordered the unit to honor the picket line. The members refused. The local, applying Guild rules, ordered 327 Guildsmen who were still working at the *Post* to stand trial before the union. "If your arm becomes cancerous, you have to cut it off," said Brian Flores, the local's administrator. The first forty *Post* employees were to face the board on January 5. There remained much bitterness between Flores, who had lost two bids for president of the union, and the *Post* members over the 1974 Guild strike. The deck was stacked against the accused *Post* people. Their request to be represented by counsel was denied; the press would be excluded from the proceedings in a midtown hotel; the names of the trial board would not be disclosed in advance. Finally, the union constitution barred anyone convicted by the trial board from nominating candidates and voting in the local's impending election. It was Catch 22 and Kafka.

The Guild's national leaders watched the cauldron boil with growing dread of the consequences. The Guild, national president Charles Perlik concluded, could not afford to lose most of the 843 members at the *Post,* the fourth largest unit in the entire union, as seemed certain if the trials proceeded. With them would go the national's share of their dues, but far worse, according to Perlik, "We would also lose the prestige of representing workers at the *Post* in organizing other papers around the country." Rather than risk a "cataclysmic rupture," Perlik stepped in and nullified the disciplinary action.

Perlik's eleventh-hour intervention only stopped the lunacy of the trials. It did not halt the civil war within the local and in the *Post* unit itself. The Washington Newspaper Union was formed at the *Post* under the leadership of national reporter Stephen D. Isaacs drawing enough support to force an election that summer in order to throw out the Guild. It won a majority in the newsroom. But the national union poured money and effort into a blitz to hold the paper, accusing Isaacs's group of being a "company union." The Guild won, largely with the votes from the commercial employees.

For some there was a deeper motivation behind the Washington Newspaper Union. It arose from the feeling of Isaacs and others that something beyond trade unionism was needed in the newsroom. The short-lived union reflected the hope of some of its champions "for something different in a newspaper atmosphere where something called 'creative tension' runs amok, where reporter stabs reporter, editor stabs editor, reporter stabs editor," Isaacs recalled. "We had a hope for a workplace that offered something other than mere cachet and status . . . dignity for the people and respect for their individual persons and opinions, and some caring for their talents." In April 1978, Isaacs, forty years old, left the *Post* to become editor of the *Minneapolis Star.* What excited him was the chance to put into practice what he had preached—to involve the entire *Star* staff in the basic decisions about the daily operation of the paper and planning for its future.*

February, the fifth month of the strike, was a corrosive time for the pressmen and their supporters. Their ranks were thinning. The mailers settled with the company, and the printers returned to the composing room. Reporter Liz Becker, who had walked out in sympathy with the strike, ran out of savings and sold her second-hand car. Fearful of her prospects at the *Post* she phoned metropolitan editor Leonard Downie

*Isaacs saw Minneapolis as a model for other newspapers faced with continuing technological changes and competition from alternatives including the delivery via the family television set of much of the information and advertising now carried by dailies. Minneapolis might point the way for newspapers to better meet the future.

to tell him that she wanted to return, and he sent her back to covering Maryland. Her colleague, editor John Hanrahan with two young children, never returned to the *Post.* Donald Graham took him to dinner and they talked, but mostly past each other about Hanrahan's future. When William Mackaye, another editor who early joined the strike, started to enter the *Post,* a picketing pressman motioned him aside and whispered, "We know we're dead, but there's nothing else to do."

Despair so overwhelmed sandy-haired John Clauss that he asked to be excused from picket duty. A quiet man, Clauss had been recruited from Springfield, Ohio, seventeen years earlier when the *Post* desperately needed pressmen. The paper gave him three hundred dollars for moving expenses. He could see no satisfactory end to the strike. At fifty-nine, still several years away from a decent retirement, he wondered where he would find other work? On the second Tuesday in February John Clauss sat alone in the living room of his green-shuttered white house in a working-class neighborhood and put a bullet through his head. He was buried in Springfield. Some said that two other striking pressmen had tried suicide. Several pressmen, who had not been involved in the pressroom melec, were refused work at newspapers in other cities simply because they belonged to Local 6. The government ruled that this denial violated Federal law.

Two days after the printers went back to work at the *Post* in mid-February, some fifty pressmen and their backers, feeling their cause abandoned by the other newspaper unions, invaded the cathedral of American unionism, the A.F.L.-C.I.O. headquarters. Their hope was to force some act in their behalf by the labor leadership. They took over the eighth floor offices of George Meany. Late in the afternoon Meany, who was in Bal Harbour, Florida, authorized helmeted police to evict the demonstrators; they refused to leave and were arrested. Prompted by this episode, however, the A.F.L.-C.I.O. executive council issued a statement condemning the *Post:* "It is clear that the *Post* management wanted a strike, hoped for a strike and long-planned to replace union members with scabs trained especially in an effort to break the pressmen's union. . . ." The council's call for final and binding arbitration was as futile a gesture as the pressmen's sit-in. Mrs. Graham had repeatedly rejected this route to a settlement. She had already won what she wanted.

"Breaking the union." "Busting the union." The charges were leveled against the *Post* throughout the strike and still are. The pressmen, Mrs. Graham said, "busted themselves." What happened was that the company used all of its power, individual courage, and ingenuity to break the union's power. Had the pressmen accepted the outcome the *Post* intended Local 6 would still be alive at the *Post.* The company and the pressmen themselves busted the union.

In mid-March three hundred pressmen, their families and friends warmed by hot cider served in a church, marched with lighted candles through Georgetown to a half-hour memorial service for John Clauss in front of Katharine Graham's darkened mansion. Some of the pressmen's wives felt that the chairman of the board of the Post Company somehow could be appealed to as a woman; if the strike were lost there was another matter in which Mrs. Graham's sympathy would help— some of their men still faced felony indictments and possible trial for their part in the strike-related disorders. Perhaps, some of the women mused, she was not responsible for what was happening.

One Sunday in the spring Mrs. Graham walked down the circular drive in front of her home to where women and children with pro-pressmen placards were standing. She shook hands and asked, "How's it going?" They took heart from the gesture.

On a windy Sunday night in early April *All the President's Men* premiered in Washington. More than one thousand persons filled the Eisenhower Theater in the Kennedy Center to watch the movie about the *Post*'s coverage of Watergate. Robert Redford, Dustin Hoffman, and Jason Robards were there with the journalists they portrayed—Bob Woodward, Carl Bernstein, and Ben Bradlee. Gerald Ford, who was president because of Watergate, invited Katharine Graham to use the presidential box because it was "her night." As the festive crowd moved from the theater to a lavish party, two hundred pressmen and their friends who had picketed the entrances to the Kennedy Center moved into the lobby, singing, "Pressmen shall overcome." No one—not even liberal Democrats like George McGovern—paid them much attention.

In July fifteen pressmen were indicted for strike-related offenses and the encounters turned more bitter and dogged. When the pressmen's wives began picketing Mrs. Graham's house, they wanted her to recognize "we're here, you're not driving us out," recalled Alice Zarbrough, a dark-haired woman whose husband had been a *Post* pressman for fifteen years. "Then, as the indictments came down and the trial approached, we wanted to draw attention to the case." When a Jewish organization honored Mrs. Graham for her humanitarian work, twenty pressmen and their wives stood in the rear of the temple. They booed when editor Ben Bradlee, one of the speakers, referred to the pressmen as "savages."

"This is a house of God," a congregant admonished.

"But he's lying in the house of God," a striker countered.

Seventy-five pressmen and their families and backers wearing T-shirts lettered "Defend the Pressmen" heckled Mrs. Graham when she stood to make the principal speech at a Bicentennial ceremony on the Ellipse behind the White House. After three luckless attempts to speak over the shouts she suggested to a large crowd, "Let's all join hands and sing 'God Bless America.'"

One September night when the publisher threw a party to celebrate the opening of Bloomingdale's branches in Washington, a major new advertiser in her newspaper, the pressmen's supporters handed out leaflets to the arriving guests, including Secretary of State Henry Kissinger. The evening party was in the garden behind the Graham house and over the agreeable sounds of the fete could be heard the chant of the demonstrators,

> Kepone Kay, Kepone Kay.
> How many people did you poison today?

The reference was to a pesticide that had severely contaminated the James River in Virginia and sickened workers in a chemical plant. Kepone was produced exclusively for Allied Chemical Corporation, which Eugene Meyer, Mrs. Graham's father, had helped establish in 1920. She was a director of Allied, which was fined for committing gross violations of environmental law. Later, after many of the guests had left, Katharine Graham came out of the house and stood on the lawn watching the women pickets. "In her chiffon dress she looks like Loretta Young," Alice Zarbrough mused wistfully.

The indicted pressmen did not stand trial. After months of legal maneuvers, they pleaded guilty to various misdemeanors in exchange for the prosecutor's dropping of felony charges. On May 20, 1977, twenty months after the melee in the *Post* pressroom, fourteen pressmen sat in Superior Court of the District of Columbia awaiting sentencing by Judge Sylvia Bacon. The windowless courtroom overflowed with their families and friends. Her face devoid of expression, Judge Bacon declared that the accused men's actions during the strike were "planned, purposeful and unjustified. These events did not erupt spontaneously." Six of the men were jailed; the rest drew suspended sentences and fines. Prosecutor Richard Chapman said the pressmen had "showed no remorse. They should not be free to walk the streets of this jurisdiction." Chapman's remarks evoked boos and hisses. When a bearded ex-pressman was sentenced to a year in jail for beating political writer Jules Witcover a woman shrieked, "There's no justice." "There's Katharine Graham," another shouted, standing and pointing at Sylvia Bacon. Marshals hurriedly cleared the courtroom of spectators who chanted, "The *Post* and the courts, hand in hand," as they filed out. Pressmen president Jimmy Dugan, his eyes welling with tears, and uncertainty etched in his face, shuffled out, too. Next morning the *Post* carried a column-and-a-half story on the sentencing. The Company declined to comment. What could it say?

About the time the pressmen were facing Judge Bacon, five New York stock analysts were discussing investment opportunities in newspaper publishing. Dark-haired Joan Berger Lappin, a senior analyst for the Dreyfus Corporation, was talking about the great prospects for the *Washington Post* as a result of vast improvements in production. "The *Washington Post* had an unfortunate situation with their pressmen foolishly setting fire and doing substantial damage to the presses which wound up being the death knell for the union," Lappin said. "And the *Washington Post* now operates without any union in that particular situation. The *Washington Post* pressmen gave a major gift to all newspapers in the country, not just to the *Washington Post* . . . the dramatic increase in the *Post*'s earnings in the years following the act revealed just what a happy strike that was for them."

Happy, indeed, for them. The gains were "staggering," the *Post*'s Mark Meagher put it. According to the company's projections, at least a decade would have been needed to win control of the pressroom through a series of contracts. Meagher snapped his fingers to indicate the speed with which the *Post* accomplished its ends: overtime worth $1.2 million was eliminated; productivity jumped 20 percent.

In 1976 the *Post*'s profits surged again. Katharine Graham once said, in all seriousness, that she wanted to win a Pulitzer Prize for management. It surely would have been hers that year.

• • •

Katharine Graham had won all the big battles: against a president of the United States; against tough unions, against family ghosts. Most of all she had, step by step, won her own independence and strengthened that of her newspaper. Over the nearly sixteen years that she guided the fortunes of the *Post* she made it powerful, rich, envied, emulated, and, by some, feared.

In 1963 when she took the leadership of the *Post,* Mrs. Graham pledged to hold it well for a new generation. On January 10, 1979, Donald Edward Graham—Eugene Meyer's grandson, Katharine and Philip Graham's oldest son—became publisher. He was thirty-three years old, the third generation of the family to command one of the nation's major institutions. He had trained faithfully and hard for this stewardship. The praise poured in. "I wouldn't hesitate to say," prophesied James Reston of the *New York Times,* an old family friend and one of his mentors, "that Donald Graham will be the most distinguished publisher of his generation in this country." Some voices at the *Post* said that was not preordained; he would have to prove himself in battles still to come. Donald Graham understood saying, "Today, as in the rest of my life, my mother has given me everything but an easy act to follow."

Notes on Sources

THE *Washington Post* ITSELF, of course, was a basic reference throughout my work. With few exceptions I have not cited *Post* articles in the following chapter notes because the dates or the period in which they appeared are evident in the narrative. Merlo J. Pusey's *Eugene Meyer* (Knopf, 1974) and Chalmers M. Roberts's *The Washington Post: The First 100 Years* (Houghton Mifflin, 1977) were particularly useful in several chapters of this book because both authors wrote from the vantage point of many years on the *Post* staff. Several persons who had intimate involvement in certain events described in this book agreed to be interviewed on condition that their remarks not be attributed to them. They were concerned that their candor would either jeopardize their careers or business undertakings, or hurt their relationships with friends and colleagues. They are highly reliable and authoritative sources. I agreed to the condition. In some cases their names are not included in the lists of author's interviews.

• • •

ONE Up From Bankruptcy

Books *Cissy* by Paul E. Healy (Doubleday & Co., 1966); *McCormick of Chicago* by Frank C. Waldrop (Prentice-Hall, 1968); *American Journalism,* third edition, by Luther Mott (Macmillan Co., 1962); *Out of These Roots* by Agnes E. Meyer (Little, Brown and Co., 1953); *Behind the Lines—The World of Drew Pearson* by Herman Klurfeld (Prentice-Hall, 1968); *The Vantage Point* by Lyndon B. Johnson (Holt, Rinehart & Winston, 1971); *The Professional: Lyndon B. Johnson* by William S. White (Fawcett World Library Edition, 1964); *The Making of the President 1964* by Theodore H. White (Atheneum, 1965); *Robert Kennedy and His Times* by Arthur M. Schlesinger, Jr. (Houghton Mifflin, 1978).

Articles and Documents On Meyer's purchase of the *Post:* reports in the *New York Times,* June 1933; article by Marquis Childs, *Saturday Evening Post,* June 5, 1943; the Eugene and Agnes Meyer file, biography division, District of Columbia Public Library; Hearings on the nomination of Eugene Meyer to be a member of the Federal Reserve Board, Subcommittee of the Committee on Banking and Currency, U.S. Senate, 71st Congress, Third Session, 1931. Congressional Record, May 29, 1933, includes McFadden's allegations. *Time,* May 3, 1943, on Agnes Meyer's wartime reporting. *Newsweek,* July 27, 1955, on Eugene Meyer's death. *Time* cover story, on Philip Graham, April 16, 1956. The *New York Times,* profile of Graham, March 10, 1961; *Time,* August 8, 1963, Graham's suicide. *Esquire,* November 1969, on *Newsweek,* article by Chris Welles. The Eugene Meyer papers in the manuscript division, Library of Congress, were extremely useful sources. I also read the Joseph Alsop papers in this library. Joseph R. Rauh, Jr., graciously made his unpublished memoir of Democratic presidential conventions available to me. I also read transcripts of interviews for the oral history project of the Lyndon Baines Johnson Library, Austin, Texas, with Katharine Graham, Carroll Kilpatrick, and Gerald W. Siegel. [LBJ archivist Tina Lawson was of great help.]

Author's Interviews Alan Barth, David S. Clark, George Frain, Alfred Friendly, Sr., Katharine Graham, Erwin Knoll, Joseph R. Rauh Jr., Chalmers Roberts, Elizabeth Rowe, Frank C. Waldrop, and Judith Viorst.

TWO Waist Deep in the Big Muddy

Books *With Kennedy* by Pierre Salinger (Doubleday & Co., 1966); *The First Casualty, From the Crimea to Vietnam: The War Correspondent as Hero, Propagandist and Myth Maker* by Phillip Knightly (Harcourt Brace Jovanovich, 1975); *Big Story: How the American Press and Television Reported and Interpreted the Crisis of Tet 1968 in Vietnam and Washington,* volume I, by Peter Braestrup (Westview Press, 1977); *Vietnam Folly* by Ernest Gruening and Herbert W. Beaser (The National Press, 1968); *The Press and the Cold War* by James Aronson (Bobbs-Merrill, 1970); *Pentagon Papers* (Bantam Books, 1971); *What Washington Said* by F. M. Kail (Harper & Row, 1973); *The Vietnam Legacy: The War, American Society and the Future of American Foreign Policy,* edited by Anthony Lake (New York University Press, 1976); *The War at Home* by Thomas Powers (Grossman, 1973); *The Haunted Fifties* by I.F. Stone (Random House, 1963).

Articles and Documents Subcommittee on Preparedness, report on air war in Vietnam, Armed Services Committee, U.S. Senate, September 1967; Intelligence Activities and the Rights of Americans, Book III, Final

Report of the Senate Select Committee to Study Governmental Operations with Respect to Intelligence Activities, April 1976; speech by Morton Mintz, May 18, 1972, on the Gruening opposition to the Tonkin Gulf Resolution; "Journalists—To March or Just Observe?" by David Shaw, the *Los Angeles Times*, February 27, 1978; on Vietnam editorials, *Time*, November 29, 1965, October 21, 1966, October 20, 1967, and *Newsweek*, October 23, 1967; on Harrison Salisbury's coverage, *Columbia Journalism Review*, winter issue, 1966–67 and January-February, 1976; Martin Luther King's antiwar speech, the *New York Times*, April 6–7, 1967; Geoffrey Wolff interview with Ward Just, the *Washington Post*, April 2, 1978; on Joseph Alsop, Nieman Reports, spring 1976, Tom Kelly, *Washingtonian*, May 1972; the *Reporter*, June 13, 1968, article by Max Ascoli; on Russell Wiggins, "The Quality of an Appointee," *Washingtonian*, November 1968. Letter from Russell Wiggins to author, November 2, 1978; Transcripts of interviews of the Lyndon Baines Johnson Library oral history project with Katharine Graham, Carroll Kilpatrick, Eugene Patterson and Russell Wiggins.

Author's Interviews Joseph Alsop, Alan Barth, Leon Dash, Philip Foisie, Alfred Friendly, Sr., Philip Geyelin, Donald Graham, Katharine Graham, Stephen Isaacs, Robert Maynard, Stephen Rosenfeld, and J.Y. Smith.

THREE Mrs. Graham Takes Charge

Books *The Opinionmakers* by William L. Rivers (Beacon Press, 1965); *Behind the Front Page* by Chris Argyris (Jossey-Bass, 1974); *My Life and The Times* by Turner Catledge (Harper & Row, 1971); *The American Challenge* by Jean-Jacques Servan-Schreiber (Atheneum, 1968).

Articles and Documents On the *Washington Star*, article by Kent A. MacDougall in *(MORE)*, December 1975, and the *Washington Post*, May 9, 1976; "Katharine Graham" by Judith Viorst, *Washingtonian*, September 1967; *Prospectus*, the Washington Post Company, 1971; on Frederick Beebe, *Business Week*, May 27, 1967, and *Fortune*, April 1973; transcript, annual stockholders meeting, May 10, 1978, the Washington Post Company; "The Katharine Graham Story" by Lynn Rosselini, the *Washington Star*, five-part series November 13–17, 1978; On Bradlee and the *Post*, articles by Joseph Goulden in the *Washingtonian*, October 1970, and by Norman Sherman in the same magazine, July 1974; on the Capote party, the *New York Times*, November 29, 1966 and "Truman Capote's World" (Part 2) by Anne Taylor Fleming, the *New York Times* magazine, July 16, 1978; Eugene Patterson letter to author, January 3, 1977; on the *International Herald Tribune*, James O. Goldsborough in the *Columbia Journalism Review*, July-August

1974, William Dowell in the *Paris Metro,* October 13, 1976, *Business Week,* June 27, 1977, and the *Sunday Times,* March 19, 1978; Karen DeYoung letter to author, April 2, 1977; "Promotion in the Family" in Post Company internal newsletter, July 9, 1965, on Bradlee's move from *Newsweek.*

 Author's interviews Ben Bagdikian, David Binder, Benjamin Bradlee, Philip Foisie, Alfred Friendly, Sr., Ben Gilbert, Katharine Graham, Dan Greenberg, Richard Harwood, Russell Warren Howe, Stephen Isaacs, Edward Khorry, Erwin Knoll, Mark Meagher, Dan Morgan, Bernard Nossiter, George Reedy, Hobart Rowen, Charles Seib, Howard Simons, J.Y. Smith, and Frank Waldrop.

FOUR Spin

 Books *America in Our Time* by Godfrey Hodgson (Doubleday, 1976); *Why Watergate,* edited by Paul J. Halpern (Palisades Publishers, 1975); *Assault on the Media* by William E. Porter (University of Michigan, 1976); Watergate: *Chronology of a Crisis,* volume 2 (Congressional Quarterly, June 1974); *Robert Kennedy and His Times* by Arthur M. Schlesinger, Jr. (Houghton Mifflin, 1978).

 Articles and Documents Internal memorandum by Richard Harwood on the problem of biased news handling, June 22, 1970; internal memorandum on ombudsman idea by Philip Foisie to Ben Bradlee and Eugene Patterson, November 10, 1969; speech by Howard Simons, Northeastern Illinois University, May 12, 1977; "The Presidency and the Press" by Daniel P. Moynihan, *Commentary,* March 1971; "Has the Press Done a Job on Nixon?" *Columbia Journalism Review,* January-February 1974; "New Voices on the Right" by Edwin Diamond, *Columbia Journalism Review,* May-June 1974, on George Will and William Safire; "Election Coverage '72," *Columbia Journalism Review,* articles by Ben Bagdikian and Jules Witcover, January-February 1973; Final Report of the Select Committee to Study Governmental Operations with Respect to Intelligence Activities, Book III, U.S. Senate, April 1976, on the FBI's operations against Dr. King; A copy of the Bradlee file on President Johnson interview, August 15, 1964, was provided the author by a recipient of the report; *Newsweek,* August 15, 1964, cover story on LBJ; David Wise interview, the *Washington Star,* November 30, 1976.

 Author's interviews Ben Bagdikian, Karlyn Barker, Carl Bernstein, Ben Bradlee, Hank Burchard, Philip Foisie, William Greider, Richard Harwood, Reed Irvine, Stephen Isaacs, Nick Kotz, Robert McCormick, Eugene Patterson, Howard Simons, Laurence Stern, Philip Stern, Nicholas von Hoffman, and Lawrence Wallace.

FIVE Awash in Lies

> **Books** *The Papers & The Papers* by Sanford J. Ungar (E. P.
> Dutton & Co., 1972); *The Memoirs of Richard Nixon* by Richard M. Nixon
> (Grosset & Dunlop, 1978); *Anything But the Truth: The Credibility Gap—*
> *How the News is Managed in Washington* by William McGaffin and Erwin
> Knoll (G. P. Putnam's Sons, 1968); *All the President's Men* by Carl Bernstein
> and Bob Woodward (Simon and Schuster, 1974); *The Great Coverup* by Barry
> Sussman (Crowell, 1974); *With Nixon* by Raymond Price (Viking Press,
> 1977); *Nightmare: The Underside of the Nixon Years* by J. Anthony Lukas
> (Viking Press, 1976); *Watergate: Chronology of a Crisis,* volume 2 (Congres-
> sional Quarterly, June 1974); *Agency of Fear* by Edward Jay Epstein (G. P.
> Putnam's Sons, 1977); *At That Point in Time* by Fred D. Tompson (Quadran-
> gle/The New York Times Book Co., 1975); *The Powers that Be* by David
> Halberstam (Random House, 1979); *The Vietnam Legacy: The War, Ameri-*
> *can Society and the Future of American Foreign Policy,* edited by Anthony
> Lake (New York University Press, 1976); *The Freedom of the Press,* The
> Granada Guildhall lectures (Hart-Davis MacGibbon, 1974); *Conversations*
> *With Kennedy* by Benjamin C. Bradlee (W.W. Norton, 1975); *Honorable*
> *Men: My Life in the CIA* by William Colby and Peter Forbath (Simon and
> Schuster, 1978); *The Politics of Lying* by David Wise (Random House, 1973).
>   **Articles and Documents** On the Pentagon Papers case: "We
> Knew What We Were Doing When We Went into Vietnam" by Henry
> Fairlie, *Washington Monthly,* May 1973; "The First Amendment on Trial"
> *Columbia Journalism Review,* September–October 1971, and "Maximizing
> Profits at the Washington Post" by Ben H. Bagdikian, *Washington Monthly,*
> January 1976. On Watergate: "Nixon's Defenders Do Have a Case" by Noam
> Chomsky *(MORE)* December 1975; "The Press After Watergate" by Stan-
> ford N. Sesser, *Chicago Journalism Review,* December 1973; Katharine Gra-
> ham speech Colby College, Waterville, Maine, Nieman Reports, Spring 1974;
> "Ethics Charges Largely Ignored" by Godfrey Sperling, Jr., the *Christian*
> *Science Monitor,* October 19, 1972; "Investigative Reporting—The Precari-
> ous Profession" by Clark R. Mollenhoff, Nieman Reports, Summer 1976;
> "Has the Press Done a Job on Nixon?" *Columbia Journalism Review,* January-
> February 1974; "The Washington Post and Watergate: How Two Davids
> Slew Goliath" by James McCartney, *Columbia Journalism Review,* July-
> August 1973; On Watergate press sources, hearings of the Special Committee
> on Intelligence, Armed Services Committee, House of Representatives, July
> 1974; Convocation, Boston University, April 23, 1975, remarks by Ben Bag-
> dikian, Carl Bernstein, Walter Pincus, and Roger Wilkins; "Agronsky at
> Large" WETA-TV, transcript of Bradlee appearance, December 3, 1976. On

the CIA and the press: "The CIA's Use of the Press: a 'mighty Wurlitzer' " by Stuart H. Loory, *Columbia Journalism Review,* September-October 1974; "Journalists as Spooks" by Howard Bray, the *Progressive,* February 1977; "It's Up to the Press, Not Congress, to Police CIA Ties" by Philip L. Geyelin, the *Washington Post,* May 21, 1978; correspondence between John A. Bross and Richard Helms and George Bush and Philip Geyelin provided the author; "Foreign and Military Intelligence" Book I Final Report of the Select Committee to Study Governmental Operations with Respect to Intelligence Activities, U.S. Senate, April 1976; "The CIA and the Media" hearings before the Subcommittee on Oversight of the Permanent Select Committee on Intelligence, House of Representatives, December 1977, January and April 1978. The narrative on the Glomar Explorer episode is largely derived from 64 documents released by the CIA in 1977 in a U.S. District Court lawsuit filed by journalist Harriet Ann Phillippi under the Freedom of Information Act; articles by Seymour M. Hersh, the *New York Times,* December 9–10, 1976; "Aftergate" by William Greider, *Esquire,* September 1975. On the Progressive case: Alicia Patterson Foundation conference, April 17, 1979, transcript; defendants' brief and affidavits filed in the Progressive case, U.S. District Court, Western District of Wisconsin.

Author's Interviews Joseph Alsop, Carl Bernstein, Benjamin Bradlee, Taylor Branch, Richard Copaken, Robert Fink, Joel Garreau, Philip L. Geyelin, Ben W. Gilbert, Katharine Graham, William Greider, Richard Harwood, Erwin Knoll, Stuart H. Loory, Victor Marchetti, David Rein, Harry Rosenfeld, Charles Seib, Carl Shoffler, Howard Simons, J.Y. Smith, Laurence Stern, Bob Woodward, and Victor Zorza.

six Black and White

Books *Report of the National Advisory Commission on Civil Disorders* (Bantam Edition, 1968); *The Choice: The Issue of Black Survival in America* by Samuel F. Yette (Berkley Publishing Corp. edition, April 1972); *America in Our Time* by Godfrey Hodgson (Doubleday, 1976); *The Negro in America* by Arnold Rose (Harper & Row Torchbook edition, 1964); *Witness to Power* by Marquis Childs (McGraw-Hill, 1975); *The American Negro Revolution* by Benjamin Muse (Indiana University Press, 1969); *Congress and the News Media,* edited by Robert O. Blanchard (Hasting House, 1974); *District of Columbia: A Bicentennial History* by David L. Lewis (Norton, 1976).

Articles and Documents *Time,* March 21, 1955, on the National Press Club; "The Black Press in America" Nieman Reports, Spring 1975; *New Republic,* December 15, 1962, on the Thanksgiving Day racial brawl; "White Papers and Black Readers" by Margaret Halsey, *New Republic,* October 16, 1965; "Strange Bedfellows: Congressmen Who Own Media" by Tracy Freedman, *Washington Journalism Review,* September-October 1978, on Senator Byrd's press connections; Remarks of Luther P. Jackson, Jr., at Columbia Journalism Award to Dorothy Butler Gilliam, May 12, 1978; "My Children Have a Right to Feel Proud" by Dorothy Gilliam, *Redbook,* August 1970; "What do Black Journalists Want?" by Dorothy Gilliam, *Columbia Journalism Review,* May-June 1972; "The News Media and Racial Disorders —A Preliminary Report", Community Relations Service, U.S. Department of Justice, October 12, 1967; correspondence and staff memoranda of Ben W. Gilbert on the *Post*'s policies towards blacks and riot coverage, November 15, August 11, 1967, December 9, 1968. Gilbert's remarks, American Press Institute, October 20, 1969. On the complaints of black journalists at the *Post:* Correspondence between black staffers and Bradlee, February 7, 8, and 14, 1972, and March 14, 1972; press release by seven complainants, March 23, 1972; "Black Sports Writers" by Tom Dowling, the *Washington Star,* March 26, 1972; the *Economist,* April 15, 1972; "Washington's Metropolitan Eight" by Bob Kuttner *(MORE)* May 1972; Post newsroom equal employment opportunity committee reports, October 23, 1972, April 8, 1975; Equal Employment Opportunity Commission determination letter, November 1, 1972: videotapes of WTOP-TV Harambee programs on blacks at the *Post,* July 1975. On black journalists: "The Black Reporters' Dilemma" by Jonathan R. Laing, the *Wall Street Journal,* March 23, 1972; Shiela Younge obituary, the *New York Times,* October 27, 1977. On discrimination against women journalists: "Covering the Women's Movement" by Peggy A. Simpson, Nieman Reports, summer 1979; Equal Employment Opportunity Commission determination letter, June 19, 1974.

    Author's Interviews Karlyn Barker, Alan Barth, Simeon Booker, Benjamin Bradlee, John Britton, Leon Dash, Herbert Denton, Ben W. Gilbert, Dorothy Gilliam, Donald Graham, Katharine Graham, Stephen Isaacs, Kevin Klose, Claudia Levy, Robert Maynard, Richard Prince, Harry Rosenfeld, J. Y. Smith, and Wallace Terry.

SEVEN Stretching the Empire

    Books *Jews and American Politics* by Stephen D. Isaacs (Doubleday and Co., 1974); *The Sovereign State of ITT* by Anthony Sampson (Stein and Day, 1973).

    Articles and Documents On Warren Buffett, "The Money Men," *Forbes,* November 1, 1969, and November 1, 1974; "Boys Town: An Expose Without Bad Guys" by Paul N. Williams, *Columbia Journalism Re-*

view, January-February 1975; annual reports, 1977 and 1978, Blue Chip Stamps; Annual report, 1978, Berkshire Hathaway. On the *Trenton Times* and the Kerney family: *Overset,* June 1979; internal report of Monty Curtis, March 1974; " 'Creative Tension' Comes to Trenton" by Dan Rottenberg *(MORE)* October 1975; "Okie from Muskogee" by Merle Haggard and Ray Edward Burris, (copyright Blue Book Music, 1969). On the Los Angeles Times-Washington Post News Service, correspondence on the dispute provided the author. On *New York* magazine: Michael Jackson's interviews with Otis Chandler, August 1977; "Clay Felker's New York" by A. Kent Mac-Dougall, *Columbia Journalism Review,* March-April 1974; "New York's Budding Beaverbrook" by Judith Adler Hennessee, *(MORE)* October 1975; "Murdoch Seems to be the Victor in Fight for *New York* Magazine" by Dierdre Carmody, the *New York Times,* January 5, 1977; "How Murdoch Mobilized His Money" by Vartanig G. Vartan, the *New York Times,* January 7, 1977; "Requeim for a Winner" by Lucian K. Truscott IV, *New Times,* March 4, 1977; "A Fistful of Dollars" by Gail Sheehy, *Rolling Stone,* July 14, 1977; "Krusty Kay Tightens Her Grip," *Time,* February 7, 1977.

    Author's Interviews   Terry Anzur, Warren E. Buffett, Norman Cherniss, Alfred Friendly, Sr., Joel Garreau, Katharine Graham, Richard Harwood, Stephen D. Isaacs, Morris Levin, Robert McCormick, Mark Meagher, Charles Peters, John Prescott, and Mike Rood.

EIGHT   The Padilla Affair

    Books   *The Information Machines: Their Impact on Men and the Media* by Ben H. Bagdikian (Harper Torchbooks, 1971); *The Kingdom and the Power* by Gay Talese (World Publishing Co., 1969); *A Union of Individuals: The Formation of the American Newspaper Guild, 1933–36* by David J. Leab (Columbia University Press, 1970).

    Articles and Documents   "The Strike at the Washington Post" by Robert G. Kaiser, the *Washington Post,* February 29, 1976, was a valuable reference in this and the following chapter. The *Post*'s model for this long report was A.H. Raskin's, "The Strike: A Step-by-Step Account," which ran in the *New York Times,* April 1, 1963, after the long newspaper strike in New York. I have referred to Raskin's article in describing Philip Graham's involvement in the New York strike; "The Failing Newspaper Act," Hearings before the Subcommittee on Antitrust and Monopoly of the Committee on the Judiciary, U.S. Senate, 1967; On automation: *Time,* July 5, 1963, and *Newsweek,* November 9, 1964; "A Craft in Crisis: Printers at the Post" by William Greider, the *Washington Post,* October 28, 1973; "Phasing Out the Wogs" by Patrick Owens *(MORE)* May 1974; On the Newspaper Guild: Joseph F.

Dineen's article in the *Saturday Evening Post,* August 3, 1940; *The Review of Southern California Journalism,* Number 11, May 1974, includes the Heywood Broun column; the *Wall Street Journal,* April 9 and 23, 1974; letter from George E. Reedy to author, July 12, 1977; letter from Edward Folliard to Eugene Meyer on profit-sharing, March 12, 1958. On Project X: "Means Change, Goals the Same in Newspaper Strikebreaking" by Roy Reck, *News and Views,* International Printing and Graphic Communications Union monthly publication, February 1976, as reprinted in the Congressional Record, March 31, 1976; "A School in Oklahoma Helps Newspapers Keep Printing When Workers Walk Out" by Douglas Martin, the *Wall Street Journal,* October 28, 1975: "School for Scabs" by Peter Pringle, the *Sunday Times* (London) December 28, 1975.

    Author's Interviews Karlyn Barker, Carl Bernstein, Benjamin Bradlee, James Dugan, Brian Flores, William Greider, Richard Harwood, James Ingraham, Lawrence Kennelly, Kevin Klose, George Ludlow, Mark Meagher, Morton Mintz, Dan Morgan, John Prescott, George Reedy, J. Y. Smith, John Waits, and Lawrence Wallace.

NINE The Pressmen's Strike

    Articles and Documents the *Washington Star,* October 1 and 3, 1975; "Striking Facts About the Post" by Eliot Marshall, *New Republic,* October 25, 1975; "High Noon at the Washington Post" by Philip Nobile, *New Times,* November 14, 1975; "Violence in the Morning" by Patrick Owens, *(MORE)* December 1975; "The Right to Manage" *Time,* December 29, 1975; "The Workers Hang Separately at the Washington Post" by Nat Hentoff, the *Village Voice,* January 5, 1976; "Lengthy Labor Strife at Washington Post Could Affect Industry" by Stephen Grover, the *Wall Street Journal,* January 23, 1976; "The Iron Lady Breaks the Pressmen" by Shirley Elder, the *Washingtonian,* March 1976; On relations with the *Star:* the Reston and Breslin columns appeared in the Star October 4, 1975; Releases, handbills, and strike bulletins were provided the author by persons who worked with the Strike Support Committee. Also of use were correspondence between *Post* employees and Katharine Graham, November 6, 7, and 17, 1975, Mark Meagher's briefing paper, December 8, 1975, the *Washington Post* 1975 financial budget documents, and unpublished interviews conducted in connection with an American University sociology research project on the strike; AFL-CIO statements, December 31, 1975, February 23, 1976; Hearings, Subcommittee on Labor-Management Relations, Committee on Education and Labor, House of Representatives, 1977, on Wackenhut. On indictments of pressmen: Paul Goldman and Marion Sherman Goldman affidavits regarding community impressions of the strike, Superior Court of the District of Columbia, Criminal Division, November 15, 1976, Government Memorandum on Sentencing, Ibid. May 17, 1977. On newsroom situation: Speech of Stephen D. Isaacs, Society of Silurians, New York, May 16, 1978. Stock analyst's views: The Wall Street Transcript, May 30, 1977.

    Author's Interviews Elizabeth Becker, James Bellows, Carl Bernstein, James Dugan, John Dower, Brian Flores, Ray Foresman, Donald Graham, Katharine Graham, Stephen D. Isaacs, Kevin Klose, William Mackaye, Mark Meagher, Roger Parkinson, Charles Perlik, Paul Pinsky, John Prescott, Carl Rauh, Joseph L. Rauh Jr., David Rein, Ben Segal, John Waits, Lawrence Wallace, and Alice Zarbrough.

Index